Wessex Cru...

Book. HH.

The Yacht Navigator's
Handbook

For *Mar Del Norte* (K318)
and her co-owner

The Yacht Navigator's Handbook

Norman Dahl

Ward Lock Limited·London

© Norman Dahl 1983

First published in Great Britain in 1983
by Ward Lock Limited, 82 Gower Street
London WC1E 6EQ, a Pentos Company.

House editor Helen Douglas-Cooper
Designed by Viv Harper
Layout by Heather Sherratt

Text filmset in Hong Kong
by Asco Trade Typesetting Limited.

Printed and bound in Spain
by Graficomo, S.A., Cordaba

British Library Cataloguing in Publication Data

Dahl, Norman
    Yacht navigator's handbook.
    1. Navigation
    I. Title
    623.89   VK145

    ISBN 0-7063-5920-8

Acknowledgments

The author and publishers would like to thank
the following for permission to use copyright
material:
Page 108 US Department of Commerce.
Pages 120, 149 and 151 reproduced by
courtesey of the Defense Mapping Agency
Hydrographic/Topographic Center,
Washington DC.
Pages 131, 133, 138–9, 141, 158 and 162
reproduced by permission of the Controller,
HM Stationery Office.
Page 178 reproduced by permission of Thomas
Reed Publications Ltd.
    The author and publishers would like to
thank the following for supplying photographs
for the book: Brookes & Gatehouse Ltd pages
36, 48–9, 110 top; Firdell Multiflectors Ltd
page 117; Lokata Ltd page 110 centre and
bottom; Sestrel/Henry Browne & Son Ltd
pages 25 top, centre and bottom, 27, 45, 163.

Line diagrams drawn by Harry Clow.

CONTENTS

As its name suggests, this book contains all the techniques that most yachtsmen are likely to need to conduct their vessels safely from one place to another, wherever on the surface of the earth those places might be. It is intended for use as a self-teaching book at home, as a classroom textbook or as a ready reference to be kept by the chart table at sea. For those seeking some form of yachtsman's qualification, the book is sufficiently comprehensive and detailed to meet the navigational syllabus of most of the various schemes now in operation in different countries.

This book differs from the normal run of yacht navigation manuals in two significant ways:

1) Wherever possible the contents are organized in what publishers call 'spreads'. This means that the words and the pictures for a particular subject are all to be found on two facing pages, so everything can be seen at a single book opening. Where a topic is too large to fit onto two pages, it has been broken up into logical sub-units, each on its own spread. The purpose of this arrangement is to make it as easy as possible for the user, who may be bucking about in a seaway, to find and use the information he wants.

2) One of the dominant themes throughout the book is the understanding and handling of errors. When I was first taught navigation (in the Royal Navy), errors were thought of as being rather disgraceful, the sole result of poor technique by the navigator. Whilst I always accepted (and still accept today) that I was not the most brilliant navigator in the world, I was disappointed to find, that, however hard I tried, errors never seemed to go away. Navigating a submerged submarine, and later yachts of many kinds in many situations eventually made me realise that errors are an integral part of navigation, and need to be studied in their own right. Professional navigators (especially those who fly) have studied errors in detail, but few books intended for the amateur consider them to any extent.

This book is intended to be a practical tool for the working navigator, and so theory has been kept to a minimum; where theory must be described, it is kept on its own 'spreads', away from the practical applications which follow. This has not been done to suggest in any way that theory is unimportant. Quite the reverse is the case; it very often happens that only by understanding the theory of a subject is it possible to understand and make use of the actual circumstances of the moment. However, many people find theory hard to swallow, and merely want to know what to do to get an answer. To help them, a step-by-step description is given so that they can just follow the instructions, 'plugging in' their own numbers to work out what they want.

The book is divided into a number of sections, each more or less independent of the others though some degree of overlap is inevitable.

The navigator's tools describes the various tools, instruments, charts and books that the navigator needs to do his job. Advice is given on the errors to which the various instruments are liable, and how they may (to some extent) be corrected.

The reckoning deals with the problem of dead reckoning, keeping track of the yacht's position by taking account of its own movement through the water and such external factors as tidal stream and current. Dead reckoning is of the greatest importance, as the foundation upon which the various position-finding techniques can be based, and with which they can be compared.

Position is all about the various ways that exist for finding a yacht's position on the surface of the earth. The basic unit is the *position line*, which when combined with other position lines leads to a *fix*.

The environment collects together information on some of the external factors of importance to the yacht – specifically weather, land- and sea-marks, tides, tidal streams and currents.

Radio aids to navigation now range from a simple hand-held medium frequency direction finder to the full-blooded microprocessor controlled satellite navigator.

Astronomical navigation Many yachtsmen think that astronomical navigation – finding your position from the sun, moon, planets or stars – is too difficult. In fact it is not difficult at all, once the basic principles have been mastered. An astronomical position line can often be worked out just as quickly and easily as many other kinds of position line. No navigator can call himself really capable until he can master these straightforward techniques.

Passage making is all about turning the bare bones of information into a practical course of action, so the yacht can sail, conduct herself sen-

sibly and eventually arrive at her destination.

Knowledgeable navigators may notice some errors of fact in this book, which have been included deliberately to make things simpler; in no case do the errors make any significant difference to the yacht navigator. For example, the sea mile and the nautical mile are terms used interchangeably, though they are not in fact the same thing. In plane sailing, mid-latitude is used instead of mean latitude. To repeat, these simplifying assumptions will not cause any appreciable errors in yacht navigation.

Finally, this book has been written to be as international as possible, to reflect the fact that the sea is still a place where nationality matters less than personal qualities. If navigators from many lands find this book useful as they roam the seas and oceans of the world, I shall be well satisfied.

NORMAN DAHL

For the newcomer, navigation can be a trial and a disappointment. Fresh from the winter navigation classes, where dead reckoning, estimated positions and fixes march in ordered progression across the chart, he finds that things are not so simple at sea. His observations never seem to match up with his estimated position; landfalls never appear when and where expected; and conspicuous objects on shore might be printed on a different chart for all the help they are to him. And whilst it is easy to stop a car and ask the way of a passing stranger, it is more difficult (and more embarrassing) to do the same at sea. There are few navigators who can truthfully claim never to have experienced the sickening feeling of being lost.

The reason for the discrepancy between the real world and the classroom is that in the real world, errors appear which can obscure or distort the truth that the navigator is seeking. A major purpose of this book is to show that errors in navigation are normal and natural, and that the most skilful navigator with the most advanced equipment will cheerfully accept that his position is in some doubt – even though the magnitude of his doubt may be only a few metres. It is relatively easy (with practice) to make observations and measurements at sea, and to plot them on the chart. A major skill in navigation lies in the ability to interpret the results in terms of the likely errors; in other words, the navigator must measure doubt as well.

The first step in this process is to analyse the types of error that can occur in an observation, whether caused by the instrument or by the observer. Four types of error are recognized:

Systematic errors

Systematic errors are errors which change very slowly (if at all) with time, so that they can be measured and corrected. They can arise from inaccurate manufacture or from improper adjustment of the instrument. The two most common types are:

Zero error, in which all readings (including the zero reading) are in error by the same amount; for example, an echo sounder may read one metre low on all readings.

Scale error, in which the error of a reading depends on the magnitude of the reading; if the scanning speed of an echo sounder is wrongly set, it may have an error of one metre at ten metres, two metres at twenty metres and so on.

Systematic errors are best corrected by adjusting the instrument, if the design allows; otherwise a correction table or graph can be drawn up, or the appropriate correction factors can be found and then applied arithmetically to each reading.

Semi-systematic errors

There is no firm division between systematic and semi-systematic errors. The difference between them is time; a systematic error varies very slowly or not at all, while a semi-systematic error varies more quickly – over a period of hours or days. One example of a semi-systematic error is the personal error that an observer may have when using a particular instrument; this can vary with time and circumstances. Another example is magnetic variation, caused by the fact that the earth's magnetic pole does not co-incide with the true pole, and is moving (see page 28). Thus the magnetic variation varies both with time and with the position of the vessel on the earth's surface.

Semi-systematic errors can be corrected in the same way as systematic errors, but the actual magnitude of the error must be checked at suitably frequent intervals.

Random errors

Random errors are errors which vary rapidly in a way that can neither be foreseen nor corrected. These errors can arise in many different ways, but the most common are:

Rounding error, where a reading falls between graduations on the scale of an instrument and is rounded up or down to the nearest graduation.

Periodic error, when an instrument is swinging from side to side of the correct reading, it is moving quickly past the correct reading and more slowly at the extremities of the swing. The correct value is less likely to be read than an incorrect one.

Backlash, when the reading lags or leads the true value, because of friction, backlash or damping.

Noise, where the sensitivity of the instrument is reduced or the reading is altered by some outside interference.

As has been said, random errors cannot be foreseen or corrected; however, it is generally true that a good quality instrument used by a practised observer will give smaller random errors than a poor instrument in untrained hands.

Gross errors

Gross errors, which are large and unexpected errors, can arise in three ways:

Blunders, where the operator makes a mistake, such as reading the reciprocal of a compass bearing.

Equipment faults, which can give large and sometimes undetected errors.

Breakdowns, where the equipment ceases to operate. In many ways it is preferable to have equipment that does not work at all rather than faulty equipment telling lies.

Gross errors can never be eliminated entirely, but they can be reduced in frequency; blunders can be avoided by careful and systematic working, and by checking whenever possible against information from some other source. Faults and breakdowns can be minimized by careful attention to installation, operation and maintenance procedures.

Because gross errors are unpredictable, the navigator must be constantly on his guard. He should not rely on one source of information exclusively, but should cross-check at every opportunity with information from some other source. And he should look for inconsistencies, by comparing the present with the past to make sure that the pattern which emerges makes sense.

Error distributions

It is possible to visualize the various types of error by means of graphs. These graphs plot the probability of an error (vertically) against the magnitude of the error (horizontally). For systematic errors, the error is fixed – it is certain that the error has a particular value. Therefore the distribution graph is a vertical straight line (Fig. 1a). For gross errors, the error may have any value with equal probability; therefore the graph is a horizontal straight line (Fig. 1b). Random errors follow the form of Figure 1c, which has been derived from experiment and experience; it approximates to the Gaussian or Normal distribution of statistical theory. The curve means that the reading will most probably be close to the truth (the hump on

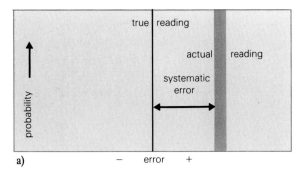

a)

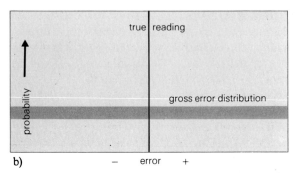

b)

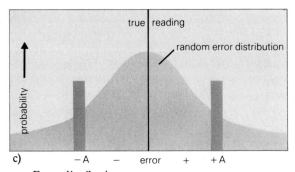

c)

1.1 *Error distributions.*

the graph), whilst it gets less and less likely that a reading will be greatly in error (the skirts of the curve). However, there is always a chance (though it may be very small) of any size of error occuring.

To make use of the idea of random errors, we must put a limit to what we consider to be likely. This we do by choosing a particular error (+A and −A in Fig. 1c), such that 95 per cent of the area of the curve lies between +A and −A. This is equivalent to saying that it is 95 per cent certain that any error will lie between +A and −A. The odds are 20 to 1 that the error is not greater than A. The value of A is known as the 95 per cent error of the instrument, and this term will be used throughout the book.

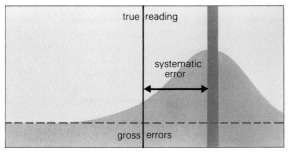

1.2 *Combined error distribution.*

Whilst the 95 per cent error is a useful value for the navigator to use, it is still true that there remains a 5 per cent chance that the error will be greater than A. The possibility must be borne in mind, but theory indicates that the chances of large errors fall very quickly, and the odds are about 1000−1 against an error of 2A.

If we combine the three distributions of Figure 1, we arrive at a picture of the total situation (Fig. 2). The 'hump' of the random component of error has been shifted sideways by the systematic error, and lifted up by the gross error. The strategy that must be followed to reduce errors now becomes obvious. Gross errors must be fought to reduce in particular the chance of large errors; the 'hump' must be re-centred by removing systematic (and semi-systematic) errors; and it must be made as narrow as possible by good quality equipment and careful operation.

Using errors

Having explored the way in which errors are likely to affect the readings that a navigator takes, the next step is to see how these can be used to help the navigator make sensible decisions about his position and future course of action.

The first case to consider is a simple position line (Fig. 3a). If, for example, a bearing of an object is taken with a 95 per cent error of 3°, then the vessel must lie (with 20−1 probability) somewhere in the 'fan' 3° either side of the measured bearing. The actual error distribution gives rise to a ridge of probability.

A fix is generally obtained by the intersection of two (or more) position lines. As each position line is not really a line at all, but rather a band of probability, the true position must lie somewhere in the region where the two bands intersect. In

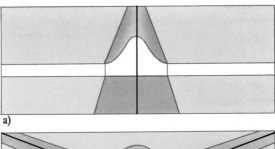

a)

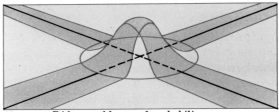

b)   **1.3** *Ridges and heaps of probability.*

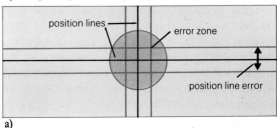

a)

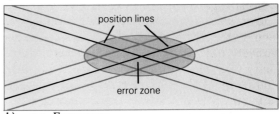

b)   **1.4** *Error zones.*

terms of probability, the two ridges of the position lines combine to give a 'heap' of probability for the true position (Fig. 3b).

If the two position lines cross at right angles and have equal 95 per cent errors, then the 'heap' can be represented on the chart by a circle, the radius of which is a little bigger (one and a quarter times) than the position line error (Fig. 4a). If the position lines have unequal 95 per cent errors or cut at an angle other than 90°, the 95 per cent error zone of the fix is an ellipse (Fig. 4b). However, unless the ellipse is very elongated, it is sufficient to assume that the 95 per cent error zone is a circle with radius rather less than the larger position line error; although this is an approximation, it is normally satisfactory and makes for easier working.

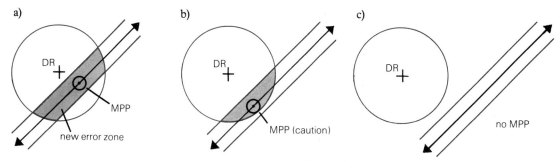

1.5 *Most probable position.*

The most probable position (MPP)

It is often necessary to estimate a most probable position by combining a position circle with a position line. The most common example is the updating of a dead reckoning position (which may have a large 95 per cent error) by means of a single position line (with its own 95 per cent error). Provided that the two error zones intersect fully, as shown in Figure 5a, then it is possible to select an MPP, with a long, thin error zone parallel with the position line and bounded by the DR error circle. If the error of the position line is less than that of the DR, it is normal to select an MPP at the closest point on the position line to the DR position; if the position line has a larger error than the DR, the navigator may prefer to use the DR position as his MPP.

Figures 5b and 5c show other possible combinations of position circle and position line;

1) The position line and the position circle do not fully intersect. A mistake is probable, either in estimating random errors or some form of gross error.

2) The position line and the position circle do not intersect at all. A gross error is most likely.

In the latter two cases, the navigator should endeavour to discover and put right any mistake that he might have made; if this is not possible, then it may be necessary to increase the error zone of his DR position to include the position line. The situation is an obvious warning that something has gone wrong, and caution will be needed until the situation resolves itself with new information.

Error magnitudes

To put the ideas in this chapter into practice, the navigator needs to arrive at some estimate of the actual magnitudes of the errors he is likely to have to use.

Gross errors By definition, these errors are unforseeable and may have any magnitude. The navigator can only be on his guard. Careful working and good maintenance will reduce their probability, and cross-checking will generally show when they have occurred.

Systematic errors These errors can be found by calibration, and either compensated within the instrument or allowed for in some other way. The sections of this book that deal with various types of equipment include notes on the correction of systematic errors; the actual procedure for an individual instrument is to be found in the maker's handbook.

Random errors These are more difficult to establish, as they are random, and vary with the type and age of the equipment and the circumstances in which they are used. It is only possible to estimate the 95 per cent error of an instrument under the various conditions in which it will be used. This book contains reasonably pessimistic estimates for the various types of instrument in common use in yacht navigation. The newcomer to navigation can use these (cautiously) for an initial estimate, but he should be prepared to revise them in the light of his own experience. Good equipment, good conditions and good operators indicate that the 95 per cent error might be reduced, and *vice versa*.

Putting errors to work

Navigators hate surprises, and any navigator who goes to sea with a clear idea of the errors he is likely to experience in all conditions is much less likely to be surprised. Before going to sea, he will have taken steps to find out what systematic errors there

1.6 *Choosing a position.*

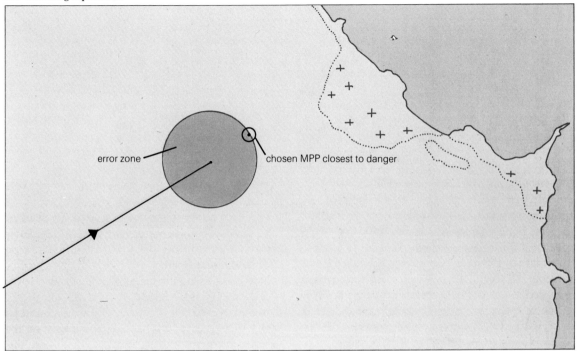

error zone

chosen MPP closest to danger

might be in his equipment, and if necessary he will have compensated for them; whilst at sea, he will take every opportunity to check that these errors have not altered. Cross-checking and tests for consistency will take care of most gross errors, and a pessimistic view of random errors, whilst giving rise to large error circles, means that the unexpected becomes much less likely. Navigation is a suspicious occupation.

When first trying to put these ideas into practice, it is a good idea to plot the error zones and circles on the chart, to help ensure that all errors are allowed for and to give an immediate picture of the scale of errors actually involved. An experienced navigator will probably carry the error information in his head rather than on the chart. The important thing is that the existence of errors and their likely magnitude is never forgotten; nor should the navigator forget the small (5 per cent) probability that he is actually outside his 95 per cent error circle.

Having established an error circle, it is not necessary (nor indeed wise) to choose the most probable position at its centre. In open waters, the centre of the circle will do as well as any other

position, but when near dangers it is best to follow that traditional practice of choosing a position within the circle closest to the danger. For example, when making a landfall, it is wise to choose a position on the leading edge of the circle (Fig. 6).

The use of the 95 per cent error should allow the cruising yachtsman to navigate with confidence that he will avoid the unexpected and be in a position to make prudent and seamanlike decisions about his future course of action. A racing navigator will need more than this, because he has the additional task of making his way from point to point in the shortest possible time. He will therefore be interested in the finer structure of the error zone, so that he can calculate the odds in favour of or against any particular tactical decision. He may choose to use a 50 per cent error zone within his 95 per cent zone, accepting the fact that there is an even chance that he is in fact outside this smaller region. The 50 per cent error is approximately half the 95 per cent error. However, the racing navigator must never forget his prime responsibility of keeping the yacht clear of danger, so he should hedge his bets where necessary by reverting to his 95 per cent errors.

THE NAVIGATOR'S TOOLS

2 Position, direction and distance on the earth

The earth

The purpose of navigation is to conduct a vessel from one place to another on the surface of the earth, so any study of navigation properly begins by considering the whole environment in which it takes place. The earth is one of the planets of the solar system, and it moves around the sun in a closed orbit once in each year; at the same time, the earth rotates on its own axis to give the familiar pattern of days and nights as each point on the surface is either exposed to or hidden from the light of the sun. A day, measured with respect to the sun is approximately 24 hours long and a year consists of just over 365 days.

For the purposes of navigation, the earth can be regarded as a sphere, though it is in fact slightly flattened at the poles. A spherical earth is much easier to deal with mathematically and the errors resulting from this assumption are rarely of any significance in the navigation of small craft.

In essence, navigation can be described as a way of answering three basic questions:

Where am I?

Which way should I go?

How far is it to my destination?

With this in mind, we need definitions of the three basic building blocks of navigation – position, direction and distance.

Direction

Directions on the surface of the earth (and indeed of any planet) are defined with respect to its rotation. The direction towards which the earth rotates is defined as *east* and the opposite direction is *west* (Fig. 1) The earth rotates on an imaginary line called its axis; the two points on the surface where the axis cuts it are called the poles. For an observer facing east, the pole on his left hand is the north pole, which lies *north* of him. The pole on his right hand is the south pole, lying *south* of him.

These rules define the four principal, or cardinal, directions at 90° intervals; but the navigator needs to be able to specify a direction much more precisely. The old seamen established a set of 32 points of the compass (see page 26), but the modern practice is to use degrees. Directions are measured clockwise from north (000), using a 360° notation. Thus east becomes 090, south 180 and west 270 (directions are always shown as three figures and the degree symbol is left out).

If the weather is clear, directions can be measured with respect to the heavens, but it is much more convenient to carry some form of directional reference in the craft. As far as yachts are concerned, this is almost invariably a magnetic compass (see pages 26–31). As is explained there, the magnetic compass does not in general point to true north (towards the pole) but towards the magnetic north pole nearby. The magnetic compass in a particular ship may also be affected by iron in the ship or other local influences, deflecting it away from magnetic north. Corrections must therefore be applied to a magnetic compass to obtain true directions.

Great and small circles

If the earth is cut by a plane (as if it were an orange being cut by a knife), a circle is formed on the surface (see Fig. 2). If the plane of cut includes the centre of the earth, the resulting circle on the surface is called a *great circle*; otherwise a *small circle* is formed. The great circle is of considerable importance in navigation: the shortest distance between two points on the earth's surface lies along the great circle which joins them.

Position

Because the earth can be considered as a sphere, a convenient way of defining the position of any point on its surface is by means of angles measured at the centre of the earth (Fig. 3). These angles are measured from two fixed axes:

Latitude is measured north or south of the *equator*, a great circle running east and west exactly midway between the poles. The equator itself is 0° latitude and the two poles are 90°N and 90°S respectively. Any other point has a latitude between these two values. Points with the same latitude lie east and west of each other on a small circle called a *parallel of latitude*.

By international agreement, *longitude* is measured east or west of the half great circle between the poles which passes through Greenwich, near London. This north-south line is called the *meridian of Greenwich*. Each point on the surface

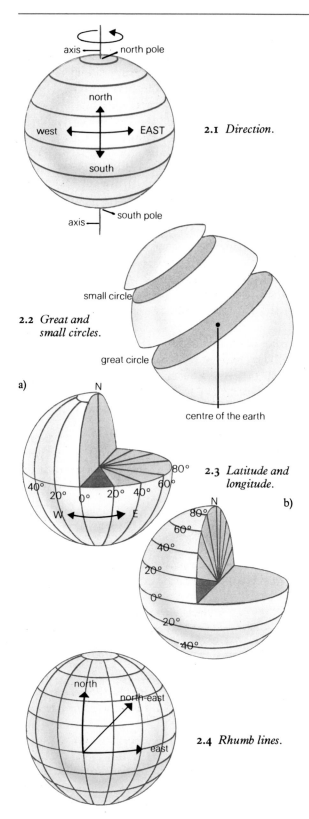

2.1 *Direction.*

2.2 *Great and small circles.*

a)

2.3 *Latitude and longitude.*

b)

2.4 *Rhumb lines.*

of the earth has its own meridian, and longitude is the angle (measured at the equator) between the Greenwich meridian and the meridian of the place. It has a maximum value of 180° east or west.

In defining the position of a point, the latitude is given first, followed by the longitude. In yacht navigation it is often sufficient to define a position to the nearest minute of arc (1 minute = 1/60 degree), but for more precise work, tenths of a minute may be quoted as well. For example:

Greenwich 51°28'.6N 0°00'.0
New York 40°45'N 74°00'W
Sydney 33°53'S 151°10'E

A minute of arc can also be subdivided into 60 seconds of arc.

Distance

There is a fixed relationship between the distance between two points and the angle between them as measured at the centre of the earth. For example, the distance between the equator and one of the poles corresponds to 90° of angle. Because of this, navigators use a unit of distance related to angle. The *sea mile* is the distance on the surface corresponding to one minute of arc at the centre of the earth. As the earth is not truly spherical, the sea mile can vary from 6046 feet (1844 m) at the equator to 6108 feet (1862 m) at the poles. To avoid this variation, the *nautical mile* has been defined as a fixed distance; the British Standard nautical mile is 6080 feet (1853.18 m), and the International nautical mile is 1852 metres. The yacht navigator can ignore these differences and regard the sea mile and the nautical mile as being the same.

The rhumb line

If a vessel travels in a constant direction, it follows a *rhumb line*. If the vessel is travelling due north or south, the rhumb line corresponds with the meridian, and if travelling east or west, the rhumb line corresponds with the parallel of latitude. In all other cases, the rhumb line spirals towards the pole (Fig. 4). As the shortest distance between two points is a great circle and a rhumb line is not (in general) a great circle, it follows that the distance between two points along the rhumb line joining them is greater than the great circle distance. Over short distances, this is unimportant, but for ocean passages it can become significant (see page 180).

3 Chart projections

Having established ways of defining position, direction and distance, the navigator needs to carry with him some form of model of the world so he can establish his present position and decide on the distance and direction of his destination. The most obvious model of the world is a globe, but this is clearly impractical, especially in a yacht! Instead the navigator uses a chart, which is a representation of some part of the earth's surface on a piece of paper. An ideal chart would be an exact model of the area without distortion of any kind; but as the earth is curved and the chart is flat, the ideal is impossible to attain. Chartmakers therefore introduce deliberate distortions by using a *projection* which preserves certain relationships at the expense of others less important for the particular application. The only two projections of any importance to the yacht navigator are *mercator's* projection which reproduces rhumb lines as straight lines, and the *gnomonic* projection which reproduces great circles as straight lines.

Mercator's projection

The course of a vessel (the direction in which it travels) is normally decided with reference to the compass, and is therefore a rhumb line. The mercator projection (first used in 1569) represents rhumb lines as straight lines on the chart, and is therefore the most generally useful projection for nautical charts. By drawing a straight line from his starting point to his destination, the navigator can measure directly the constant course he needs to follow from start to finish.

The mercator projection is derived mathematically, but the principle is shown in Figure 1. A transparent globe with a bright light at the centre is enclosed by a cylinder of paper, touching only at the equator. The details on the surface, including the graticule of latitude and longitude, are projected onto the paper.

The properties of the mercator chart are:
1) Rhumb lines are straight.
2) The direction of a rhumb line is not altered.
3) The equator is a straight line.
4) Meridians appear as equally spaced straight lines.
5) Parallels of latitude appear as straight lines, but their spacing increases as the latitude increases.
6) The poles themselves cannot be shown on the standard mercator chart.
7) The straight line between two points (the rhumb line) is not the shortest distance between the points. This is given by the great circle track, which appears curved towards the nearer pole on a mercator chart.

The gnomonic projection

The second projection of interest to yachtsmen is the gnomonic projection, in which great circles appear as straight lines. The principle of this projection is shown in Figure 2. A flat sheet of paper touches the globe at one point only, called the

3.1 *Mercator's projection.*

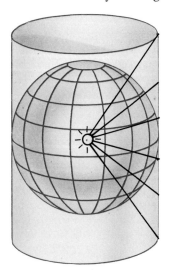

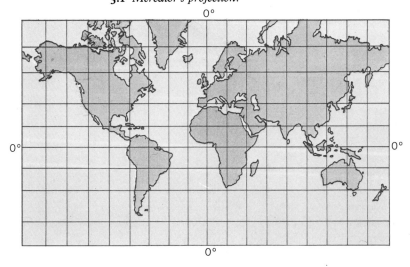

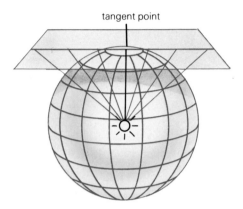

tangent point

3.2 *Gnomonic projection.*

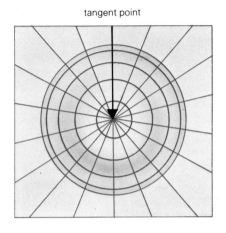

tangent point

tangent point. Very often a pole is chosen as the tangent point for an ocean passage planning chart, but this is not essential.

The properties of a gnomonic chart are:

1) Great circles appear as straight lines.
2) Rhumb lines are curved.
3) Parallels of latitude (small circles) are curved.
4) Meridians (great circles) are straight lines which converge towards the poles.
5) Distortion increases with distance from the tangent point.

The gnomonic chart is most often used in ocean passage planning, where the differences between the great circle and the rhumb line tracks become important (see page 180). It is often used for charts of the polar regions (of little interest to yachtsmen) and in a modified form for harbour plans.

Scale and distance on a mercator chart

Because latitude is measured along a great circle (in fact, a meridian), the angle subtended at the centre of the earth by one sea mile is one minute of latitude, and so the scale of latitude and the scale of distance are one and the same. The same is not true of longitude; at the equator, one minute of longitude is indeed equivalent to one sea mile, as the equator is a great circle (Fig. 3). But as the meridians converge, a minute of longitude becomes shorter and shorter on the surface, until at the pole it disappears entirely.

A problem exists with small-scale mercator charts because the parallels of latitude become more widely spaced as the latitude increases. This distortion is an essential part of the projection as it helps to preserve the shape of the land on the chart, but it means that the latitude scale changes over the chart. The navigator should take care to use the latitude scale adjacent to the position of interest for measuring distance, or considerable errors may arise. This effect is not important on medium or large scale charts (i.e. with a natural scale of 1 : 150,000 or less).

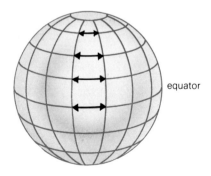

equator

3.3 *Convergence of the meridians.*

4   The chart

A chart is one of the basic tools that a yacht navigator needs to plan and conduct his passage from one place to another. At first sight, it is a complicated and confusing document, but it contains a wealth of information about the part of the world it covers. The difference between a chart and a map is obvious at the first glance; a map deals with the land and there is little or no detail shown of the sea. A chart is exactly the reverse; a navigator is not much interested in the land, except to know where the shoreline runs and to see where prominent objects are for the purpose of fixing his position. On the other hand, he needs to know about buoys and beacons, the nature of the bottom, the depth of water and about underwater hazards that cannot be seen. So a chart is filled with detail over the sea, whilst much of the land area covered by a chart is left blank.

Almost all the charts offered to the mariner are precisely and beautifully produced, but for any particular purpose there are good charts and bad; and as charts are by no means cheap, it is worth considering carefully before buying. A good chart is accurate, comprehensive, easy to use, easy to correct, robust and covers the area of interest at a suitable scale. So, what factors should be considered in choosing a chart? To a large extent, this will depend on the individual navigator and the individual chart under consideration, but there are a number of indicators which can help in making a choice.

Official or commercial?

All maritime countries of any importance maintain a hydrographic service which produces charts for their own mariners and for the rest of the world to use. Most of this information is pooled for the benefit of other countries, so that, for example, a British chart of the River Tagus (Tejo) would be based upon Portuguese government surveys. Apart from these official charts, a number of commercial companies produce charts for a specialized use – for fishermen or for yachtsmen. These commercial charts can vary widely in quality, though those produced by a reputable company are thoroughly trustworthy. They are in general an edited and re-arranged form of the official charts of the area,

concentrating on aspects of particular interest to the user and omitting detail that is irrelevant. Examples of different kinds of chart are given on pages 61–4. In deciding between official and commercial charts, the key point is that official charts are based on official surveys. *Ipso facto*, the official chart ought to be more accurate, though not perhaps as easy to use.

Scale

Scale is the relation between distance on the chart and distance on the surface of the earth. A large scale chart covers a small area of the earth.

The scale of a chart can vary from 1 : 1,000,000 or more for passage planning to 1 : 10,000 for a harbour plan. For coastal passages, a suitable scale is somewhere between 1 : 50,000 and 1 : 150,000, depending on the complexity of the coastal features. The largest scale chart available should always be used, for two good reasons; the larger scale chart carries more detail, and it is generally the first to be up-dated as the topography alters.

Country of origin

If possible, it is best to use charts prepared and produced by the country concerned, rather than by some other country. Thus a Finnish chart of Helsinki is likely to be more satisfactory than an American or British or French chart, especially as the foreign charts are almost certainly based on the same survey as the original. When using foreign charts, problems of correction and language arise, but the balance is firmly in favour of the local article.

Soundings

For popular and well-travelled areas almost all charts are equally reliable, but for the more remote regions, the pattern of soundings on a chart can often give an idea of its reliability; scattered soundings with gaps in the coverage and incomplete depth contours are both warning signs. Even in well-surveyed areas it is entirely possible for a small, isolated danger to escape detection. In poorly-surveyed areas the risk is all the greater.

Date of survey

The date of survey, which is given on all good charts, can be a useful guide when considered with the type of country involved. Solid, rocky regions change very slowly and an old survey may be quite acceptable; on the other hand, a river estuary with shifting sand- or mudbanks requires a modern survey. The date of a survey may also affect the quality of the soundings; before the 1930s, soundings were all made by hand, using a lead and line. Later surveys have used echo sounders and (nowadays) side-scan sonar, with more systematic results. Modern position-fixing methods have also vastly improved the quality of surveys.

Corrections

It is essential that any chart purchased should be up-to-date with the latest information available to the charting authority or his agent. New editions are brought out from time to time, incorporating any corrections known to date; subsequently, small corrections are published at regular intervals so that chart users can correct them by hand (see pages 20–1).

Appearance

A chart that looks full and 'interesting' is likely to be better than one that is sparse and bare. Charts of remote regions are likely to be bare, and a yachtsman should remember that he may well be testing such a chart for the first time since the original survey. Very considerable caution is required, particularly in the first approach to the coast.

5   Looking after charts

A chart properly cared for is a very accurate and useful guide to the mariner; a chart which is damaged or has been allowed to get out-of-date is a danger. Some yachtsmen choose to buy new copies of charts at frequent intervals, but charts are not cheap and an outfit can represent a substantial investment. It makes good sense to care for your charts for both safety and financial reasons.

The physical care of charts

Charts are printed on strong, stable paper of good quality, but they can still be damaged quite easily if care is not taken. A few common-sense rules can extend the life of a chart considerably.

1) Draw lightly with a good quality soft pencil.
2) Rub out lines with a good quality soft eraser, but not when the chart is wet.
3) Keep the chart as dry as possible. In a yacht in bad weather this may well be impossible, but at least remove a dripping hat and keep the chart sheltered.
4) Protect the edge of the chart nearest you; wet oilskins rubbing on a wet chart can destroy it in seconds.
5) Do not fold a chart into new creases if you can help it. If essential to make it fit the chart table, then fold it carefully. Take the folds out before putting the chart away.
6) Do not keep charts rolled up, as this makes them difficult and annoying to use. Stow them flat, under the mattress of a bunk if nowhere more suitable is available.
7) When you have finished with a chart, rub off all old work (if the chart is dry), so that it is immediately ready for use next time.
8) In general, treat the chart as a valuable document; protect it from falling on the sole, spilt coffee, dropped food and the other detritus of shipboard life.

Chart correction

There is no need for a chart to get out-of-date within its lifetime (before a new edition is published). Corrections are published by all charting authorities at frequent intervals, and are generally available free of charge (except perhaps for postage). If tackled regularly and systematically, correcting even a large outfit of charts takes little time, though it can become a daunting task if corrections are allowed to accumulate. Chart agents may offer a correction service, maintaining and correcting a yacht's outfit of charts during the off season.

Chart corrections are published in a number of ways:

Urgent navigational warnings are broadcast by coast radio stations on marine frequencies. These warnings are normally temporary in nature, concerning unlit navigational buoys, new wrecks and the like. Any such warnings received should be noted on the chart in pencil until either cancelled or confirmed in a *Notice to Mariners*.

The majority of chart corrections are published at regular intervals (often weekly) by charting authorities, as *Notices to Mariners*. These Notices contain details of new charts or new editions of charts which have just been published, together with corrections to existing charts and publications. If a notice is described as 'Temporary' or 'Preliminary', the details should be noted on the chart in pencil until cancelled or confirmed.

The process of correcting a chart is reasonably straightforward, though it requires a good knowledge of chart symbols (pages 41–2). Corrections should be made neatly and legibly in waterproof ink using a fine pen (violet is the conventional colour for the ink). An example of a *Notice to Mariners* and the resulting chart correction is given in Figure 1. Neatness should be a matter of pride, and an excellent example to follow is the meticulous work of professional correctors who keep charts up-to-date between the time they are printed and the time they are sold. Having made a correction it is *very important* to make a note of the fact in the appropriate place on the chart so that another user can have confidence that the chart has been corrected. Templates of chart symbols exist (e.g. DMAHTC No. 9998 for US charts). These can help keep your work neat.

Sometimes a correction may be so extensive or complicated that it is difficult to describe in words. In this case, a block is produced; this consists of a reprint of the appropriate section of the chart with all the necessary corrections made. The block should be carefully cut out with scissors and offered up in the right place on the chart to ensure

5.1 *Correcting a chart.*

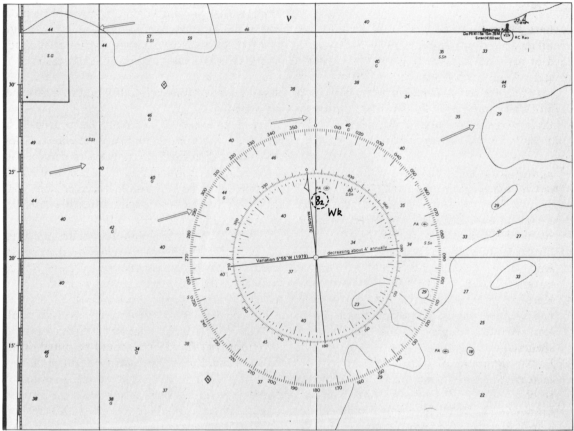

FRANCE, North coast — Bassurelle — Amendment to wreck South-Westward

(1) A depth of 8 metres surrounded by a danger circle ⦂⦂, Wk, is to be inserted in position 50°23′.80N., 0°40′.05E.

(2) The dangerous wreck ⧓ PA close E. is to be deleted.

Chart [*Last correction*] – **9999** [*1395/81*]
French Notice 11/27/81

that it fits. A few pencil strokes across the block and the chart will help in fixing the block later. When you are satisfied that the block fits as well as possible (paper distortions sometimes prevent a perfect fit), the block can then be pasted into place.

A *Notice to Mariners* may well affect several charts of different scales; when making corrections, put in the same quantity of detail as is already shown on the chart. Large-scale charts contain as much detail as possible. As the scale gets smaller, more and more information is left out to keep the chart from getting cluttered. For ex-

ample, the details of buoys inside a harbour are generally omitted from a chart intended for coastal passage making; on ocean charts, only the major landfall lights are shown, and so on.

Commercial charts are not as easy to correct as those published by a charting authority. Most publishers do their best to ensure the chart is correct when sold, but few have any facilities for publishing corrections. *Notices to Mariners* can of course be used, but there is a difficulty if a correction is published as a block, which will not fit the commercial chart.

6   Books and tables

A vast number of books have been published to give the navigator information he needs. The more important of these are described below. It would be a very unusual yacht that would need all these books at one time, so this list should not be considered as a recommended library; it is rather a guide to what is available for any particular purpose.

The pilot

The most important of the books available to the navigator is the *Pilot*, or *Sailing Directions*. A *Pilot* is a narrative description of coastlines, dangers, harbours and facilities, and is an invaluable supplement to the chart. *Pilots* have a history as old as seafaring itself, as they are descended from the verbal account of a coast that one mariner would give to another, even before charts were dreamed of. The modern *Pilot* is the distillation of many years experience by many seamen and contains a wealth of information that is difficult to find elsewhere.

Pilots are of two kinds; official *Pilots* are published by charting authorities, and yachting *Pilots* are published commercially. Each has its advantages and its disadvantages. Official *Pilots* are thorough and detailed, and cover most parts of the world, but they are written with the larger ship in mind; a safe and pleasant haven may be dismissed with the words 'suitable only for small craft with local knowledge'.

Yachting Pilots are a very mixed bunch; some are excellent and others are awful. With a little experience it is not too difficult to form an opinion about the worth of a particular book; if it has been through several editions at regular intervals, it ought to be more up-to-date and better maintained than one that has been re-published only rarely. Perhaps the best way to choose a yachting *Pilot* is on the recommendation of someone you trust.

The advantage of a yachting *Pilot* over an official one is that it has been written with the yachtsman in mind, and it supplies much valuable information that the bigger *Pilot* leaves out. However, there is a major problem of correction. Official *Pilots* are normally supplied with correc-tions in the form of a supplement, which is revised every year or so. Very few yachting *Pilots* offer this service. The more reputable publishers will reprint at frequent intervals so that recent information can be included. It should also be remembered that yachting *Pilots* are only published for popular sailing areas, and do not cover places off the beaten track.

List of lights and fog signals

The *Light List* supplements the information on the chart, in that it gives full details of a light or fog signal, rather than the 'shorthand' version printed on the chart. A description of the structure housing the light is also given for daytime recognition. The details of buoys, light floats and lightships over a certain size are also recorded.

List of radio signals

This document (which may be in several volumes) gives information about the use of radio in navigation, including radio and radar beacons, direction-finding services, weather information services, time signals, radio position-fixing systems and details of port radio stations and pilot vessels.

Tide tables

Tide Tables are published for all areas of the world where tide is significant. Predictions are normally made for a number of 'Standard Ports'. In simple cases the height of the tide at a 'Secondary Port' can be established by applying a simple set of corrections to the data for the nearest Standard Port, but in some parts of the world more elaborate techniques are needed (see page 102).

Pilot charts and ocean passage planning aids

The function of these books or charts is to link together the *Pilots* of different parts of the world by giving recommended tracks between ports, distances, details of weather, currents and potential hazards (such as ice) and much other useful information.

Distance tables

Tables are published of the distances (by the most practical route) between the major ports of the world. This book is of little use to yachtsmen.

Nautical Almanac

The *Nautical Almanac* (published annually) is essential for the practice of astronomical navigation. It gives details of the movements of the sun, moon, major planets and brighter stars, together with the times of sunrise, sunset, moonrise and moonset. Calendars and eclipse predictions are included.

Nautical tables

Several volumes of mathematical tables specially prepared for navigators have been published. The more important of the tables normally included are *Traverse Tables* (see page 177), *Distance Tables* and tables for obtaining a position line from observations of heavenly bodies.

Sight reduction tables

Sight Reduction Tables offer another, simpler way of getting a position line from astronomical observations. The tables chosen for use in this book are the *Sight Reduction Tables for Air Navigation* (US Pub 249, British AP3270) in three volumes. The use of these tables is described in detail on page 148 and following.

Combined Almanacs

Some nautical publishers gather together as much of the above information as they consider their customers will need, and publish it all in one (rather fat) volume. These books can save both space near the chart table and money, but it should be remembered that they must of necessity be more limited in their scope than full-size tables.

Tidal stream atlases

For areas where tidal streams are important and complex, atlases are published giving chartlets which show the direction and strength of the tidal streams for each hour of the tide. Though less exact than the tidal stream information given on the chart, these atlases give an excellent overall impression of the way in which the water moves. They are therefore especially useful for passage planning.

Chart catalogues

When planning a passage, a *Chart Catalogue* gives a rapid view of the scale and coverage of available charts.

7 Drawing and plotting instruments

Chartwork consists essentially of plotting and drawing points (representing positions) and lines (representing directions), and measuring distances. To help the navigator do this quickly and accurately, a number of instruments have been evolved for measuring distances and angles, and for drawing parallel lines. As with many aspects of navigation, there is more than one way of killing a cat, and the same job can often be done with a variety of instruments. Which one to use depends more on the training and preference of the user than any inherent advantage. Each navigator will develop his own approach, but he should at least be familiar with other methods, in case he finds himself navigating a boat which does not carry his favourite tools. Plotting instruments should be purchased on the basis of their quality and accuracy; it is a mistake to buy cheap, flimsy and inaccurate instruments.

Pencils

Pencils should be of good quality, with soft leads (grade 2B is perhaps best). Hard leads dig into the chart and are difficult to erase; on the other hand, soft leads wear down quickly and need frequent sharpening. They can also smear and make the chart messy. Fine lead propelling pencils (0.5 mm) are very convenient as they do not need to be sharpened, but their life tends to be rather short in the adverse surroundings of a small boat at sea. Always carry plenty of spare pencils.

Erasers

Carry a good stock of soft, good quality artists erasers for rubbing out old work. Keep them as dry as possible, and avoid using them on wet charts as this tends to rub off the top layer of the paper and the print.

Dividers

Dividers are used for measuring distances. They should be well made, and smooth and firm in operation without being stiff. It should also be possible to take them to pieces for cleaning and lubrication. Most good dividers for marine use are made of brass with stainless steel points. The points should be sharp enough to catch the surface of the chart

without digging in and making holes; they will need sharpening from time to time. Dividers are inconvenient if they are too short; arms of about 6 in (15 cm) are very suitable. As Figure 1 shows, there are two kinds of dividers; the conventional straight-armed type, and a bowed version which has the advantage that it can be either opened or closed with one hand. Good quality 'straight' dividers can also be used with one hand, given a little practice.

Parallel rulers

Parallel rulers are used for drawing parallel lines (though protractors can also be used – see below). The most common material for these nowadays is clear perspex, though boxwood and brass are also used. It is obviously essential that the two sides of the ruler are parallel with each other and that the ruler moves with a truly parallel motion. A good test is to use the ruler to compare the opposite borders of a chart; if the instrument can carry a line right across the chart, it is clearly satisfactory. There are two types, as shown in Figure 2. Both have their disadvantages; the rolling type is more difficult to use if the boat is moving violently and is likely to roll all over the place when not in use, unless it is properly stowed. The opening type of parallel ruler has to be 'walked' across the chart and is very likely to twist if it catches in a fold or an obstruction under the chart (such as a hinge). The opening ruler shown in Figure 2 is of Captain Field's Improved Pattern, which incorporates a protractor.

Protractors

Because protractors are used in navigation as much for drawing lines as for measuring angles, square or triangular shapes are more useful than round or semi-circular. It is possible to draw on the reverse side of this instrument for plotting fixes by horizontal angles (see page 82). The triangular protractor is illustrated in Figure 3.

Proprietary plotting instruments

A bewildering variety of more or less complicated plotting instruments are offered to the yachtsman, each claiming to make his life easier. Many of them consist of some form of square protractor with a hinged plotting arm attached. All too often these

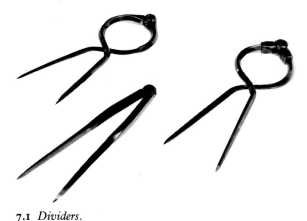

7.1 *Dividers.*

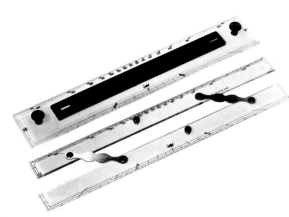

7.2 *Parallel rulers.*

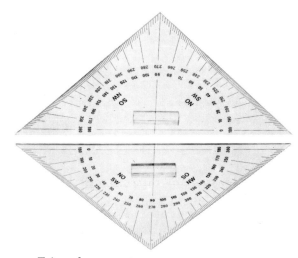

7.3 *Triangular protractors.*

devices are flimsy, clumsy and difficult to stow. It is advisable to try such devices out at sea (by borrowing one) before putting your hand in your pocket.

The station pointer

The station pointer is a protractor with three arms (two of them adjustable). It is used only for horizontal angle fixes (see page 83); on grounds of size, cost and infrequency of use it cannot be recommended for yachts.

Compasses

There are occasions when a pair of compasses is useful for drawing arcs or circles; as with all instruments, a good quality pair should be chosen.

The chart table

The chart table, as the field on which the navigator works, requires some comment, though very few yachtsmen are in a position to have their navigating position designed and built for them. Most yachtsmen have to put up with the arrangements, good or bad, that happen to exist in the boat they buy or are invited to crew in. However, the chart table should be one of the factors in judging a boat. It is difficult to be specific, because a chart table for a fifty-footer would be absurd in a twenty-footer and *vice versa*. The chart table should be as big as practicable with good stowage nearby for books, charts and instruments. It should be protected from the weather, but within easy contact of the helm. It should be strong, with a comfortable seat; some form of restraint should be provided to hold the navigator in place while he works with both hands. And it needs a light which can illuminate the chart at night without troubling off-watch crew members or dazzling the navigator or helmsman.

The techniques for using plotting instruments are described on pages 54–5.

8   The magnetic compass

A compass is a device carried in a vessel to indicate north, so that the heading of the vessel can be known. There are two principal types of compass – the magnetic compass and the gyrocompass. Because of price and a continuous need for electrical power, the gyrocompass is only found on a few large, luxury power yachts. For all practical purposes, the yachtsman's compass is a magnetic compass.

The origins of the magnetic compass are obscure, but it came into general use in European ships in the late Middle Ages. In its earliest form, it consisted of a piece of magnetic iron ore (lodestone) suspended by a thread. The magnetic axis of the stone took up a north-south line. It was later found that this magnetic property could be transferred (by rubbing) to an iron needle. The needle was at first floated in a bowl of water on a piece of cork; later it was suspended from a card, pivoted at the centre. Though vastly improved in materials, construction and accuracy, the modern magnetic compass has altered little in principle.

A typical yacht compass is shown in Figure 1. A number of magnets are suspended below a light

8.1   A yacht compass.

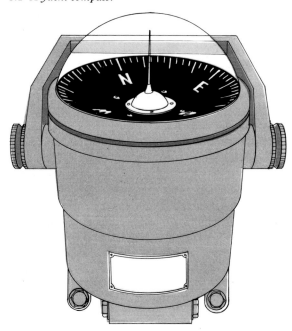

card. The card is free to revolve on a very carefully made pivot. The bowl of the compass is filled with a liquid which helps to damp down oscillations in the card, and which supports much of the weight of the card and needles, thus reducing wear on the pivot. The bowl is fitted with bellows so that the liquid in the bowl may expand and contract in differing temperatures without causing a bubble to form or bursting the bowl.

The compass card
As well as supporting the magnets, the compass card carries graduations to allow the direction of the ship's head to be read. When the compass is installed, a line inside the bowl, called the lubber's line, is lined up with the ship's head. The heading is indicated by the graduation opposite the lubber's line.

Having established the cardinal points of the compass, north south east and west, the early navigators divided the card into half, and half again, and then once more to give the traditional card divided into 32 points, each $11\frac{1}{4}°$. Modern compasses are graduated in degrees clockwise from north; a yacht compass may only have graduations at 5° intervals.

Choosing and installing a compass
Modern yacht compasses are available in many different styles; some have internal gimbals to keep the card level, while some have external gimbals; some are designed for bulkhead mounting, others have to be mounted on a bracket; some carry internal correcting magnets, while others have to be corrected by magnets outside the compass. A steering compass should be selected mainly for its quality; it can be (literally) fatal to make a false economy by buying a cheap, inaccurate and unreliable compass. From different styles of compass, a choice should be made to suit the particular boat and your own preferences; if you are uncertain, the advice of a knowledgeable friend can be invaluable.

The ideal steering compass position is one where the card can be seen easily by the helmsman (on either tack in sailing yachts). It should be remote from any bodies of iron which may cause errors (see page 29), and protected from accidental damage from feet, bodies or equipment. It should also be out of the way. Fairly obviously, the ideal is generally impossible, but any compass installation should be carried out with a great deal of careful thought, together with expert advice if available.

Hand bearing compasses

The navigator often wishes to take a compass bearing of some object, which means that he wants to measure the direction in which the object lies from him. This can sometimes be done by using the steering compass, but often this is not possible. A hand bearing compass is a small compass which can be held in the hand and taken to any convenient part of the deck to take a bearing. A typical hand bearing compass is shown in Figure 2. It incorporates a prism or some other optical device to allow the navigator to look at both the object and the compass card at the same time, so he can record the bearing. As with a steering compass, the hand bearing compass must be carefully chosen. It can be a sobering experience to compare hand bearing compasses at the door of a chandler's shop. A variation of 10° or 15° is not uncommon among cheap compasses.

Transmitting compasses

A transmitting compass consists of a master compass unit which can be mounted almost anywhere, with one or more repeater units to indicate the ship's heading wherever desired. Transmitting compasses are inevitably more expensive than normal compasses of the same quality, and they require continuous electrical power; this can be a problem in a sailing craft. The advantages are the ability to mount the master unit in a position remote from magnetic interference (even up the mast), and the ability to position repeaters without having to worry about magnetic influences.

The gyrocompass

Though the gyrocompass is rarely found in a yacht, it may be found in some large power yachts. The principle is related to the child's gyroscope toy. A spinning wheel is made to interact with the rotation of the earth and the force of gravity to cause the axis of the wheel to point to north. The essential difference between a gyrocompass heading and a magnetic compass heading is that a gyrocompass *points to true north*, whereas a magnetic compass points to magnetic north (see pages 28–9). A gyrocompass takes about 90 minutes to settle after it is first switched on; thereafter, the error should not exceed 1–2°. An adjustment has to be made to the gyrocompass as the latitude of the vessel changes. The gyromagnetic compass is a combination of gyrocompass and magnetic compass; it is often used in aircraft, but rarely at sea.

8.2 *A hand bearing compass.*

9 Using the magnetic compass

The entire earth can be considered to be a magnet, probably because the molten iron core of the earth sustains powerful electric currents as a form of generator. Like an ordinary bar magnet, the earth has two magnetic poles, north and south, connected by lines of force along the surface and in nearby space. The magnets of a compass align themselves with these lines of force to give an indication of direction.

The first problem in using a magnetic compass arises from the fact that the magnetic north pole does not coincide with the geographic north pole; therefore, in general, the magnetic compass does not point to true north. The difference between magnetic north and true north is called the *variation* (see below), which varies in an irregular way with time and with position on the surface of the earth. At present, the north magnetic pole is in about 75°N, 95°W – some 1,000 miles from the true pole. It revolves around the true pole about once every 500 years.

Variation

Variation is a semi-systematic error of the magnetic compass (page 9). It varies both with position on the earth's surface and with time; in areas likely to be visited by yachts, it is unlikely to exceed 30° east or west of the true meridian.

The variation at a particular place can be obtained from two sources. A chart showing curves of equal magnetic variation is called an isogonal chart (Fig. 1). Such a chart will also give information about the rate of change of variation with time. The second and more convenient way to discover the variation is to consult a chart of the area. This will contain (probably in or near the compass roses printed at intervals across the chart) a notice in the following form:

['Variation 6°22′W (1979) increasing about 10′
annually.']

Note that the variation will vary across the chart, and in certain areas the change can be quite marked. For example, when approaching Halifax, Nova Scotia from Newfoundland, the variation will change 10° in less than 500 miles. Small scale

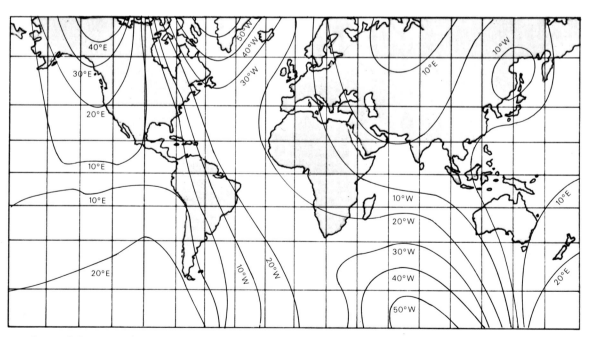

9.1 *Isogonal chart.*

ocean charts often have isogonic lines (lines of equal magnetic variation) printed on them. If the chart has been in circulation for some time without a new edition, the change in variation with time (called the secular change) may also be appreciable.

Variation is expressed as the number of degrees (and minutes) east or west of the true meridian. The navigator often needs to convert a true direction to a magnetic direction and *vice versa*. This is done by applying the variation according to the following rule: (Fig. 2)

Magnetic to true – add easterly variation
True to magnetic – subtract easterly variation
For example:
True direction 155
Variation   6W
Mag direction 161M

True direction 266
Variation   12E
Mag direction 254M

Mag direction 091M
Variation   9W
True direction 082

In certain places, the magnetic variation is disturbed by geological features; details of these local magnetic anomalies are given on charts and in pilot books where they are known. Intense electrical storms can also cause temporary derangement of the magnetic compass.

Deviation

A magnetic compass may also be disturbed by magnetic influences close to it – in a steel vessel, the hull and decks and in wooden or glassfibre boats, the engine or other fittings of ferrous metal (in general, marine grade stainless steels are non-magnetic). These disturbing influences, if they exist, give rise to a systematic error (page 9) called deviation. It varies with the actual heading of the vessel with respect to magnetic north, and can alter with time. Deviation is measured east or west of magnetic north and the process of calibrating a particular compass installation to discover the deviation is called swinging the compass (see page 32). It is most important that a compass is swung periodically (at least once a year), and that

9.2 *Correcting for variation.*

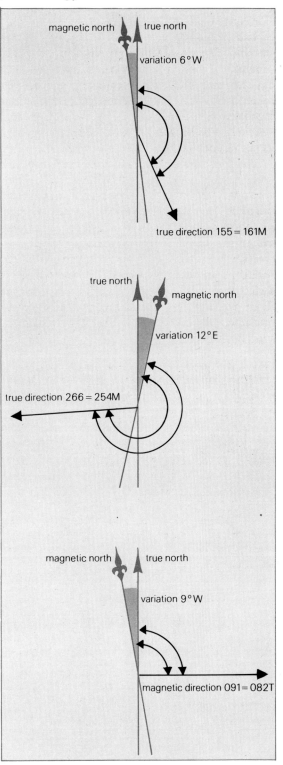

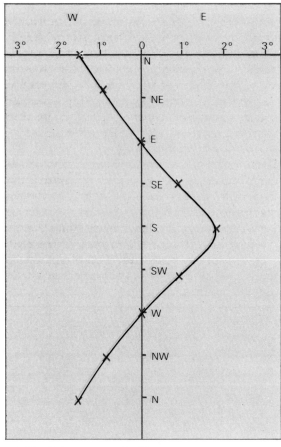

9.3 *Deviation curve and table.*

Ship's Head by Compass		Deviation
N	(000)	$1\frac{1}{2}°$W
NE	(045)	$1°$W
E	(090)	$0°$
SE	(135)	$1°$E
S	(180)	$1\frac{1}{2}°$E
SW	(225)	$1°$E
W	(270)	$0°$
NW	(315)	$1°$W

frequent checks are made to ensure that no unsuspected change in deviation has occurred. The deviation on any heading is normally shown as a table or as a curve (Fig. 3).

If the deviation on any heading is found to exceed 2–3°, the compass should be adjusted by placing small magnets at suitable locations close to the compass. For the majority of wooden or glass-fibre yachts this is a straightforward operation well within the capacity of the owner, but for more difficult installations (steel or ferro-cement boats, or if the engine is close under the compass) a professional compass adjuster should be engaged. The simple procedure is described on page 33.

Converting between compass, magnetic and true headings

Where both variation and deviation exist, it is necessary to convert between true, magnetic and compass headings. To convert a true heading to a compass heading, first apply the variation (from the chart) to obtain a magnetic heading; then look up the deviation for that heading, and apply it following the same rules as for variation, to obtain the compass heading. To convert the opposite way, from compass to true, this procedure is reversed.

Two examples will show the principle:

True heading	154
Variation	3E
Mag heading	151M
Deviation	2E (from deviation table)
Compass heading	149C

Compass heading	357C
Deviation	4E
Mag heading	001M
Variation	11W
True heading	350

Note the use of the suffixes M and C to indicate magnetic and compass headings respectively; true headings are given without a suffix.

If a bearing of an object is taken from the steering compass, the deviation must be applied to the result; this should be the deviation appropriate to the course of the yacht, *not* to the direction of the bearing. Most bearings, however, are taken with a hand bearing compass. If this is held well clear of possible magnetic influences, it can generally be assumed that any deviation will be negligible; in a steel or ferro-cement yacht, hand bearing compasses should be used with caution and held at least three feet (one metre) above deck level.

Heeling error

A large body of iron below the compass can lead to heeling error, which varies in magnitude according to the angle of heel. This can cause an unsteady compass in a rolling vessel, and a sailing yacht may experience different deviations on different tacks for the same heading. Heeling error can only be corrected by a professional adjuster with the proper instruments.

Acceleration errors

Acceleration errors can affect the compass of a high-speed craft making a tight turn, causing the compass either to lag or lead during the turn. The error will disappear as the craft steadies on its new heading.

Summary of errors

Gross errors A good quality compass, overhauled every five years or so, is a thoroughly reliable instrument. Wear in the pivot can cause a sticky card. A bubble in the bowl can cause gross unsteadiness. The most likely cause of gross errors is the careless placing of magnetic objects near the compass; the most common offenders are drink cans and cameras (which have a magnet in the automatic exposure meter).

Systematic errors Apart from variation and deviation, the most common systematic error is misalignment between the lubber line of the compass and the fore-and-aft line of the ship.

Random errors The inherent random errors of a properly adjusted compass are small (1° maximum on 95 per cent of occasions). They are masked by the errors in using the compass in a seaway, discussed on page 52.

10 Swinging and adjusting compasses

Swinging a compass

Swinging a yacht's compass to establish a table or curve of deviation is a relatively quick and easy procedure, which should be done at least once a year. It should not be attempted in a marina, where steel fittings on the pontoons may give unwanted errors. Many different ways of swinging a compass have been described, most of them requiring the use of a pelorus, or dumb compass card, for taking relative bearings of shore objects or a heavenly body. The method described below, whilst marginally less accurate than the best, has the overpowering merit of being both simple and practical*. It can even be done single-handed, if necessary.

The principle is shown in Figure 1. The boat is taken to a convenient location, in smooth water and with land at a reasonable distance off (certainly not less than a mile); then:

1) Head north by compass.
2) Identify *any* object which is right ahead on this heading – a tree, a house, a telegraph pole or anything else that may be readily kept in the mind's eye. If there is no such object right ahead on the heading, then move the boat to a position where there is one.
3) Take a careful bearing of the object with a good quality hand bearing compass.

   The hand bearing compass should be used standing well up and clear of any magnetic influences on the yacht.

   Whilst taking this magnetic bearing, there is no need to keep the boat exactly on the original heading.
4) The difference between the original heading with the object right ahead (north) and the compass bearing of the object is the deviation; if the magnetic bearing is to the left of the heading, deviation is easterly and *vice versa*.
5) Repeat the process on the remaining cardinal points and on the inter-cardinal points (NE, SE, SW, NW). Again, if no object conveniently presents itself on any heading, move to another position where it does.

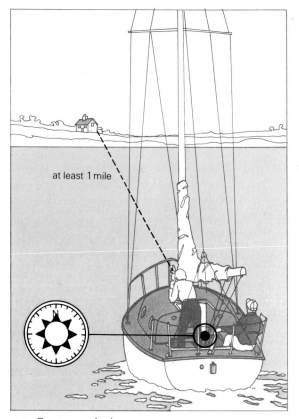

at least 1 mile

10.1 *Compass swinging.*

6) From the results thus obtained, a deviation table or a deviation curve (whichever is preferred) can be drawn up as shown in Figure 2.

   If the deviations are large (more than a few degrees), or appear to follow an irregular pattern, the compass needs to be adjusted. An owner can often do this himself as described below, but if he is in any doubt or difficulty, he should engage a professional compass adjuster.

Steering Compass	Hand Bearing Compass	Deviation
N	357	3°E
NE	044	1°E
E	090	0°
SE	137	2°W
S	183	3°W
SW	226	1°W
W	269	1°E
NW	313	2°E

10.2 *Drawing up the deviation table.*

*This method was suggested by I. McLaren of the City of London Polytechnic's School of Navigation.

Adjusting the compass

In most cases, the owner of a wooden or glassfibre boat should be able to adjust his own compass, assuming that a swing shows this to be necessary. The owner should be careful if the compass installation is close above the engine (say two feet or 0.6 metres); if so, heeling error may be present, which can only be removed by a qualified compass adjuster. Steel boats and ferro-cement boats (which have large quantities of steel in the reinforcing mesh) are more complicated to adjust, and should be left to the professional.

A theoretical study shows that a deviation curve can be broken down into five components, but the 'do-it-yourself' adjuster assumes that only two of these are of any importance.

Coefficient B is caused by hard iron fore and aft of the compass. It produces a deviation which is zero on north and south headings, and at a maximum (with opposite signs) on east and west (Fig. 3).

Coefficient C is caused by hard iron on either which is zero on east and west headings, and at a maximum (with opposite signs) on north and south (Fig. 4).

To correct for the effects of coefficients B and C, it is necessary to steady the yacht in turn on the four cardinal points (magnetic this time, not by compass). This can be done in a similar way to the swinging of the compass, as follows:

1) Using a hand-bearing compass, identify an object on shore which is exactly due north (magnetic) from the yacht; if necessary, move the yacht until you find one.
2) Point the yacht at the object so that it is right ahead.
3) Adjust the compass so that it reads north by means of magnets pointing *athwartships*. Some compasses contain built-in correcting magnets on a special mechanism which can be adjusted by a screwdriver; others have little pockets into which small magnets can be put by 'cut and try' until the deviation disappears. If the compass has no facility at all for correction, it should be rejected as unfit to take to sea.
4) Repeat steps 1, 2 and 3 for a magnetic heading of east, this time adjusting the compass by

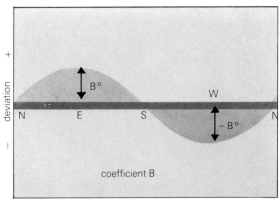

10.3 *Coefficient B deviation.*

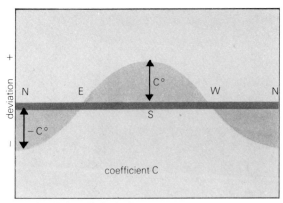

10.4 *Coefficient C deviation.*

means of magnets pointing *fore-and-aft*. This will compensate for coefficient B, in the same way that step 3 compensated for coefficient C.
5) Steady the boat on south (magnetic) and check the deviation; in theory it should be zero but in practice a small deviation may remain. Adjust the athwartships magnets to remove *half* the deviation.
6) Now steady the boat on west (magnetic) and, if necessary, remove half the remaining deviation with the fore-and-aft magnets.
7) Finally swing the ship again to obtain the final deviation table; by now the deviations should be small (no more than 2°).
8) Note that when adjusting a compass, it does not matter which heading is used initially, or which way round the compass the adjustments are made, provided the basic sequence is followed.

Checking a compass

Every opportunity should be taken to check the compass on a variety of headings. Along the coast this can be done by pointing the boat at a known shore object from a known position, and comparing the compass with the magnetic bearing extracted from the chart. A better way is to point the boat along a transit (*range* in US terminology) formed by bringing two charted objects into line (Fig. 5). The opportunities for taking transits are less frequent, but the accuracy is better. Out of sight of land, the compass can be checked by taking bearings of the sun and computing its azimuth (bearing) using the techniques described on page 162. A simpler way is to take the bearing of the sun at sunrise or sunset (when the bottom edge of the sun is about half the sun's diameter above the horizon). Using the boat's latitude and the declination of the sun (from the *Nautical Almanac*), it is possible to work out the azimuth of the sun. A table for this purpose is given in this book (p. 193) and similar tables are published in other books.

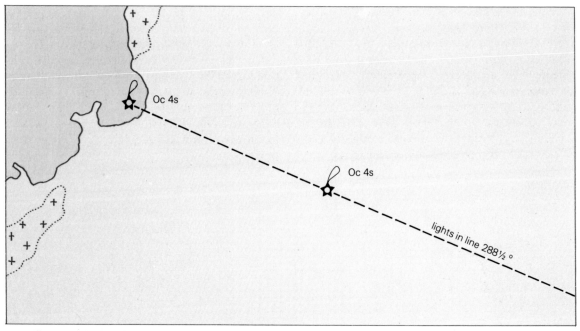

10.5 *Compass checking by transit (range).*

11 Logs and distance measurement

A log is primarily a device for recording the distance travelled through the water by a vessel; most yacht logs now incorporate a speed indicator, which is of more value to the helmsman than to the navigator. The *common log* was invented at the end of the sixteenth century; before then, seamen had estimated the speed of their ship by eye. The common log is shown in Figure 1. It consists of a log-ship of wood, in the form of a quadrant, attached by a bridle to a long line. The log was cast over the stern, and the log line was paid out as the ship sailed away. The line was marked at equal intervals by pieces of knotted cord, and the number of these 'knots' paid out in a fixed time (measured by a sandglass) represented the speed of the ship. At the end of the run, the line was jerked, pulling a pin on one leg of the bridle so that the log-ship lay flat in the water and could be recovered. It is from the common log that the knot, or one nautical mile per hour, is named.

The towed log was invented at the beginning of the nineteenth century and in a developed form is still in use. This consists of a carefully shaped rotor which revolves as it is dragged through the water astern of the ship. The rotation is transmitted along the towing line to a recording device mounted at the stern. Though rather less convenient than other types of log, it is the most accurate.

The majority of modern yacht logs are designed to be fitted to the hull of the yacht. While this is convenient, it leads to the major cause of inaccuracy in such logs. As the hull of the yacht moves through the water, it tends to carry with it a thin layer of water, called the *boundary layer* (Fig. 2). Thus close to the hull (the region in which most hull logs work) the speed of the water past the hull is not the same as the speed of the bulk of the water away from the hull. As the thickness of the boundary layer varies with speed, it is not always possible to correct the log thoroughly for the entire speed range of the boat.

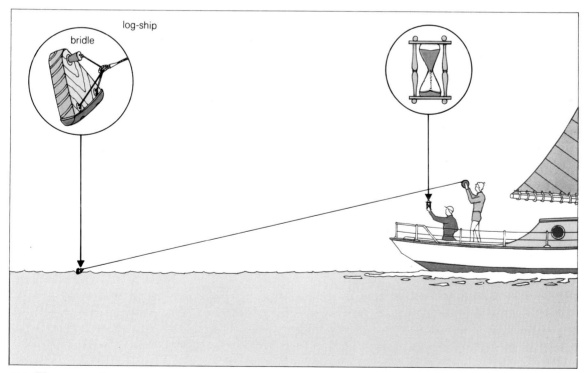

log-ship

bridle

11.1 *The common log.*

Yacht logs are constructed on a variety of physical principles, but it cannot be said that any one type has overwhelming advantages over the others. As with any instrument, accuracy and reliability are related to price and quality.

Impellor logs These consist of a small rotor or paddlewheel projecting into the water through the hull (Fig. 3). The rotation of this device is transmitted to an indicator – sometimes by flexible cable like the speedometer of a car, but more commonly by electronic circuitry. The impellor log tends to be more reliable than other types, but is very prone to fouling by floating weed and marine

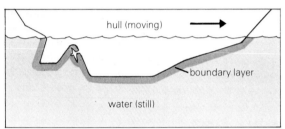

11.2 *Boundary layer.*

growth in spite of the protective measures taken by the manufacturers.

11.3 *Impellor type hull log.*

Electromagnetic logs These work on a principle first discovered by Faraday, that a voltage is induced across the ends of a conductor moving in a magnetic field. In the case of a log, the magnetic field is produced by an electromagnet mounted flush with the skin of the boat and the conductor is the seawater itself (Fig. 4). As the boat moves through the water, a tiny voltage proportional to speed is picked up by two electrodes. This voltage is amplified and applied to the indicating instruments.

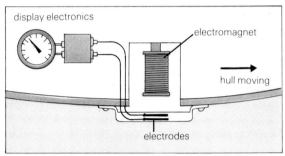

11.4 *Principle of the electromagnetic log.*

Doppler logs These logs use the well-known doppler effect, whereby the pitch of a sound is lower if the source is moving away from the hearer, and higher if the source is moving towards him. In the doppler log, a transducer emits very high frequency sound waves (ultrasound), and a receiver detects the change in pitch caused by the speed of the boat.

Pitot logs The pitot log works in the same way as the air speed indicator in an aircraft. It consists of two tubes (Fig. 5). One tube is bent so that the opening at its end points into the flow of water past it; the other tube has its opening at right angles to the flow. The speed of the boat causes a difference of pressure in the two tubes, which is used to drive a pointer over a scale.

11.5 *The Pitot type log.*

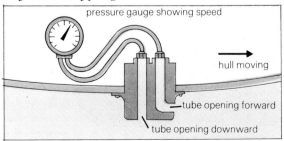

The Dutchman's log This is a way of measuring the speed of a boat when no other means is available. A piece of paper, an empty can or any other scrap object that will float is thrown over the side near the bow, and a stopwatch is used to measure the time it takes this object to pass between two marks a known distance apart on the ship's side. From this, it is easy to calculate the speed of the boat.

For example, if it takes five seconds for the object to move 30 feet, then the speed is given by:

$$\frac{30}{5} \times \frac{3600}{6080} = 3.55 \text{ knots}$$

Or if the object moves ten metres in five seconds,

$$\frac{10}{5} \times \frac{3600}{1852} = 3.9 \text{ knots}$$

Hull logs compared

The impellor type of log is at present the most common; it tends to be more reliable than the other types, though it can be expected that purely electronic logs like the electromagnetic and the doppler type will improve in reliability as development proceeds. In spite of careful design and (in some cases) the fitting of weed deflectors, the impellor log is liable to fouling by floating weed which stops the impellor and makes the log useless until it is cleared. It is also possible for marine growth to slow or stop the rotation. For these reasons, it is essential that an impellor log should be capable of withdrawal into the boat for cleaning. The electromagnetic log is flush with the hull and must be kept clear of marine growth. The doppler log, too, must be kept clean; it can be difficult to find a suitable place for installation, but once that has been done it seems to work satisfactorily. The pitot log has a non-linear scale and only works well at high speed; it is therefore best suited to high-speed motor craft.

Installing a log

A hull log should be installed in a place where it will remain well submerged whatever motion is experienced, and where the flow of water is smooth and undisturbed. For a sailing yacht, a position on the centreline near the forefoot is good. For power yachts, a position well aft but out of the direct slipstream of the propellors is generally best.

Calibration

A good quality towed log will probably not need any calibration, though its accuracy should be checked over a measured distance. All types of hull log *must* be calibrated before they are trusted for navigation. The manufacturer's instructions will explain any adjustments that can be made. The principle is to compare the distance recorded on the log with the distance actually covered. In still water, this can be merely the distance between two known objects, but if a current or tidal stream is running, then two runs should be made, one in each direction.

For example: On the first run over a measured distance of one mile, the log recorded 0.88 miles. On a second run in the opposite direction, it recorded 1.06 miles.

Total distance covered 2 miles
Total distance logged 1.94 miles
Error is 0.06 miles in 2 miles or 3 per cent low.

Summary of errors

Gross errors Any form of impellor log, whether towed or mounted in the hull is liable to fouling by floating weed or debris; it has also been reported that towed log impellors can be swallowed by sharks! Any form of electronic log can suffer serious errors if the batteries driving it are allowed to go flat.

Systematic errors As it works in the boundary layer, any form of hull-mounted log may suffer systematic errors, which may vary with speed. These errors can be corrected by calibration, but only for one speed; it is wise to check for remaining errors at different speeds.

At low speeds, any form of impellor log tends to under-read, due to friction; in rough conditions, the towed log (and probably other types) tends to over-read, as the boat has to travel further over rough seas than it would if the sea were flat.

Random errors The long-term random error of a towed log is probably of the order of 1 per cent on 95 per cent of occasions. A properly calibrated hull log will have an error of 2–5 per cent on 95 per cent of occasions.

12   Depth measurement

One of the primary functions of the navigator is to keep his boat safely afloat in sufficient water, so the measurement of the depth of water is of great importance. The early teachers of navigation used to refer to the three 'Ls' – lead, log and lookout – as the fundamentals of safe navigation. The sounding rod, later replaced by the lead and line, was the first navigational instrument ever devised, and can be seen in use in ancient Egyptian pictures. Depths were traditionally measured in fathoms (1 fathom = 6 feet or 1.8 metres). Most charting authorities now show depths in metres, but many charts marked in fathoms, or fathoms and feet, still remain.

Apart from making sure that there is enough water to float the boat, sounding (the measurement of depth) can also give valuable information to the navigator. The 100 fathom (180 m) line has for centuries been used to warn of the crossing of the continental shelf and the approach of land. On a smaller scale, yachts can use the crossing of chosen depth contours to help fix their position. When doing this, there are two cautions to observe:

1) As is explained on page 100–1, charted depths are referred to as chart datum, a level below which the water rarely falls. Depending on the state of the tide, soundings will generally be deeper than the charted depth (this is a deliberate safety factor). Before it can be compared with a charted depth, a sounding must be *reduced* (see page 104).

2) The value of a sounding for navigation depends very much on the nature of the bottom. If the bottom is irregular, soundings can be difficult to interpret, if not downright misleading.

The lead and line

Every boat should carry a lead and line, even if only for insurance against the failure of an echo sounder. The line should be about ten fathoms (eighteen metres) long, with a seven to eight pound (three and a half kilogram) lead weight on the end. The lead should have a hollow in the bottom for *arming* (see below). After stretching, the line should be accurately marked in feet, fathoms or metres. Any clear system of marking the navigator cares to devise will do, but for interest

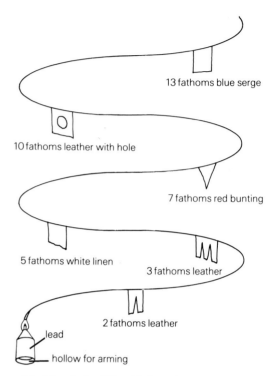

13 fathoms blue serge

10 fathoms leather with hole

7 fathoms red bunting

5 fathoms white linen

3 fathoms leather

2 fathoms leather

lead

hollow for arming

12.1 Marking the lead line (fathoms).

the traditional markings are shown in Figure 1. These marks were carefully chosen; they were easy to remember and the different textures of leather, linen and bunting could be felt in the dark. The leadsman would deduct the 'drift', or distance between his hand and the waterline when sounding at night.

Heaving the lead is an operation which requires practice. When reading off the depth, the line must be vertical; so if the boat is moving ahead, as it generally is, the lead must be heaved ahead (Fig. 2). This process leads the beginner very quickly into a tangle. Running a line of soundings also leads to a soaked and aching arm.

Arming the lead

The lead and line offers one advantage over the echo sounder, in that it can bring up a sample of the bottom for examination. This is done by arming the lead, or filling the hollow in the bottom with tallow or stiff grease. A sample of sand, mud, shingle or broken shell from the sea bottom can often be tied in with information on the chart or in the *Pilot*.

12.2 *Using the lead and line*

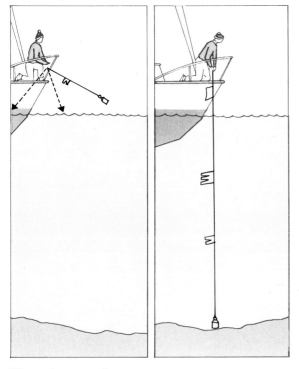

12.3 *Principle of the echo sounder.*

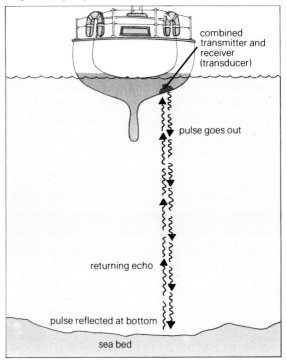

combined transmitter and receiver (transducer)

pulse goes out

returning echo

pulse reflected at bottom

sea bed

The echo sounder

With the advent of modern electronics, the small echo sounder is now both cheap and reliable. For many kinds of sailing they are so convenient as to be almost indispensable. They work by sending out a pulse of sound energy from a transducer mounted in the bottom of the boat. This pulse is reflected off the sea bed, and the echo is detected as it returns to the boat. The time interval between the outgoing pulse and its echo is a measure of the depth of water (Fig. 3).

All echo sounders work on this principle, but there are several different types of display (Fig. 4).

Rotating lamp display A lamp is made to spin around a circular scale in synchronism with the sound pulses. The lamp is made to flash at the zero mark as the pulse is sent out, and it flashes again when the echo is received; the depth can then be read off the scale. This type of display is cheap and simple, but it can be hard to read in bright sunlight.

Meter display This display makes use of a conventional pointer moving over a scale. There is generally provision for a repeater meter to be fitted where the helmsman can see it.

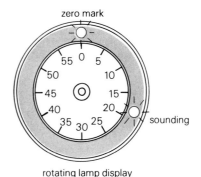

zero mark

sounding

rotating lamp display

12.4 *Types of echo sounder display.*

meter display

12.4 *Types of echo sounder display (cont.).*

depth in metres

digital display

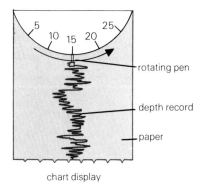

rotating pen

depth record

paper

chart display

quite simple, and the manufacturer's instructions should be followed. In a glassfibre hull, it may be possible to mount the transducer inside the hull with no significant loss of performance. The transducer should be mounted where it has a good 'view' of the seabed and as near the centreline as possible. In a sailing yacht, it may happen that the transducer comes too close to the surface when the yacht is steeply heeled; the solution to this problem is to fit two transducers, one on each side, and to select the 'downhill' transducer with a manual or automatic changeover switch. The more expensive echo sounders can be adjusted to read the depth below the waterline, the depth below the transducer or the depth below the keel. The navigator is free to choose whichever he prefers, but the indicator *must* be clearly marked accordingly.

The principal control in operating an echo sounder is the sensitivity control; this should be adjusted to the minimum level that gives consistent and reliable soundings. Some models are fitted with variable depth alarms, which can be very useful, especially if short-handed.

When using a powerful echo sounder in deep water, it is possible for the echo to be delayed until after the next transmission pulse; the result is a sounding which appears very much shallower than it really is. This can cause considerable alarm until the situation is recognized.

Digital display The depth is displayed in numerical form on a light-emitting diode or liquid crystal display.

Paper recorder Some echo sounders produce a semi-permanent record of the depths measured on a paper chart. This rather more expensive equipment is of great value for fishermen, and it can help in establishing a profile of the bottom when trying to run a line of soundings.

Video display Echo sounders are now appearing which mimic the paper chart recorder by storing digital information to produce a record of the past few minutes' soundings.

Installation and operation

The installation of an echo sounder is normally

Summary of errors

Gross errors Flat batteries; second-time echoes (see above); using the wrong datum (below waterline, transducer or keel).

Systematic errors The two most likely systematic errors are related. On one hand, the timing speed of the recording device may be wrong; on the other, the velocity of sound through the water may differ from the nominal 1500 metres/sec, which is the agreed average value. The best way of establishing if either of these errors exists is by comparing a depth on the echo sounder with that obtained from a carefully marked lead and line. In general, correction of the scanning speed must be carried out by the maker.

Random errors Most echo sounders are surprisingly accurate, and an error of two to four per cent on 95 per cent of occasions is about right.

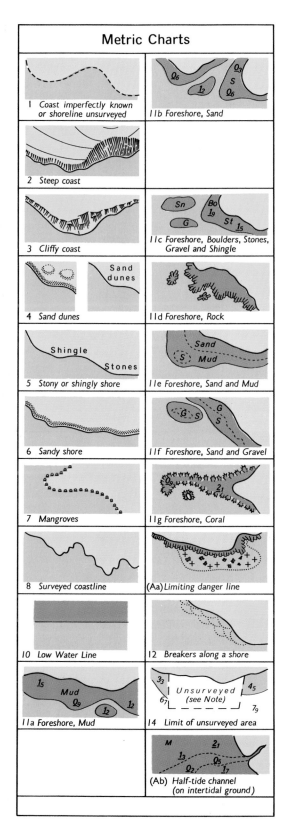

Metric Charts

1 Coast imperfectly known or shoreline unsurveyed	11b Foreshore, Sand
2 Steep coast	
3 Cliffy coast	11c Foreshore, Boulders, Stones, Gravel and Shingle
4 Sand dunes	11d Foreshore, Rock
5 Stony or shingly shore	11e Foreshore, Sand and Mud
6 Sandy shore	11f Foreshore, Sand and Gravel
7 Mangroves	11g Foreshore, Coral
8 Surveyed coastline	(Aa) Limiting danger line
10 Low Water Line	12 Breakers along a shore
11a Foreshore, Mud	14 Limit of unsurveyed area
	(Ab) Half-tide channel (on intertidal ground)

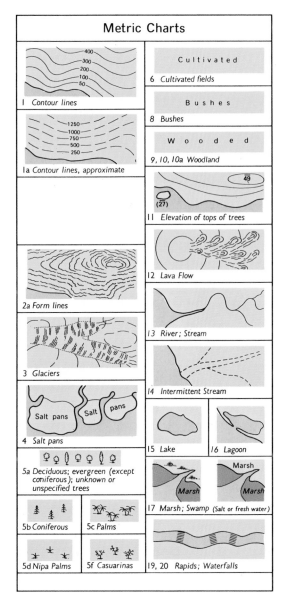

Metric Charts

1 Contour lines	6 Cultivated fields
1a Contour lines, approximate	8 Bushes
	9, 10, 10a Woodland
	11 Elevation of tops of trees
2a Form lines	12 Lava Flow
3 Glaciers	13 River; Stream
	14 Intermittent Stream
4 Salt pans	15 Lake 16 Lagoon
5a Deciduous; evergreen (except coniferous); unknown or unspecified trees	17 Marsh; Swamp (Salt or fresh water)
5b Coniferous 5c Palms	
5d Nipa Palms 5f Casuarinas	19, 20 Rapids; Waterfalls

Selection of symbols used on British Admiralty charts: 'The Coastline' (left) and 'Topography: Natural Features' (right).

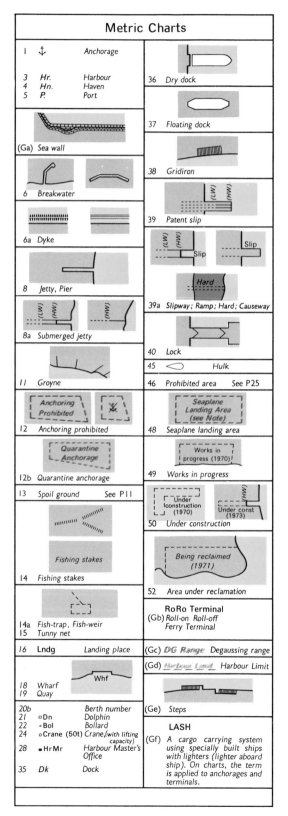

Metric Charts

1	⚓	Anchorage		36		Dry dock
3	Hr.	Harbour		37		Floating dock
4	Hn.	Haven		38		Gridiron
5	P.	Port		39		Patent slip
(Ga)		Sea wall		39a		Slipway; Ramp; Hard; Causeway
6		Breakwater		40		Lock
6a		Dyke		45		Hulk
8		Jetty, Pier		46		Prohibited area See P25
8a		Submerged jetty		48		Seaplane landing area
11		Groyne		49		Works in progress
12		Anchoring prohibited		50		Under construction
12b		Quarantine anchorage		52		Area under reclamation
13		Spoil ground See P11		(Gb)		Roll-on Roll-off Ferry Terminal
14		Fishing stakes		(Gc)	DG Range	Degaussing range
14a		Fish-trap, Fish-weir		(Gd)		Harbour Limit
15		Tunny net		(Ge)		Steps
16	Lndg	Landing place		(Gf)		LASH A cargo carrying system using specially built ships with lighters (lighter aboard ship). On charts, the term is applied to anchorages and terminals.
18		Wharf				
19		Quay				
20b		Berth number				
21	▫Dn	Dolphin				
22	◦Bol	Bollard				
24	◦Crane (50t)	Crane (with lifting capacity)				
28	▪HrMr	Harbour Master's Office				
35	Dk	Dock				

Selection of symbols used on British Admiralty charts: 'Ports and Harbours'.

2. LATERAL MARKS

2.1. Definition of "conventional direction of buoyage"

The "conventional direction of buoyage", which must be indicated in appropriate nautical documents, may be either:
2.1.1. The general direction taken by the mariner when approaching a harbour, river, estuary or other waterway from seaward, or
2.1.2. The direction determined by the proper authority in consultation, where appropriate, with neighbouring countries. In principle it should follow a clockwise direction around land masses.

2.2. Buoyage Regions

There are two international Buoyage Regions A and B where lateral marks differ. These buoyage regions are indicated in Section 8.

2.3. Description of Lateral Marks used in Region A

2.3.1. Port hand Marks

Colour :	Red
Shape (Buoys) :	Cylindrical (can), pillar or spar
Topmark (if any) :	Single red cylinder (can)
Light (when fitted) :	
Colour :	Red
Rhythm :	Any, other than that described in section 2.3.3.

2.3.2. Starboard hand Marks

Colour :	Green
Shape (Buoys):	Conical, pillar or spar
Topmark (if any) :	Single green cone, point upward
Light (when fitted) :	
Colour :	Green
Rhythm :	Any, other than that described in section 2.3.3.

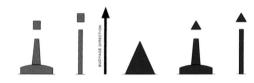

2.3.3. At the point where a channel divides, when proceeding in the "conventional direction of buoyage", a preferred channel may be indicated by a modified Port or Starboard lateral mark as follows:

2.3.3.1. Preferred channel to Starboard :

Colour :	Red with one broad green horizontal band
Shape (Buoys) :	Cylindrical (can), pillar or spar
Topmark (if any) :	Single red cylinder (can)
Light (when fitted) :	
Colour :	Red
Rhythm :	Composite group flashing (2 + 1)

2.3.3.2. Preferred channel to Port :

Colour :	Grmen with one broad red horizontal band
Shape (Buoys) :	Conical, pillar or spar
Topmark (if any) :	Single green cone, point upward
Light (when fitted) :	
Colour :	Green
Rhythm :	Composite group flashing (2 + 1)

2.4. Description of Lateral Marks used in Region B

2.4.1. Port hand Marks

Colour :	Green
Shape (Buoys) :	Cylindrical (can), pillar or spar
Topmark (if any) :	Single green cylinder (can)
Light (when fitted) :	
Colour :	Green
Rhythm :	Any, other than that described in section 2.4.3.

2.4.2. Starboard hand Marks

Colour :	Red
Shape (Buoys) :	Conical, pillar or spar
Topmark (if any) :	Single red cone, point upward
Light (when fitted) :	
Colour :	Red
Rhythm :	Any, other than that described in section 2.4.3.

2.4.3. At the point where a channel divides, when proceeding in the "conventional direction of buoyage", a preferred channel may be indicated by a modified Port or Starboard lateral mark as follows:

2.4.3.1. Preferred channel to Starboard :

Colour :	Green with one broad red horizontal band
Shape (Buoys) :	Cylindrical (can), pillar or spar
Topmark (if any) :	Single green cylinder (can)
Light (when fitted) :	
Colour :	Green
Rhythm :	Composite group flashing (2 + 1)

2.4.3.2. Preferred channel to Port :

Colour :	Red with one broad green horizontal band
Shape (Buoys) :	Conical, pillar or spar
Topmark (if any) :	Single red cone, point upward
Light (when fitted) :	
Colour :	Red
Rhythm :	Composite group flashing (2 + 1)

2.5. General Rules for Lateral Marks

2.5.1. Shapes
Where lateral marks do not rely upon cylindrical (can) or conical buoy shapes for identification they should, where practicable, carry the appropriate topmark.

2.5.2. Numbering or lettering
If marks at the sides of a channel are numbered or lettered, the numbering or lettering shall follow the "conventional direction of buoyage".

3. CARDINAL MARKS

3.1. Definition of Cardinal quadrants and marks

3.1.1. The four quadrants (North, East, South and West) are bounded by the true bearings NW-NE, NE-SE, SE-SW, SW-NW, taken from the point of interest.

3.1.2. A Cardinal mark is named after the quadrant in which it is placed.

3.1.3. The name of a Cardinal mark indicates that it should be passed to the named side of the mark.

3.2. Use of Cardinal Marks

A Cardinal mark may be used, for example:

3.2.1. To indicate that the deepest water in that area is on the named side of the mark.

3.2.2. To indicate the safe side on which to pass a danger.

3.2.3. To draw attention to a feature in a channel such as a bend, a junction, a bifurcation or the end of a shoal.

3.3. Description of Cardinal Marks

3.3.1. North Cardinal Mark

Topmark[a] :	2 black cones, one above the other, points upward
Colour :	Black above yellow
Shape :	Pillar or spar
Light (when fitted) :	
Colour :	White
Rhythm :	VQ or Q

3.3.2. East Cardinal Mark

Topmark[a] :	2 black cones, one above the other, base to base
Colour :	Black with a single broad horizontal yellow band
Shape :	Pillar or spar
Light (when fitted) :	
Colour :	White
Rhythm :	VQ(3) every 5s or Q(3) every 10s

3.3.3. South Cardinal Mark

Topmark[a] :	2 black cones, one above the other, points downward
Colour :	Yellow above black
Shape :	Pillar or spar
Light (when fitted):	
Colour :	White
Rhythm :	VQ(6) + Long flash every 10s or Q(6) + Long flash every 15s

3.3.4. West Cardinal Mark

Topmark [a] :	2 black cones, one above the other, point to point
Colour :	Yellow with a single broad horizontal black band
Shape :	Pillar or spar
Light (when fitted):	
Colour :	White
Rhythm :	VQ(9) every 10s or Q(9) every 15s

IALA Maritime Buoyage System: Lateral Marks (Regions A and B) and Cardinal Marks.

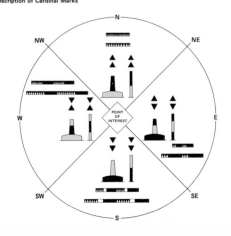

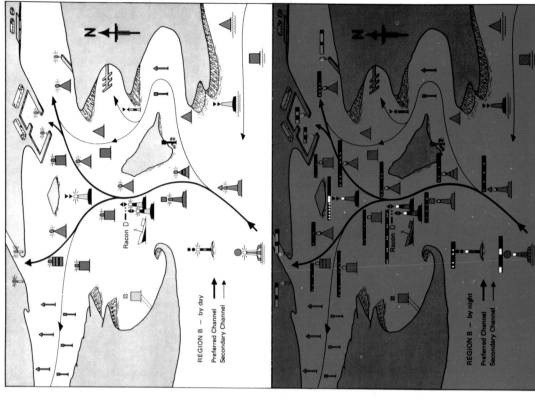

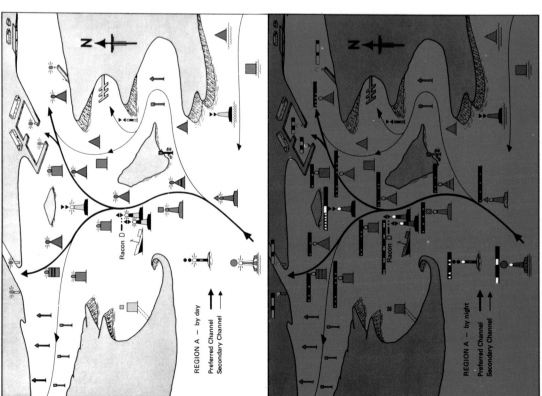

IALA Maritime Buoyage System: Region A and Region B by day and by night.

13 The sextant

The sextant is an instrument for measuring angles with great accuracy; it is indispensable for astronomical navigation, where it is used to measure the angle between a heavenly body and the horizon, and it can also be of great value for accurate coastal navigation. The sextant was invented in the eighteenth century by Hadley, though an unpublished design for a very similar instrument was later found amongst Sir Isaac Newton's papers. Hadley's instrument was known as a quadrant, though it is better described as an octant (Fig. 1). This means that the scale covers one eighth of a circle (45°). The sextant has a scale covering one sixth of a circle (60°), which means that it is capable of measuring larger angles than the octant; apart from this, there is no practical difference between them. The quintant (one fifth of a circle) was popular at one time.

13.1 Hadley type quadrant.

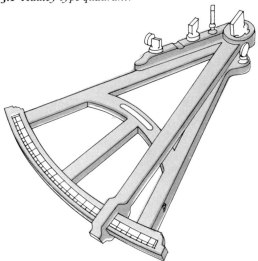

Construction and principle of the sextant

The principle upon which the sextant works is shown in Figure 2. A mirror, called the index glass, is pivoted at the top of the instrument, and the angle to which it has been set is indicated on a scale. A second mirror, called the horizon glass, is only half silvered, so the observer can both look through it to see the object directly in front of him, and at the same time see a second object reflected in the silvered portion of the horizon glass and the

index glass. If the observer adjusts the index glass so that the images of the two objects co-incide, then it can be shown that the angle between the two objects is exactly twice the angle between the two mirrors. The 60° scale of the sextant is therefore capable of measuring angles between objects of up to 120°, and the scale is graduated accordingly.

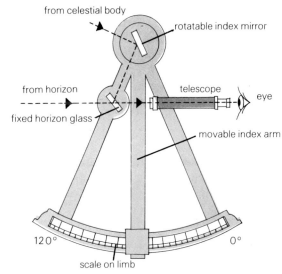

13.2 The principle of the sextant.

The construction of a modern sextant is shown in Figure 3. The frame of the instrument carries the scale, marked to 120°. The index glass is

13.3 A modern sextant.

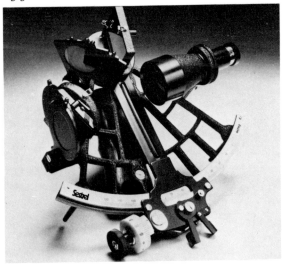

mounted on a pivoted arm, with an indicating mark that moves over the scale; a micrometer device is fitted to allow angles to be read off with great precision (0.1 minutes of arc in the best sextants). The actual observations are made through a telescope mounted on the frame, with the horizon glass in front of it. Both the horizon glass and the index glass are fitted with shades which can be used to reduce the light entering the telescope (for example, when observing the sun). The radius of the scale is usually about six inches (ten centimetres). A light is sometimes provided to illuminate the scale at night.

For accurate work, a good quality, metal-framed sextant with a good telescope is essential, but it costs a lot of money. Plastic sextants are now on the market, and the better ones can be quite satisfactory for use in a yacht; they are rather more difficult to use and adjust (and of course less accurate), but cost only a fraction of the price. A beginner would do well to consider buying a plastic sextant for his first attempts, and the experienced navigator might carry a plastic sextant as a spare in case his good one gets smashed.

Figure 4 shows how to read the scale of the sextant; in general this is easy enough. The degrees are read from the scale along the bottom of

13.4 *The micrometer scale of a sextant.*

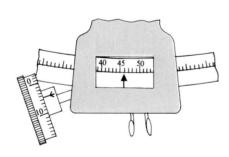

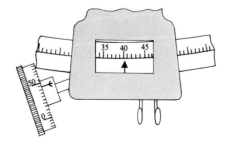

the instrument, and the minutes of arc are read from the micrometer drum. It is easier to estimate fractions of a minute by eye, though a small vernier is provided for accurate interpolation. Care is needed when the reading is close to an exact degree; it is not difficult to get confused about the number of degrees and record, for example, an angle of 49°59′ as 50°59′.

Care of the sextant
Though remarkably robust, a sextant is a precision instrument and should be handled with care; avoid bumps and bangs which can put the sextant out of adjustment. Keep it in its box except when actually using it, and make sure that the box is securely stowed. Fit a lanyard to the handle or the frame so that you can hang it around your neck to prevent it going over the side if you lose your balance in a seaway. It is not a bad idea to keep it buttoned inside a jacket except when actually making observations; this will protect it against knocks and help to keep it dry. If the sextant should be knocked or dropped, it is *essential* to check the calibration (see below) before it is used again.

A sextant should be protected from seawater as much as possible. A little spray is not too bad, provided that the instrument is carefully cleaned and dried before being put away (take care when cleaning the mirrors lest they are put out of adjustment). If conditions are such that the sextant is likely to get soaked, then it should be left in the box until the weather moderates.

Mirrors and telescope lenses should be cleaned with a lens cloth or soft tissue; the scale and micrometer rack can be coated with a thin film of petroleum jelly, and the moving parts can be given a tiny drop of light machine oil occasionally.

The Royal Air Force arranged for their sextant boxes to be marked 'handle like eggs'. It is an excellent principle.

Errors of the sextant
The sextant has a number of systematic errors, which must be corrected as described below. They are:

Perpendicularity error: in which the index glass is not at right angles to the plane of the scale.

Side error: in which the horizon glass is not at right angles to the plane of the scale.

Index error: in which the two mirrors are not parallel when the scale reading is zero.

These errors must be corrected in the following order:

Perpendicularity error This can be checked by setting the arm to about half-way along the scale, and then looking into the index glass from the top of the instrument. By moving the eye, it is possible to find a position in which the edge of the scale and its reflection in the mirror can be seen. If they are not co-incident, then perpendicularity error exists. It is removed by carefully adjusting the adjusting screw on the index glass mounting.

Side error This is corrected in conjunction with the index error (see below). It can be seen by looking at a point (e.g. a star) or a vertical line (a mast, or the horizon if the sextant is held on its side) with the arm set at zero. If the reflected image falls to one side of the direct image, then side error exists (Fig. 5). It is corrected by the outer adjusting screw on the horizon glass mounting.

Index error This is shown by the two images failing to co-incide when the sextant is set to zero. It is corrected by the inner adjusting screw on the horizon glass mounting.

When adjusting side error and index error, the two adjusting screws interact, so the procedure is to remove half the side error, then half the index error, then half the remaining side error and so on. Side error should be removed entirely, but some index error may remain; it should not be allowed to be more than a few minutes of arc.

Index error should be checked every time the sextant is used. Bring the two images of the horizon into coincidence and look at the reading (Fig. 6). Index error may be *on the arc*, in which case it should be subtracted from all readings taken. If it is *off the arc*, it should be added.

Random errors

The random errors inherent in the sextant itself are so small that they are entirely submerged by personal and observational errors, such as the quality of the horizon or the motion of the vessel. These errors are discussed in the sections which describe the actual methods of using the sextant.

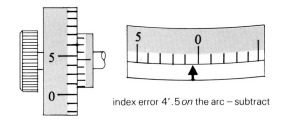

index error 4′.5 *on* the arc – subtract

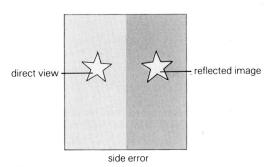

direct view — reflected image

side error

13.5 *Side error.*

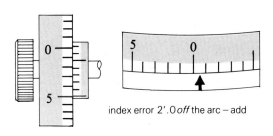

index error 2′.0 *off* the arc – add

13.6 *Index error.*

14 The use of radio in navigation

Though they are entirely a twentieth century development, radio aids to navigation are now of the utmost importance, even to the yacht navigator. They vary in cost and complexity from the very cheap and simple to the present limits of technology, and span a very large section of the electromagnetic spectrum (Table 1). Each radio aid of importance to the yacht navigator is discussed in detail later in this book, but this section summarizes what is available.

A domestic radio receiver capable of working on MF and LF can be used for receiving time signals and weather information near the coast. Some broadcasting organizations transmit special weather forecasts for shipping, but even forecasts intended mainly for shore consumption can give valuable indications of the weather to come at sea.

A communications receiver covers LF, MF and HF bands, and can be used to receive information specially broadcast for the mariner, such as continuous time signals, weather information and navigational warnings. These sets require a properly installed antenna to be effective, but are capable of world-wide reception.

Marine communications equipment (Fig. 1) working on MF, HF or VHF channels, is primarily intended for communications, but is a useful source of weather forecasts and navigational warnings.

Facsimile equipment works with a suitable communications receiver to produce synoptic charts and other weather information, transmitted by national meteorological authorities. Its price makes it very much a luxury item, but it can be found in some larger yachts.

Radiobeacons are perhaps the most useful radio navigational aid for the yachtsman, as they require relatively simple and cheap equipment. A radiobeacon is a transmitter sited at some point of navigational interest, such as a lighthouse or lightship. It transmits on an LF frequency, either continuously or at regular frequent intervals. The ship carries a suitable receiver connected to a directional antenna, with which the operator can

	Band	Frequency Range	Wavelength Range	Use at Sea
VLF	Very Low Frequency	3–30kHz	100km–10km	Omega. Submarine Communications
LF	Low Frequency	30–300kHz	10km–1000m	Radio beacons, time signals, Decca, Loran C, Consol
MF	Medium Frequency	300kHz–3MHz	1000–100m	Morse and voice communications, radio beacons, weather broadcasts, domestic radio
HF	High Frequency	3MHz–30MHz	100–10m	Long range communications, weather broadcasts, time signals, facsimile, CB radio
VHF	Very High Frequency	30MHz–300MHz	10–1m	Communications, radio lighthouse, satellite navigation, VOR, domestic radio broadcasts
UHF	Ultra High Frequency	300MHz–3GHz	1m–10cm	Satellite navigation
SHF	Super High Frequency	3GHz–30GHz	10cm–1cm	Radar

1kHz = 1 kilohertz = 1000 cycles per second
1MHz = 1 megahertz = 1,000,000 cycles per second
1GHz = 1 gigahertz = 1,000,000,000 cycles per second

Table 1 *The electromagnetic spectrum.*

take a bearing of the transmitter. This gives him a position line (see page 68) which can be used to help him fix his position. Though useful at any time, radiobeacons are of particular value in poor visibility when visual fixing is not possible.

Consol and the radio lighthouse are methods of giving the navigator a bearing of the transmitter without requiring him to have a directional antenna. Consol operates on LF, and the (experimental) radio lighthouse on VHF. The transmitted signal is made to appear as if it comes from a rotating aerial, so that the navigator can work out his bearing from the transmitter by a simple counting or timing process.

Hyperbolic navigational systems provide navigational information by measuring time delays between signals received from pairs of special transmitters. There are a number of different systems, but they all require special equipment and are uncommon in yachts on the grounds of cost and complexity; as electronic equipment becomes progressively cheaper, this situation may alter.

The major hyperbolic aids are:

Omega operates on VLF and offers global coverage with a network of eight transmitters. Accuracy is of the order of one mile, when properly corrected.

Loran C also works on LF, with a range of some 1,500 nautical miles. The coverage is good in the North Atlantic, near the United States, and in much of the Pacific Ocean. Accuracy depends on a number of factors, but is of the order of a few miles at 1,000 miles from the chain. The earlier Loran A system on MF is now becoming obsolete.

Decca is another LF system, but intended for greater accuracy at shorter ranges. Decca chains are established in many strategic areas of the world, and have a maximum range of about 250 miles. Accuracy is very high, less than 100 yards (100 m) under ideal conditions.

VOR (VHF omni range) is a radio aid primarily used by aircraft. A single transmitter sends out a signal which is received and decoded in the aircraft to operate a pointer giving the magnetic bearing of the transmitter. Where VOR beacons are suitably sited, they can also be of value to yachtsmen.

Radar can be of great value both for navigation and for collision avoidance in poor visibility. A rotating aerial on the ship sends out a pulse of energy in the SHF band (a wavelength of about three centimetres). A big enough object in the path of the beam will reflect back sufficient energy to be detected by the radar receiver. The time taken by the returning echo, allied to the direction in which it was sent, is displayed as a form of electronic map on a PPI (plan position indicator). The maximum range depends mostly on the height of the aerial and the size of the object to be detected. The accuracy of the range displayed is high, of the bearing less so. Some important buoys and lightships are fitted with a *Racon*, a device to enhance and mark the echo so that the object may be positively identified.

Satellite navigation requires a special VHF or UHF receiver and a microcomputer (Fig. 2). It uses a network of earth satellites which transmit information to the receiver; from this data, the computer can calculate a position to within a quarter of a mile with simple equipment or a few metres with the best available. Although a very sophisticated system, the price has recently fallen enough to make it attractive to the better-off yachtsman.

14.1 *Marine radio receiver display unit.*

14.2 *Satellite navigator display unit.*

15   Records

Records of various kinds are essential to good navigation, for a number of reasons:

1) It is unwise to rely upon memory in a yacht at sea. A sudden change in circumstances can drive an important piece of information out of your mind, or the significance of some seemingly unimportant fact may be overlooked. If facts are recorded, they will not be forgotten, and can be reviewed later if necessary.
2) No navigator can be on duty for 24 hours a day, so the watch on deck must keep records of the ship's progress while the navigator is resting.
3) Scribbled notes on the chart or on scraps of paper can be rubbed out or thrown away by mistake.
4) As this book stresses throughout, errors are an integral part of the navigation process. Accurate and complete records are the only way of checking and backtracking when things have gone wrong, as they inevitably will from time to time.
5) Apart from its value in navigation, a well-kept log is an invaluable reminder of past enjoyment, and makes evocative reading in times to come.
6) In some cases, the keeping of a log is a legal requirement.

The deck log

The deck log is the most important of the navigational records, as it contains (or should contain) a full record of courses and distances sailed, and notes of any event of navigational importance, such as the raising of a light or the passing of a buoy. The deck log, kept by the watch on deck, is the raw material from which the dead reckoning (see page 56) is determined.

Many of the pre-printed logs offered for sale to yachtsmen carry lines and columns which are not really suitable for the purpose. It is often better to choose a suitably stout notebook and to rule up columns as you wish. A form of log which has proved useful at sea is shown in Figure 1. Most of the columns are obvious and self-explanatory, but the two columns 'course ordered' and 'course steered' may cause surprise. The purpose is to acknowledge the fact that a sailing yacht is controlled by the wind direction; when sailing on the wind, for example, a small change in wind direction may make it impossible for the helmsman to keep on the compass course ordered. If the wind shift was a major one, then clearly the skipper and navigator must be told, but a minor shift only needs a suitable entry in the 'course steered' column. Similar problems may occur when running square to a shifting wind.

The log should be written up frequently; any significant event should be recorded at once; and regular entries of course, distance run, wind, weather and barometer should be made at least once an hour, even when ocean sailing hundreds of miles from land. This is necessary because a close watch must be kept on the barometer; in the tropics, suppression of the diurnal variation of the barometer or a fall of three millibars (0.09 in) may herald the approach of a tropical revolving storm (see page 92).

In coastal waters, it is better to fill in the log at half-hourly intervals and when racing, quarter-hourly intervals may be appropriate. Provided the navigator is firm about keeping the log, crews generally welcome the need to write up the log as a regular incident in their watch. It also helps if the crew are encouraged to use the log to record anything of interest or amusement such as marine life seen, comments on the cooking, or a description of a hilarious misadventure on the foredeck.

Navigator's work book

The navigator should keep his own work book, in which he writes down information from the deck log, and any calculations he may make such as the times and heights of high water, times of sunrise and sunset, details of fixing information and passage notes. The format for this work book is entirely a matter of choice, but some clear and consistent scheme should be adopted and every entry should include the date and time.

Sight book

Many navigators choose to keep the records and calculations for astronomical sights in a special book, though they can equally well be kept in the work book if desired. In either case, a suitable format is given on page 157.

15.1 *Layout for a yacht's log.*

Time	Course Ordered	Course Steered	Log Reading	Wind & Weather	Barometer	Remarks

Barometers and barographs

The importance of keeping a record of barometer readings has already been mentioned in the section on the deck log. In conjunction with other meteorological data, the barometer can give warning of the weather to come; in tropical regions it is often the first sign you get of impending bad weather.

A barograph can be used to keep a continuous record of barometric pressure on a paper chart for a week. A barograph must be suitably designed for use at sea in a small yacht, as the motion of the vessel can otherwise shake the recording pen to such an extent as to obliterate the record. The instrument should always be mounted on a resilient bed with the recording arm lying athwartships. It should be firmly secured in position as befits any delicate instrument.

16 Boat and crew

As the object of navigation is to guide the vessel on her way from place to place, the performance of the boat and the crew is obviously of great importance; if either differ from that expected, then errors in navigation will arise. It is necessary to monitor and 'calibrate' the boat and the crew, in particular each individual helmsman.

Leeway Unless the wind is coming from right ahead or right astern, it exerts a force which tends to push the boat (sail or power) sideways. The extent to which it succeeds depends upon several factors:

1) Obviously, the strength of the sideways component of the wind.
2) The underwater profile of the boat. Deep keel sailing yachts and displacement power craft will resist leeway better than shoal draught cruisers or power boats with little sideways 'grip' of the water.
3) Boats with high freeboards offer more windage than those without.
4) Large or confused seas increase leeway by checking the forward component of the vessel's progress.

Various methods of measuring leeway have been suggested, such as measuring the angle at which the line of a towed log streams astern, or by watching the bearing of floating objects thrown over the stern; however these measurements are not easily taken and are unreliable. An educated guess is perhaps the best approach, and as the navigator gains experience in different conditions, these guesses will improve in accuracy. Because of the wide variation in boats and conditions, it is not possible to give much guidance in a book, but noticeable leeway can be expected if the wind and sea cause the boat to labour (see page 60).

Leeway is normally allowed for as an error in the heading, as shown in Figure 1.

Weather helm and lee helm Sailing yachts are generally trimmed to give some weather helm, so that the boat tends to luff up into the wind. An experienced helmsman will allow for this effect and steer the course that he is given, but the majority of helmsmen will actually make good a course somewhat to weather of the course they have been given. By a happy coincidence, it very

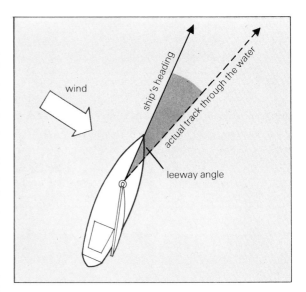

16.1 *Allowing for leeway.*

often happens that the weatherway made in this manner cancels out the leeway described above. Trimming the boat to give lee helm should be avoided, not only because it makes the boat more difficult to handle, but also because additional leeway is generated by inexperienced helmsmen.

Broaching If the wind and sea are such that the boat tends to broach from time to time, the actual course achieved will be somewhat to weather of that ordered; again, the effect is not so marked if the helmsman is experienced.

Dead running In a sailing yacht with the wind right aft, most helmsmen will flinch away from a possible gybe, and so make good a course to weather. The best thing to do in these circumstances is to alter course to put the wind on the quarter. Not only does this give the helmsman peace of mind; it also increases boat speed to a useful extent. Otherwise, rig a strong preventer on the main boom.

Helmsman errors It is not easy to steer a proper course in a yacht when the compass card is swinging about all the time; an inexperienced helmsman will often fail to ensure that the boat swings equally on either side of the desired course, so that an error accumulates while he is steering. Equally, such a helmsman will often report a course which is not in fact his actual mean course. The solution to this problem is to study (unobtrusively) the performance of each helmsman and apply a suitable correction when necessary. It sometimes helps to restrict the choice of courses to even 5° intervals, as indifferent helmsmen find it easier to steer on a prominent mark on the compass card.

It is not uncommon for helmsmen to steer the wrong course, generally because of a blunder in handing over from one helmsman to the next. This often takes the form of transposed digits, so that he steers 335 instead of 353 for example. Some navigators like to write the course to be steered on a slate beside the compass, but this in itself can be a source of error if it is not kept up to date at all times.

Another point to watch, with experienced sailing helmsmen, is that they will generally try to sail the boat to its best speed by altering course to follow changes in the wind. This is a good thing if they are punctilious about recording what they do in the deck log; otherwise it can lead to serious errors in the reckoning.

THE RECKONING

17 Plotting techniques

Plotting navigational information on a chart is a very straightforward process, though the techniques depend upon the actual equipment used; English-speaking navigators tend to prefer a parallel ruler for laying off directions and parallel lines, whilst European navigators often use a pair of triangular set squares for the same purpose. Various types of protractor and proprietary plotting aids are also on the market, each with its adherents. The newcomer is advised to experiment with as many of these devices as he can, to find out which suits him best.

It must always be remembered that a chart is a precise and valuable document and it must always be treated with care; when plotting, a soft-leaded pencil should be used, with as little pressure as will lead to a distinct line.

Some of the more common plotting tasks are illustrated, using different types of plotting aids.

1) Chart graduations at different scales.
2) Plotting and recording position in latitude and longitude.
3) Ways of drawing a line parallel to another.
4) Drawing a line in a given direction; measuring the direction of a line.
5) Position by direction and distance; direction and distance between two points.

17.1 *Chart graduations.*

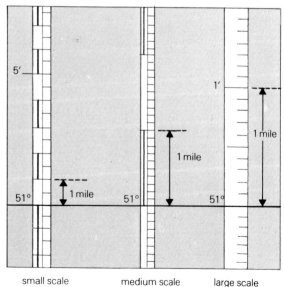

small scale   medium scale   large scale

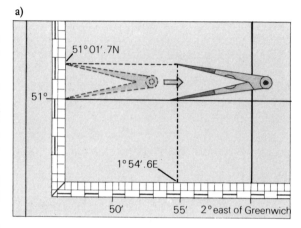

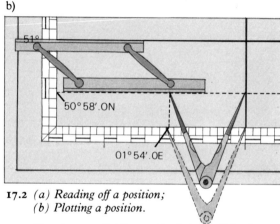

17.2 *(a) Reading off a position;*
(b) Plotting a position.

17.3 *Drawing parallel lines with: (a) parallel ruler;*
(b) protractor.

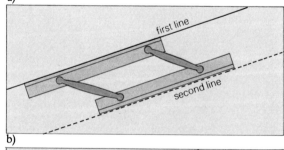

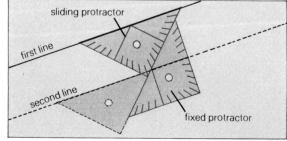

17.4 *Drawing or measuring directions with: (a) parallel ruler; (b) protractor.*

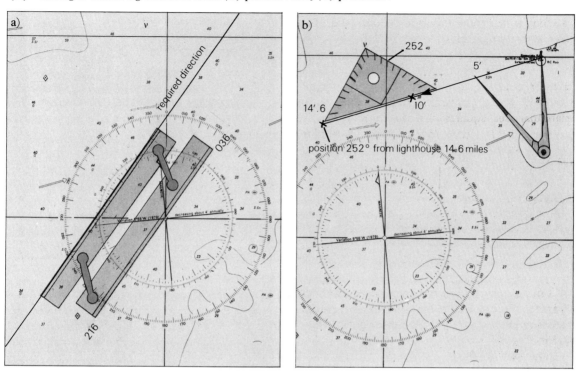

17.5 *(a) Position as a bearing and distance; (b) Course and distance between two points.*

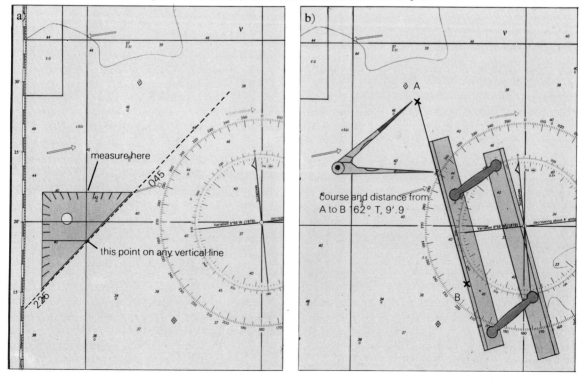

18 Dead reckoning

Dead reckoning is the name given to the process of estimating the position of a vessel by taking account of the direction and distance that the vessel travels, together with other factors such as estimations of current, tidal stream and leeway (see Note, page 67). At one time the dead reckoning position was also known as the *position by account*, which expresses the situation very well; the position is derived by accounting, rather like a book-keeper, for all the factors that have affected the progress of the ship. The term *dead reckoning* is generally thought to be a corruption of ded (= deduced) reckoning.

Dead reckoning is an essential corner-stone of the whole edifice of navigation, because it is the only way in which an estimate can be made of the position without any reference to the world outside the vessel. Whatever the conditions, a DR can always be kept up, using the simple and almost totally reliable instruments of compass, log, chart and pilot book. Obtaining a position by observing outside objects requires objects to observe and instruments and visibility with which to observe them; these may not be available when they are most wanted, but a DR is.

If dead reckoning could be made totally accurate, then there would be no need for any other form of navigation (except perhaps as a check). Inertial navigation is merely a very sophisticated automatic DR system; the inertial navigation equipment in inter-continental ballistic missiles can guide them to within a few tens of metres of a chosen point across a distance of thousands of miles. Manual DR, especially at sea in a small craft, is very substantially less accurate than this, and unless outside objects can be observed at suitable intervals, the errors of the DR will rapidly grow to a point where it becomes difficult to make sensible decisions. Despite this drawback, a navigator should always maintain a dead reckoning plot, for the following reasons:

1) As has been said, a DR is derived from sources within the vessel and is always available.
2) Because it is totally independent of outside observations, it acts as an invaluable check on such observations. Consistency between independent sources of information is a great comfort.

3) For some types of observation (e.g. astronomical position lines), a dead reckoning position is needed as a starting point for the calculations.

The simplest aspect of dead reckoning is illustrated in Figure 1. In this example, account is taken only of the direction and distance travelled by the yacht, as recorded in the log. A starting position is needed to begin the process; when setting off on a passage, this could be typically a pinpoint fix on the fairway buoy or some other mark near the harbour entrance. A fix is marked as a dot with a small circle around it, the time and (generally) the log reading.

In Figure 1, the deck log records that the departure fix was taken at 0800, at which time the log was set to 0.0 (Beware the confusion between log or deck log, a document, and log in the sense of an instrument for recording distance travelled.) The yacht set off on a course of 075 compass. With a variation of 6°W and a deviation of 2°E, this represents a true course of 075 − 6 + 2 = 071 (see page 30). A line can now be drawn on the chart from the departure point in the direction 071 true, to represent the course of the yacht across the sea.

At 0900, the deck log records that the log read 5.6 miles; therefore in the hour since the fix, the yacht has travelled 5.6 nautical miles. This distance can be measured off with dividers against the latitude scale of the chart and pricked off along the course line. A tick across the line represents the DR position at 0900.

At 1000, the log read 11.7, whilst the course has been held constant at 075 compass or 071 true. In the hour since 0900, the yacht has travelled 11.7 − 5.6 = 6.1 miles. This distance can now be pricked off along the course line to give the 1000 DR position.

At 1025, course was altered to 150 compass (variation still 6°W, deviation now 1°W), with the log reading 14.5. The yacht therefore continued past the 1000 DR on the original course of 071 true a distance of 14.5 − 11.7 = 2.8 miles; the DR position for 1025 can now be plotted. From this point a new course line can be drawn in the direction 150 − 6 − 1 = 143 true.

At 1100 the log read 17.5, which represents a distance travelled along the new course line of 3.0 miles since the alteration at 1025; the 1100 DR can now be plotted.

18.1 *Basic DR plotting: log entries and resulting plot.*

Time	Course Ordered	Course Steered	Log Reading	Wind & Weather	Barometer	Remarks
0800			0·0	NW 4		Position 235M Bassurelle L.V 4·5 mi Set course 260M
0900	260	260	5·6	NW 4		
1000	260	255	11·7	WNW 5		Headed off by windshift
1025	260	255	14·5			Tacked to 350M
1100	350	350	17·5	WNW 4		
	NB: Variation 6°W throughout.					

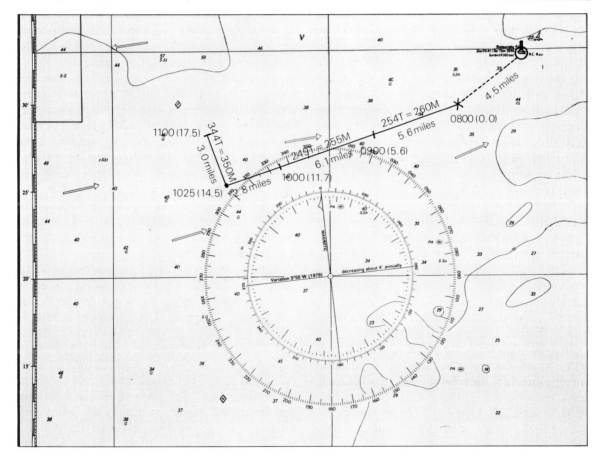

At its simplest, dead reckoning navigation requires no more than this – the meticulous recording of courses, times and log readings, followed by a very simple plotting exercise. There are many areas, notably in the Mediterranean and the Baltic, where the procedure described above is often all that is required; however in general it is necessary to allow also for external influences on the boat, notably those caused by tidal streams or currents. This is described overleaf.

19 Allowing for tides, currents and leeway

Two main factors generally complicate the plotting of a dead reckoning position. They are:
1) Movement of the water in which the boat floats.
2) The effect on the boat of the wind.

Water movement – tidal streams and currents

The simple dead reckoning so far described plots the movement of the boat through the water under the influence of its sails or its engine. But the navigator needs to know his position relative to the land, rather than the water; the positions of harbours, rocks, shoals and navigational marks of all kinds are defined with respect to the land. If the water in which the boat moves is itself moving, then the navigator will not know where he is unless he makes a suitable allowance.

The body of water which supports a boat may move under one of two influences (sometimes, but rarely, found in combination). These are:

1) Currents, caused by the long-term circulation of water around the globe, or by winds blowing in the same direction for a prolonged time.
2) Tidal streams, caused by the gravitational influence of the sun and the moon. Tidal streams are cyclic in nature, continually varying in strength and direction.

In order to make allowances for the effects of tidal streams or currents, the navigator must be able to find out their likely magnitudes and directions. For currents, the best place to find this information is in a suitable pilot book for the region. Methods of discovering the forecasted tidal streams are described on pages 106–9. In both cases, more accurate information for the moment can sometimes be obtained by direct observation – for example by watching the flow of water past some fixed object such as a navigational buoy.

If a boat is moving through water which is itself moving, the resulting motion will be a combination of the two (Fig. 1). In air navigation it is common to combine the two influences (in this case the aircraft's velocity and the wind velocity)

19.1 *Combined effect of boat and water movement.*

19.2 *Boat and water movement treated separately.*

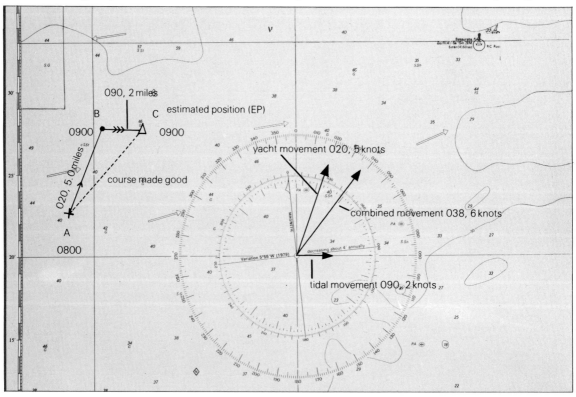

by using an instrument such as a Dalton computer. The normal approach at sea is to consider the two velocities as acting separately, as shown in Figure 2. In this example, it is assumed that the vessel is steering a course of 110 at five knots; after one hour, the yacht will have moved five miles from its starting position at A to position B. However, during this same hour, the water itself will have moved one mile in a direction of 220. If this movement is plotted from B, it leads to the corrected DR position (C); this is the position that the yacht would reach under the combined influences of its own motion and the tidal stream. Of course, in the real world these two influences are acting together so that the ship follows the line AC directly, rather than travelling along two sides of a triangle – from A to B to C. It is a convenient fiction to pretend otherwise.

The effects of both tidal streams and currents can be estimated in this way; the difference is that it will normally be necessary to revise the estimate of tidal stream every hour, whereas a current will set in much the same direction and speed for days

19.3 *Sailing into a fair or foul stream.*

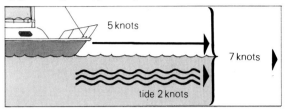

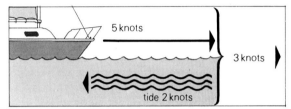

or weeks (in some cases, permanently). Sometimes it is possible to simplify the procedure; if a yacht is steaming directly into a foul stream, the position can be derived merely by subtracting the speed of the water flow from the speed of the boat (Fig. 3). On the other hand, if the boat is travelling exactly with the flow, the speeds can be added.

19.4 *Setting course to allow for the stream.*

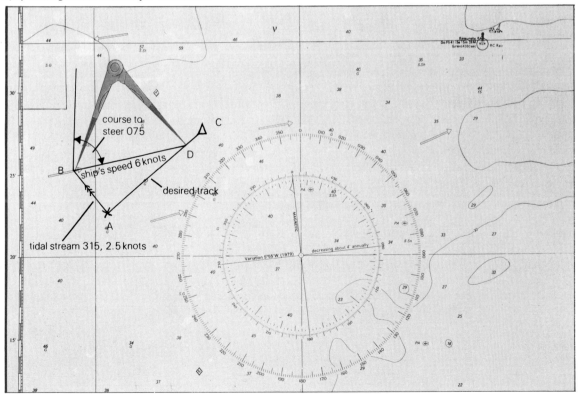

The effect of a current or tidal stream, unless it is directly fair or foul, is to set the vessel to one side or the other of its chosen course. Frequently the navigator will wish his craft to follow a particular line across the sea bed, and wants to know what course to steer so that the resulting movement is correct (Fig. 4). To do this, he must plot the tidal triangle 'in reverse'. He knows the direction in which he wants to go (AC in the diagram), the speed and direction of the stream, and the speed at which his own boat will travel. The first step is to plot the tidal stream or current for a suitable interval (say, an hour) *backwards* from C to B. This is equivalent to saying that a floating object dropped at B will get to C after the given interval of time, solely by virtue of the water movement. The next step is to take a pair of dividers set to a distance corresponding to the boat's speed (for the same time interval as that chosen for the water flow). One point is set on position B, and an arc is struck to cut the line AC (at position D). The course to steer is given by the direction DB; even though he starts from A, he will track along the line AC if he steers in that direction.

Leeway

The wind, acting on the topsides of a yacht, can also affect its progress. A wind directly ahead or astern will simply slow down or speed up the boat – an allowance very easily made. If, however, the wind is blowing from the side, then the vessel will be blown downwind of her proper course (Fig. 5).

It is difficult to say how much allowance should be made for leeway, as circumstances can vary so much. Clearly, the stronger the wind, the more it is on the beam and the surface area of the topsides and superstructure will all tend to increase leeway; so will the underwater shape of the vessel, as it controls the 'grip' of the boat on the water. Sea state is also a factor, because a boat that is continually stopped by an awkward sea will make more leeway than one that is sailing smoothly. Very strong winds also cause a surface drift (the beginnings of a current) which can be significant, and a

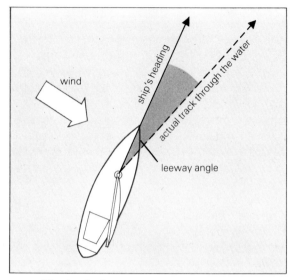

19.5 *Allowing for leeway.*

boat that slides down the face of a breaking wave will also be pushed to leeward. The following suggestions may be useful: (wind on the beam, sea state appropriate to wind)

Craft	Moderate	Gale
Offshore racer	none	5°
Motor sailer	5°	10°
Displacement power boat	5°	10°
Semi-displacement boat	5°	15°

In very severe conditions, leeway can become very marked; a total set of two and a half knots under the influence of windage, surface water drift and breaking seas has been observed, in Force eleven storms in the Bay of Biscay.

No satisfactory way of measuring leeway, other than guessing it, has yet been devised. Suggestions have included observing the angle between the trailing line of a towed log and the ship's fore-and-aft line; measuring the angle of the wake similarly; watching the progress of floating rubbish thrown over the side; and various instruments of differing impracticability. None of these approaches seems to offer much advantage over an educated guess.

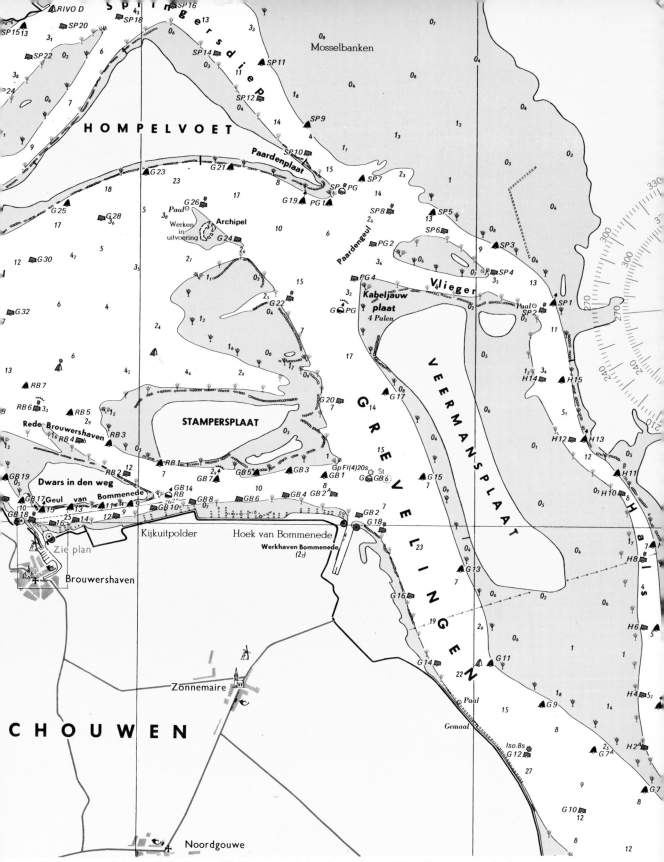

Extract from Netherlands Hydrographic Bureau yachting chart 1807.1 (Grevelingenmeer). Scale 1 : 50,000.

Reproduced from a portion of Chart No. 1807.1 by permission of Netherlands Hydrographic Bureau.

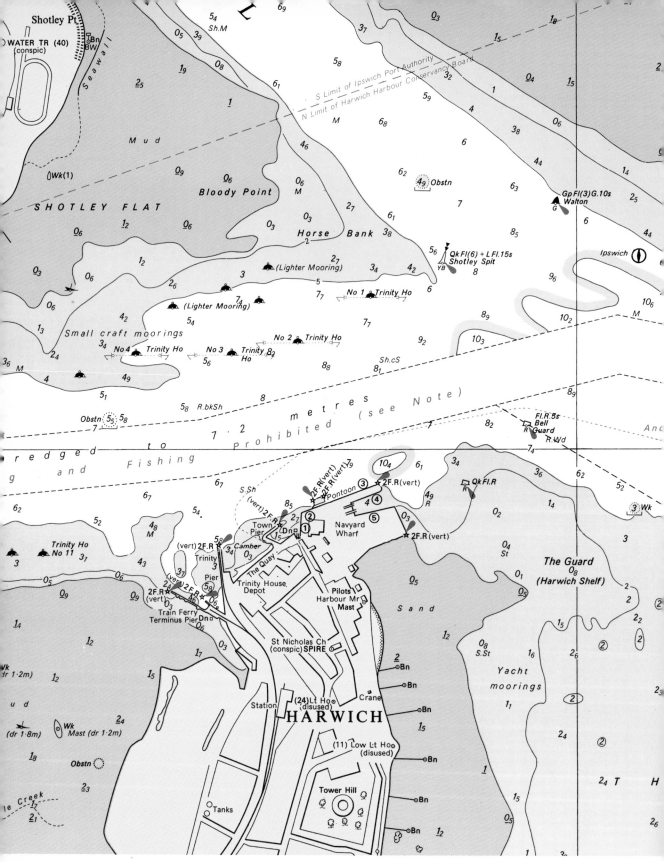

Extract from British Admiralty chart 1491 (Harwich Harbour). Scale 1 : 10,000.

Reproduced from a portion of BA Chart No. 1491 with the sanction of the Controller, HM Stationery Office and of the Hydrographer of the Navy.

Extract from a French commercial chart: Editions Cartographiques Maritimes chart 1014 (Iles Anglo-Normandes).
Scale 1 : 100,000.

63

Extract from Brazilian Government chart 110 (Baia de Todos os Santos). Scale 1 : 65,000.

20 Dead reckoning accuracy

Whilst a carefully maintained dead reckoning position is the bedrock on which sound navigation is based, it is essential to understand very clearly the errors involved in the process. These are generally quite large and errors accumulate as time passes, so there may come a time when the position becomes so uncertain as to cause problems. The navigator would hope to reduce these uncertainties by making observations of objects on shore or in the heavens, but this is not always possible at the time the navigator would like them most.

Before dead reckoning can even be attempted, systematic errors in the equipment must be removed; the compass must be properly adjusted (or at least swung), and the log must be calibrated. The correct magnetic variation appropriate to the date and the ship's position must be used; on a long passage, the variation can alter markedly from beginning to end.

Each of the components used in plotting the DR position makes its own contribution to the error of the final position:

Compass and steering errors Random errors in the compass and in the steering of the yacht will result in her being to one side or the other of the chosen track.

Log error The random error in the log results in the vessel being either ahead or astern of the calculated position.

Tidal stream or current errors Errors in the estimation of the direction or the strength of the flow velocity will affect the final position.

Leeway estimation error Errors in estimating leeway will result in an across-the-track error rather like compass error. When the actual leeway is small, then any error in estimation will have little effect, but in bad conditions this factor may become significant.

It is possible to make separate allowances for these different errors but the process would be laborious. A more practical approach is to lump all the errors together in the form of a radial error, such that the boat is known to lie (with 95 per cent probability) within a circle centred on the DR position. As all the errors tend to increase with the distance travelled, it is convenient to express the radius of this circle as a proportion of the distance run since the last fix.

Table 1 offers some suggestions for 95 per cent DR errors under various conditions. Rough seas will tend to increase certain errors, and the speed of the craft will affect the relative influence of tidal stream or current errors. There may be circumstances which cause these errors to be smaller than the table indicates; if the passage is an out-and-home run, then certain heading errors will cancel out. On a longer passage, errors in assessing tidal streams will tend to diminish because of the cyclic nature of the flow.

Table 1 *95 per cent dead reckoning errors*

Error	Magnitude		Percentage	
	Calm	Rough	Calm	Rough
Five knot yacht				
Compass and steering	3°	5°	5	8
Log	2½ %	5 %	2½	5
Tidal stream or current	¾ kt	¾ kt	15	15
Leeway	2°	5°	3	8
Combined error			*16*	*19*
Ten knot yacht				
Compass and steering	3°	5°	5	8
Log	2½ %	5 %	2½	5
Tidal stream or current	¾ kt	¾ kt	7½	7½
Leeway	2°	5°	3	8
Combined error			*10*	*14*

20.1 *Dead reckoning – an example.*

Time	Course Ordered	Course Steered	Log Reading	Wind & Weather	Barometer	Remarks
14 30	—	—	81·2	SW5	1005	Position 240°. Lt. Vess 4mi. Co.270C (port tack). Deviation 3°E Leeway 5° Tidal stream 1400-1500 112°T. 1·9 kts
1500	270	270	84·3	SW5	1004	Tidal stream 1500-1600 125 1·5 kts
1600	270	265	90·1	SW5	1003	Tidal stream 1600-1700 210 1·0 kts
1625	270	265	93·3	SW5	1003	Tacked to 175C Deviation 1°W Leeway still 5°
1700	175	175	96·5	SW5	1002	(Estimated position 241°. Lt. Vess 15.1mi

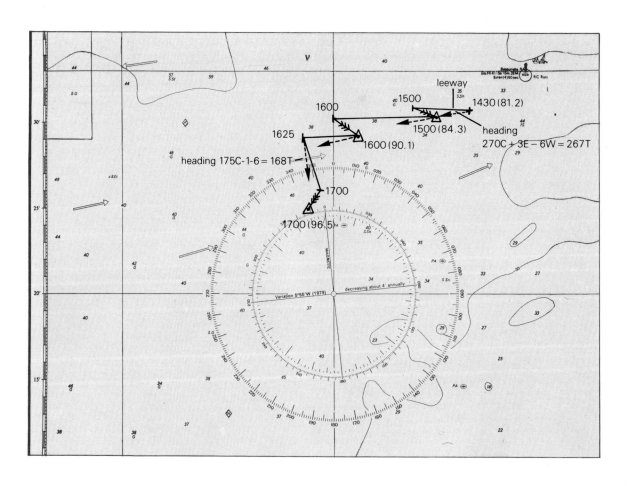

Experienced navigators may consider the figures in Table 1 to be far too pessimistic. They should firstly remember that the errors are the 95 per cent (20 : 1) errors and that the most likely error is about half as big. They might also reflect on how often they have found themselves very much further from their dead reckoning than they thought possible; a gloomy view of errors avoids nasty surprises.

Example of DR navigation

Figure 1 gives an extract from a deck log, together with the plotted dead reckoning and estimated positions. The reader may care to plot these figures as an exercise on a spare chart or plotting sheet, to confirm that the principles and techniques have been mastered.

However, mastering the techniques of DR navigation in the classroom or on the dining-room table is only part of the story. The problem takes on a different dimension at sea; the chart table is likely to be small and cramped; the motion may be violent; the navigator may be wet, cold, tired and possibly seasick; and the boat's actual progress through the water may be fitful and erratic, especially if under sail. The result of all these factors is that work at the chart-table becomes very slow and prone to blunders. The track on the chart soon begins to look like the ramblings of a drunken spider, and everything seems to take longer than you expect. In consequence it is all too easy for the navigator to lose confidence in what he is doing. Only by a firm effort of will can he maintain a grip on what is happening, and preserve his trust in the information he is using (a trust tempered by an understanding of the likely errors). And when anxiety does set in (as it inevitably will), the rest of the crew must never be allowed to see it.

Note: Experienced navigators will notice that the definition of dead reckoning given in this book differs from that in most text books – this is a deliberate step as I feel it reflects the actual situation exactly.

THE POSITION

21 The position line

The position line is one of the most important and useful concepts in navigation; it can be defined as follows:

> A position line is a line on the surface of the earth on which the navigator knows, from some observation, his vessel must lie.

In the USA, the term 'line of position' (LOP) is used.

The importance of the position line concept is that it can be used to complement the other fundamental idea in navigation, the dead reckoning. The DR position is derived from a knowledge of the direction and distance the yacht has sailed, with allowances for external factors such as tidal stream and leeway; but the errors in the DR position grow rapidly with time (see page 65), so the position becomes more and more uncertain. If the navigator can observe some external object whose position he knows, he can use the measurements he makes to correct his DR position or reduce his uncertainty. It does not matter what object is observed, provided that the navigator knows where it is at the time he observes it; it can be on land, attached to the sea bed (like a buoy), in orbit round the earth (moon, navigation satellites), part of the solar system or a distant star. Equally, it does not matter how the observation is made, provided the navigator can estimate its accuracy; he can use visible light, radio waves (radio beacons, radar etc), or sound (echo sounder). The instruments he uses can range from the incredibly advanced (such as a navigational satellite receiver) to the centuries-old simplicity of a weight on a piece of line for measuring the depth of water; some position lines can be observed without any instruments at all.

Position lines can therefore be derived in many ways, the most likely of which to come the yacht navigator's way are described below.

Transits (Ranges) (Figure 1)

The simplest of all position lines can be obtained when the navigator sees that two objects, whose positions he knows, are in line with each other. All he has to do is to draw a line on the chart through the two positions, and he knows that he must lie somewhere on the extension of that line, which is known as a *transit* or *range*. A transit has the great

21.1 *The transit (range).*

advantage that it can be observed without any instruments at all (except, perhaps, binoculars), but the drawback is that transits only appear at variable and unpredictable intervals; the navigator should keep his eyes open to take advantage of any transits that appear, and train his watchkeepers to do the same. If a compass bearing is taken of two objects in transit, it can be used to check the accuracy of the compass.

Accuracy The accuracy of a transit depends upon the relative positions of the objects and the ship; it will be least when the two objects are close together and the ship is a long way away. However the transit is likely to be the most accurate position line that a navigator will find, and he should use them whenever possible.

Compass bearings (Figure 2)

A compass bearing of an object is taken by observing the object across a suitable compass card and noting the direction in which the object lies; it

21.2 *The compass bearing.*

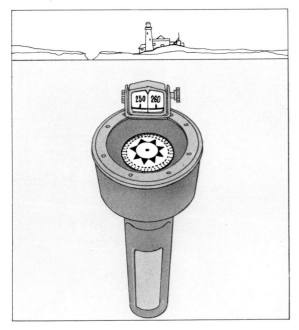

follows that the vessel must be on a line in the *opposite* direction from the object. For example, if the object is north of the ship, then the ship must be south of the object. Compass bearings are generally taken with a hand bearing compass (see page 27), but may also be taken with the steering compass if suitably sited, perhaps with the aid of an attachment known as an *azimuth ring*. Compass bearings must be corrected for variation and deviation (see pages 28–30); for the steering compass, deviation can be obtained from the deviation table (*Caution*: use the deviation that applies to the ship's head, not the deviation that applies to the observed bearing). Hand bearing compasses can be assumed to be free of deviation if used well away from magnetic influences; this may prove difficult in steel or ferro-cement yachts. Compass bearings are quick and easy to take, and are the most common type of position line in yacht navigation, though the accuracy can be poor in bad conditions. **Accuracy** The 95 per cent error of a bearing taken with a good quality compass and properly corrected for variation (and deviation if appropriate) will be of the order of:

Good conditions $+/- 2°$
Moderate conditions $+/- 5°$
Rough conditions $+/- 10°$

Relative bearings (Figure 3)

A *relative* bearing of an object is one that is taken using the ship's head as a reference, using a device known as a *pelorus*. This looks very like a compass card, but it is fixed on the fore-and-aft line of the ship, rather than north. A relative bearing is given as red or green (depending on whether the object is to port or starboard), followed by the number of degrees from ship's head; thus an object exactly on the port beam has a relative bearing of red 90 and an object almost right astern on the starboard side may have a relative bearing of green 175. (US practice is to measure relative bearings on a scale of 0°–360° from ship's head.)

Before the navigator can use a relative bearing as a position line, he has to convert it to a compass bearing; this is done by adding or subtracting the relative bearing to the ship's compass course – red bearings (on the port side) are subtracted and green bearings (starboard side) are added.

For example:	1	2
Ship's head	125	335
Relative bearing	R90	G 175
Compass bearing	035	510 − 360 = 150

Having obtained a compass bearing, the navigator must correct it for variation and deviation in the same way as any other compass bearing (*Caution*: use the deviation that applies to the ship's head, not the deviation that applies to the compass bearing derived from the relative bearing).

21.3 *The relative bearing.*

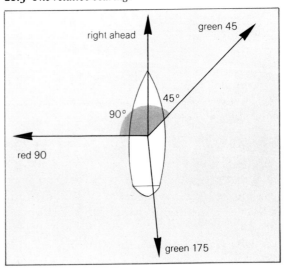

When taking relative bearings for navigational purposes, it is necessary to record ship's head at the same time as each of the relative bearings; the helmsman should be instructed to call out the exact heading at the moment that the bearing is taken. Given the marked tendency for yachts to yaw, even in a moderate seaway, the headings called out may not be the same for each bearing, or the same as the course the helmsman is steering.

Accuracy As a relative bearing involves the additional operation of recording the ship's compass heading at the moment of observation, the resulting position lines are somewhat less accurate than compass bearings taken directly. The 95 per cent errors of properly observed and corrected relative bearings will be of the order of:

Good conditions   + / − 4°
Moderate conditions + / − 8°
Rough conditions   + / −15°

Horizontal angle (Figure 4)

A position line can be obtained if the angle between two objects is measured. From simple geometry, it can be shown that the resulting position line is an arc of a circle. The advantage of such a position line from a horizontal angle is that it is substantially more accurate than a compass bearing, especially if a sextant (see pages 45–7) is used to measure the angle in question. It is not usual to plot a single position line of this kind as the work involved, though simple, is tedious. It is more usual to plot a *horizontal angle fix*, using two measured angles between three objects. Methods of plotting this type of fix, potentially the most accurate visual fix available, are given on pages 82–3.

21.4 *Horizontal angle position line.*

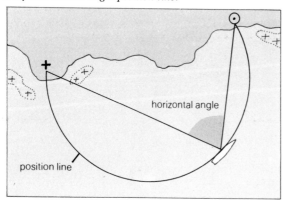

Range by narrow horizontal angle (Figure 5)

An alternative way of getting a position line from the angle between two objects is to use trigonometry to compute a range; for best results, the two objects should be at approximately the same distance from the vessel. A typical opportunity to use this type of position line is when both the left- and right-hand edges of a small island are visible at a distance; knowing the width of the island and the angle between the two edges, the range of the mid-point of the island can be calculated.

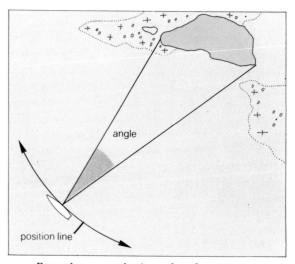

21.5 *Range by narrow horizontal angle.*

Calculation Using a calculator with trigonometric functions or trigonometric tables, the range is given by:

$$R = \frac{D}{2 \cdot \tan \cdot (A)} \quad \text{or} \quad \frac{D}{2}\cot \cdot (A)$$

where D is the distance between the objects
A is the measured angle
R is the range of the mid-point between the objects

A rule of thumb, accurate within 2 per cent for angles between 1° and 25° is:

Range (n miles) =
$$\frac{28 \times \text{distance between object (n miles)}}{\text{measured angle (degrees)}}$$

Accuracy The accuracy of the resulting position line will depend upon the accuracy with which the angle can be measured, and on the accuracy with which the distance between the two objects can be determined. Using a sextant, a 95 per cent accuracy of better than 5 per cent should be obtainable even in the case of small angles; 2 per cent might be a more typical figure. If the angle is measured by a less precise technique the accuracy will be substantially impaired.

Range by vertical sextant angle (Figure 6)

If the angle between the top and the bottom of an object of known height can be measured, then simple trigonometry makes it possible to calculate the distance of the object from the observer. Whilst this approach can be very useful, it is not always possible to see the base of an object (particularly from the low height of eye of a yacht's deck), as the base of the object will be below the sea horizon.

Another complication can be atmospheric refraction, which tends to bend rays of light and alter the measured angle. The tables published for finding range by vertical sextant angle vary in their scope from those intended for short-range work only to others that can give a useful range of a distant mountain peak; the table on pages 187–91 can be used for any type of observation, and includes corrections for atmospheric refraction.

As the angles to be measured are frequently small (perhaps only a few minutes of arc), an accurate measuring device, such as a sextant (see pages 45–7) must be used.

The height of shore objects is generally given with respect to mean high water springs or mean high water (see your chart title to find out which); depending on the state of the tide when an observation is made, the actual height of the object will probably be greater than the charted value; for accurate results, the charted height should be corrected to allow for the height of the tide. If this is not done, it will appear that the vessel is closer to the object than is actually the case; many navigators use this fact as a sort of in-built safety margin. When taking an angle of a lighthouse, the charted height refers to the height of the lantern itself, not the top of the structure.

Calculation Most books of nautical tables and yachtsman's almanacs contain tables to convert angles to distances; an alternative table is given on pages 187–190 of this book. The formula on which this table is based is given on page 184. It is laborious, but could be used on a programmable calculator.

Accuracy The accuracy of a vertical sextant angle position line depends upon a comparison between the accuracy of the sextant observation and the angle actually measured; the smaller the measured angle, the less reliable the results. The 95 per cent accuracy of a vertical sextant angle observation by an average user is probably one minute for a metal sextant and five minutes for a plastic one. Thus, if the angle measured is 50 minutes of arc, the 95 per cent error of the resulting distance would be about 2 per cent if using a metal sextant, or 10 per cent if using a plastic sextant. It would be unwise to expect a 95 per cent error of less than 2 per cent under normal circumstances.

Lights dipping or raising (Figure 7)

A special case of the vertical angle position line is of great value to the navigator; it happens when the angle to measure is zero, i.e., when the top of the object is exactly on the horizon. It is of most value at night, when approaching or leaving a coastline. Most navigational lights can be seen when the actual lantern is below the horizon, as the beam is scattered by the air to give what is called the *loom* of the light – a bright patch over the position of the light. It is immediately obvious when the light itself comes over the horizon; the loom is replaced by clear, bright flashes. Approaching the coast, the transition from loom to bright flash is called *raising* the light; when the opposite happens on leaving the coast, the light is said to *dip*. Given the height of the light above sea level, a simple table can be used to obtain the distance of the light at the moment of raising or dipping. The observation is

21.6 Range by vertical sextant angle.

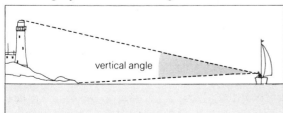

21.7 Range by lights dipping or raising.

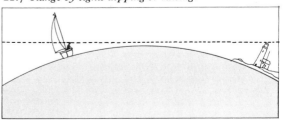

quick and simple, as it needs no instruments; it is merely necessary to know the height of the light and the height of eye of the observer.

The actual moment of raising or dipping a light can only be established in good visibility. It can be confirmed by changing the height of eye; if it is raised (by standing on the coachroof, for example), the light should be visible. Lowering the height of eye should make the light disappear, to be replaced by the loom.

Calculation Appropriate tables are printed in most books of nautical tables and yachtsman's almanacs; a version is given on page 192 of this book. The table is entered with the height of the light above sea level and the height of the observer's eye above sea level.

Accuracy Most lights will raise or dip at a range between ten and 25 miles, depending on the height of the light. The 95 per cent accuracy is about a quarter of a mile.

Important The raising or dipping of a light is one of the most valuable position lines available to the navigator making a landfall or taking a departure. It is simple and accurate, and the watch on deck should be trained to look out for the opportunity to take one.

Range by rangefinder or distance meter (Figure 8)

Various optical devices for measuring distance are available. They are either based on the rangefinder principle of binocular vision, or on an image-splitting principle. In either event, such instruments are unlikely to be of much use to the navigator; the maximum accurate range of either type is little over a mile (perhaps less), and at this sort of range the 95 per cent error may be as much as 10 per cent. The reason for this poor performance is one of cost – the yacht market could not afford to pay for the very high quality optics needed by an accurate rangefinder that works up to five miles or so. Better results can be obtained from a sextant (even a plastic one) which can also be used in many other ways.

Sounding (Figure 9)

A sounding, or a line of soundings can provide a position line provided that the shape of the sea bottom is sufficiently distinctive. Soundings can

21.8 *Range by rangefinder.*

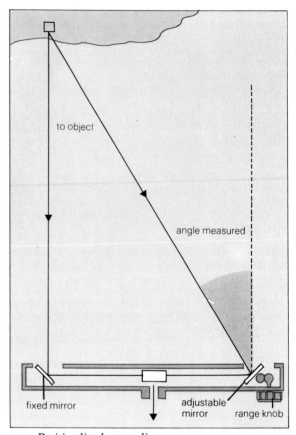

21.9 *Position line by sounding.*

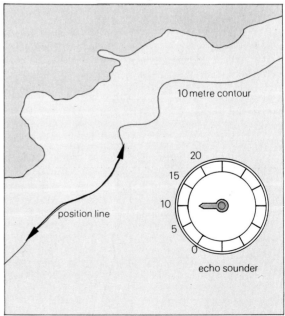

be taken by an echo sounder or (in shallow water) by means of a lead and line (see page 38).

An example of a position line from a single sounding is the traditional indication of the approach of land after an ocean passage. The 100 fathom (180 metres) contour marks the edge of the continental shelf; whilst its distance off shore varies, it offers invaluable landfall information. It also gives a useful departure line when setting off on an ocean passage.

A similar position line may be obtained by crossing a particular depth contour, provided that the sea bed is sufficiently regular for the correct contour to be identified without ambiguity.

If the seabed is irregular, a position line can sometimes be obtained by running a line of soundings. This involves recording soundings at regular intervals whilst the ship proceeds in a straight line; after a sufficient interval (perhaps an hour), a selection of the soundings can be plotted on a piece of paper, using the same scale as the chart in use (Fig. 10). This line of soundings is lined up on the chart to correspond in direction with the course steered by the ship, and the paper is moved about the chart near the DR position, to try and find a match between the depths on the chart and the line of soundings on the paper. Again, it is important to be on your guard against ambiguities caused by an

21.10 *Running a line of soundings.*

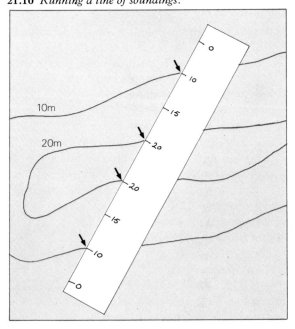

10m

20m

irregular bottom, and confirmatory information should be sought if at all possible.

Reduction to soundings A sounding taken in tidal waters will differ from the charted depth by reason of the rise of the tide; the sounding must be *reduced* by the height of the tide above chart datum. It is almost always sufficient to estimate this correction, because it is laborious and time-consuming to calculate for a slight improvement in accuracy. For those occasions when it is needed, the procedure is described on page 104.

Accuracy The 95 per cent error of an echo sounder will be about 2–4 per cent depending on the range in use (deep ranges will tend to be less accurate). A further error should be allowed if it has been necessary to reduce the sounding.

Bearing by radio direction finding
(see pages 110–4)
By using a suitable radio receiver and directional aerial, it is possible to take radio bearings of beacon transmitters to obtain a position line. The process, together with errors and corrections, is described on pages 112–4. Radio bearings are very useful when making a landfall or sailing out of sight of land, and they can be invaluable in poor visibility; but the accuracy is not particularly good, and can be distinctly poor in certain circumstances. Best results are obtained with radio bearings when they are used with caution, understanding and practice.
Accuracy The 95 per cent accuracy of a bearing from a properly installed and calibrated MFDF set, properly operated will be about:

    Good conditions   5°
    Moderate conditions 10°
    Poor conditions   15°

Under certain conditions, MFDF bearings will be so unreliable as to be unusable, particularly near sunrise and sunset (see page 114).
Half convergency When taking MFDF bearings at long range, an allowance may be needed to convert the great circle bearing given by the set to a rhumb line bearing (see page 15). This correction is known as half convergency; it can be obtained from most books of tables, lists of radio signals or yachtsman's almanacs, or from the table on page 191. The correction is applied to the measured bearing *towards* the equator. An equation for calculator use is given on page 184.

Bearing by directional radio beacons

Certain types of radio beacon give directional information without the need for a specialized receiver; two of these systems, Consol and the radio lighthouse, are described on pages 122–3, which also describes VOR for which a special receiver is needed.

Another type of radio directional beacon, known as a *radio range*, is occasionally found (Fig. 11). Its function is not to provide a position line but rather a path along which a craft can travel. Radio ranges are commonly used in aviation but their use is much less common at sea. One example of a marine radio range is to be found at Boulogne (France), where the beacon lays down a path in the direction $101\frac{1}{2}°$ to guide shipping into the harbour. If the vessel lies to the north of the beam, a succession of morse letter 'A' (.−.−.−) can be heard. On the beam itself, the signal is a continuous note and to the south it becomes a succession of morse letter 'N' (−.−.−.). The beam width of the continuous note is 5°, so the radio range is not a precision aid by any means; however the effect of this wide beam becomes less as the beacon is approached so it still can provide valuable homing information.

21.11 *Radio range.*

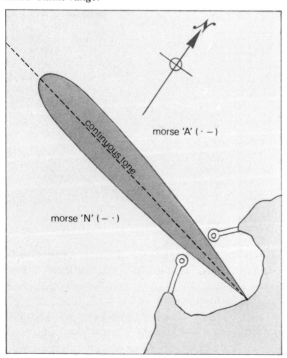

morse 'A' (· −)

continuous tone

morse 'N' (− ·)

Range differences and hyperbolic position lines

A number of radio aids to navigation have been devised which measure the difference in distance between pairs of special radio transmitters. These aids are described fully on pages 120–1. The position lines produced by these aids are families of hyperbolae which require the use of special charts over-printed with a lattice, or a specially programmed computer in some modern equipment. The various systems offer different coverage areas, accuracies and costs; they all tend to be expensive and all require special receivers and signal processors. In sailing yachts, the electrical power demand can also be significant.

Radar range

The use and limitations of radar are described on pages 115–9. From a navigational point of view, radar can provide two types of position line – the range of an object and its bearing. Of these, the range is very much the more accurate. In radar terms, the measurement of range involves the measurement of a time interval between the transmission of a radio pulse and the reception of an echo from the target; electronic techniques make this a very simple and accurate process. Bearings from a radar set are very much less accurate (see below). If at all possible, radar ranges should be used in preference to radar bearings.

Accuracy In normal yacht radar sets, the range of an echo is estimated, using fixed range rings as a guide; there are normally four range rings across the width of the screen. A practiced operator should be able to estimate a range to within about 2 per cent of the total range in use (95 per cent). Many radars now offer a device called a *variable range marker* as an optional extra; this device provides a single range ring which can be moved across the screen by means of a knob. A display then shows the exact range to which the range ring is set. Using the variable range marker, the 95 per cent error of a radar range should not exceed 1 per cent of the range in use.

Radar bearing

The use and limitations of radar are described on pages 115–9. A radar set can provide the navigator with the range and the bearing of an echo; of these two, the range is very much more accurate and should be used whenever possible in preference to a radar bearing. However, radar bearings can be used provided that their limitations are always borne in mind. These limitations arise from a number of factors, connected with the fact that the radar aerial has to rotate, at a fairly low speed, with respect to the ship's head. Because the rotation is with respect to ship's head, any bearing measured is a *relative bearing* (see page 69), and hence needs the addition of the ship's course to give a compass bearing; and because the rotation is slow, the effect of the yacht's yaw can be pronounced. Another factor leading to poor radar bearings is the relatively wide beam produced both by transmitting and receiving aerials (3° is typical). It is difficult under the best circumstances to measure a bearing with an accuracy smaller than the beam-width.

Accuracy Taking all factors into account, the 95 per cent accuracy of a radar bearing taken in good conditions is probably no better than 6°; in poor conditions this may increase to 15° or even more.

Astronomical position lines

A section of this book explains how to obtain astronomical position lines and how to assess the likely errors; it may help to relieve the mystique traditionally ascribed to astronomical navigation to stress that its major function is to provide the navigator with a position line (possibly when no other source of position lines is available). Whilst the techniques of astronomical navigation may appear unusual at first glance, the end result (the position line) is now familiar. The accuracy of such a position line is discussed on page 132.

Unusual position lines

The position lines so far described may be called conventional, in that most navigators know about them and will use them when the opportunity arises; however, position lines may be obtained from the most unusual of sources, if the navigator keeps his eyes open and his wits about him. A good navigator never lets a position line escape him; some of the following ideas may lead to very inaccurate position lines, but the good navigator will realize this, and make use of any information he can acquire with due allowance for its quality.

Sectored lights In many parts of the world (for example Scandinavia), navigational lights are often sectored, showing different colours over different arcs of the compass (Fig. 12); a position line can be obtained by observing the colour of a particular light or (more accurately) by observing the change from one colour to another.

Clouds In tropical waters it is common for the heating effect of the sun to cause clouds to form over land during the late forenoon. These clouds can often be seen for a considerable distance, marking for example the position of an island below the horizon. In temperate latitudes, similar effects can occur but are less predictable.

Waves and swell Experienced seamen can detect the disturbance of a wave train caused by the presence of land – this is one of the major clues used by Polynesian navigators.

Shipping lanes Commercial shipping tends to follow certain clearly defined routes, and the presence of merchant ships can often give valuable

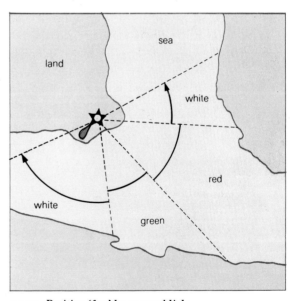

21.12 *Position 'fan' by sectored light.*

navigational information; the information can be even more precise if it is known that traffic separation schemes are in force, confining the ships to narrow traffic lanes.

Ferry routes The sighting of a ferry on a known route can tell the navigator a lot, especially if he knows the ferry's timetable as well.

Aircraft Similarly, a knowledge of the air routes within the vicinity of the yacht can also give useful indications of position.

Birds Certain birds feed at sea and roost on shore; they fly out from the land at dawn, and return to the land at dusk. If such birds can be recognized and their flight directions identified, then the direction of the nearest land is established.

Garbage In the absence of shipping, the floating garbage it leaves behind can be helpful; such garbage is sometimes marked at a distance by scavenging seabirds.

Sound The ears can offer useful information; a dull roar on an otherwise still day may indicate surf on a reef; a barking dog signals land. In fog, ships can sometimes hear echoes from their sirens reflected from cliffs; given the sort of sound signalling equipment on a yacht, it may only be possible to detect the echo of a cliff at half a mile or so, but that might still make all the difference between a safe passage and a stranding.

Rule of thumb Very roughly, the distance of an object detected by echo (in cables = 0.1 miles) is equal to the number of seconds between signal and echo; i.e., if an echo is heard five seconds after the signal, the object is five cables, or half a mile away.

Smell The nose is a very sensitive organ, and it may well happen that it will detect a smell which gives a clue to position. Typical smells that might be useful are fumes from an oil refinery or production platform, the smell of growing plants on shore, or rotting seaweed on the shoreline.

22 The transferred position line

A position line is only valid at the instant of observation, because the vessel moves away from the position line as time goes by; however, it is not always possible to obtain a position line at the exact moment that it is wanted, so it would be very helpful if we could extend the useful life of a position line in some way. This can be done by using the techniques of dead reckoning, and the result is known as a *transferred position line*.

Assume, in Figure 1, that a position line is observed at 0900 – a lighthouse (L) bears 015 degrees true. The vessel must lie somewhere along the position line, but it is not known where. Let us pick three of the infinite number of possible positions at random, A1, B1 and C1, and see what happens as the vessel proceeds on its way.

If the ship's course and speed are 090, seven knots, then one hour later (at 1000) it will be seven miles east of its original position. If that position had been A1 at 0900, then it will be A2 at 1000; if it had started from B1, then it would arrive at B2; and if C1 had been the 0900 position, then at 1000 the DR position would be C2.

The essential point to observe is that the line A2 B2 C2 is parallel to the original position line A1 B1 C1, and displaced from that line by a distance and direction exactly equal to the movement of the ship during the time interval since the original observation. Of course, the ship may not have actually been at A1, B1 or C1 at 0900, but whatever position was actually correct, the DR at 1000 must lie somewhere along the line A2 B2 C2, which is the original position line *transferred* by the movement of the ship in the interval.

An alternative way of looking at this very important concept is to imagine that the original position line has a physical existence, like a thin rod connecting the ship and the lighthouse at 0900; the ship can be imagined to pick up this rod and carry it along, keeping it parallel with its original direction. At any subsequent moment, the actual position of the ship must lie somewhere on this imaginary rod, the transferred position line (Fig. 2).

The original position line was established with reference to the earth's surface, and if it is to be transferred correctly then allowance must be made

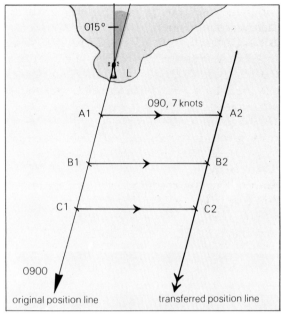

22.1 *Principle of the transferred position line.*

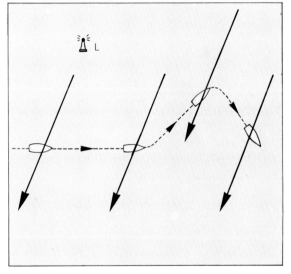

22.2 *Carrying the position line along.*

for the ship's progress over the ground; therefore full allowance must be made for such factors as tidal stream, current and leeway as well as the ship's course and speed. All the appropriate techniques of DR navigation must be used. The transferred position line is therefore an interesting combination of the two major concepts of position finding, dead reckoning and position line observation.

22.3 *Transferred position line – complete example.*

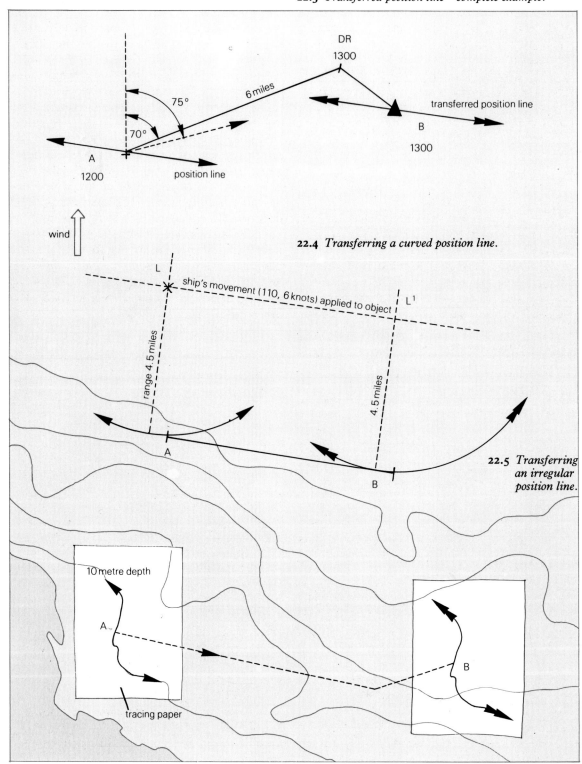

DR
1300

75°

6 miles

transferred position line

70°

A
1200

position line

B
1300

wind

22.4 *Transferring a curved position line.*

L

ship's movement (110, 6 knots) applied to object

L¹

range 4.5 miles

4.5 miles

A

B

22.5 *Transferring an irregular position line.*

10 metre depth

A

B

tracing paper

Figure 3 shows the full process of DR navigation applied to a position line (this time assumed to be an astronomical position line). The starting point (initial DR position) is assumed to be at A; the vessel is steering 075 at six knots, and 5° of leeway is allowed because of the fresh southerly wind. The tidal stream is setting 120 at two knots. After one hour, the estimated position of the ship is at B, with the transferred position line running through it, parallel with the original. It is conventional to mark a transferred position line with a double arrow head.

The majority of position lines are straight lines, and can be transferred as has been described. If the position line is an arc of a circle (from a radar range, for example), then the simplest way to transfer it is to move the centre of the circle according to the DR (Fig. 4). A transferred position circle can then be struck from the new centre, using the same radius as the original. An irregular position line, such as a depth contour, can also be transferred (Fig. 5); in this case, the simplest technique is to make a tracing of the original line and then move the tracing paper appropriately, pricking the transferred line through onto the chart.

A transferred position line has just the same validity as any other position line. Due allowance must be made for the fact that a transferred position line is necessarily less accurate than the original line (see below), but apart from this there is no difference between them.

Accuracy A transferred position line will have a larger error than the original, because of the errors in the DR. The original position line would have its own 95 per cent error, the magnitude of which depends on the type of observation and the circumstances of the moment. As the line is transferred, the errors of the DR are added to the original error (Fig. 6). The navigator must keep an eye on the error of a transferred position line, which grows with time, and make his own decision on the line's usefulness.

22.6 *Transferred position line accuracy.*

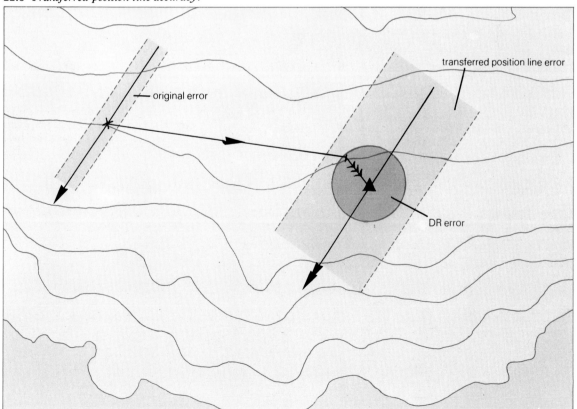

23 Using single position lines

Position lines are of restricted value in themselves, as they only give limited information about the position of the vessel; they are normally used in combination to provide a fix (see page 84). However, there are circumstances when a single position line can be of great use to a navigator.

Leading line A position line can be used to indicate a safe course for the vessel to follow. A common example is the use of a transit to indicate the safe approach to a harbour (Fig. 1). Beacons are often erected for this special purpose, and in more important harbours these beacons will be lit for use at night. Such lights may be sectored so as to show more brightly when on the transit (or range), and the lights are sometimes synchronized to aid identification. The nearer light or beacon is normally lower than the further. When steering a ship along a transit, any deviation from the correct line causes the transit to open; the ship should be turned towards the *nearer* beacon (*lower* light) to bring it back onto the correct line. A transit makes a convenient and accurate leading line, but any position line will do; Figure 2 shows the use of a compass bearing as a leading line.

23.1 *Leading line.*

23.2 *Compass leading line.*

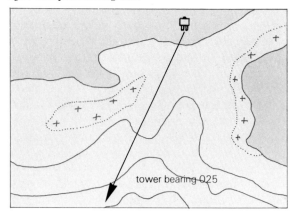

tower bearing 025

Clearing line Another way of using a position line is as a way of avoiding a danger. In Figure 3, a clearing bearing of 060 has been chosen to avoid a shoal. Provided that the bearing is 060 or less, it is known with certainty that the ship will pass clear of the shoal.

23.3 *Clearing line.*

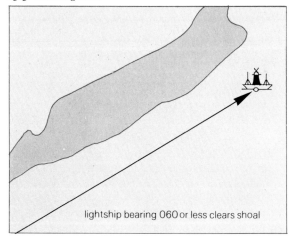

lightship bearing 060 or less clears shoal

Finding a channel or haven A transferred position line can be used to find a channel or haven when no other navigational information is available (Fig. 4). In the example, a single position line was obtained by means of the compass bearing of a headland. If this position line is transferred to pass through the destination, the ship can first run the required distance and then alter course along the transferred position line. Within the limits of accuracy of the position line, this will lead the ship to the desired point.

23.4 Finding a haven with a transferred position line.

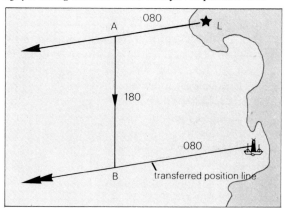

Track checking A single position line can be used to estimate a position relative to the desired track (Fig. 5). A position line which crosses the track at right angles (or nearly so) gives an indication of how far ahead or astern of the DR the ship actually is; a position line parallel (or nearly) to the track indicates the extent to which the ship has been set to port or starboard of the track. Astronomical position lines are often used for this purpose, when it may be possible to select the time of observation to yield the desired direction of position line.

23.5 Track checking.

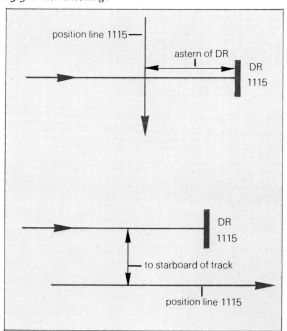

Danger approaching A single position line can be used to warn of approaching danger; when making a landfall, for example, it may be possible to select a limiting sounding (Fig. 6). Even though the position of the vessel may be in doubt, it is safe to continue the approach until the limiting sounding is reached; thereafter, the ship must be navigated with extreme caution until the true position can be established. A common strategy is to alter course to follow the position line, therefore using it as a clearing line.

23.6 Danger limit line.

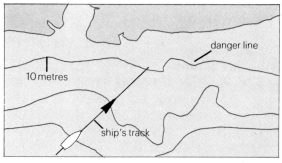

Danger circle A variation on the idea of a clearing line is so common as to be worth special mention; this is the danger circle (Fig. 7). In the example, it has been decided that it would be unsafe to go within a mile of the lighthouse (height 25 metres). This distance corresponds to a vertical angle of 47 minutes of arc on a sextant. Provided that the actual vertical angle observed is 47 minutes or less, it is certain that the ship is outside the danger circle. A similar technique can be used with radar. Provided that the echo of the lighthouse is not permitted to come inside the one-mile range ring, then the ship is at a safe distance.

23.7 Danger circle.

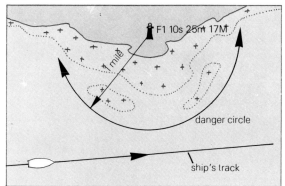

24　The fix

If dead reckoning navigation could be made perfect, then no other technique would ever be needed from start to finish of a passage. However, DR is far from perfect and the errors grow with time so that after a period the DR can become so vague as to be of little value. The navigator must continually seek to remove or reduce the error in his estimation of the ship's position by using observations to find out where he actually is. A position established by observation is called a *fix*.

A fix can be obtained in a variety of ways, of which the fix by intersection of position lines is by far the most common:

Pinpoint A pinpoint is established by passing very close to some object (e.g., a navigational buoy) whose position is known.

Electronic fix Certain electronic aids to navigation (Satnav, some Loran C sets) carry out internal processing on the position lines that they derive to present an output in the form of a fix (latitude and longitude).

Outside help A fix can sometimes be obtained from an outside source. A blue water yachtsman can often get a position from a merchant ship that he may happen to encounter, though it is by no means certain that such a position will be any more reliable than the yachtsman's own opinion – big ships make mistakes, too. Closer to shore, a more reliable position can sometimes be obtained from traffic surveillance and harbour control systems which use shore-based radar; the most common and practical means of communication with such bodies is by vhf radiotelephone. For example, the Dover Strait Information Service monitors traffic in the very crowded waters of the Dover Strait, using powerful and precise radar sets on the French and English coasts and vhf direction finding equipment. On request, the coastguards are able to identify your echo on their screen and tell you your position; they may also be able to offer advice on safe manoeuvres to avoid other shipping. A navigator who takes pride in his work would normally be reluctant to seek outside help, but there may be circumstances (especially in fog) when prudent seamanship would indicate that this was a sensible thing to do.

When coasting in fog, any position obtained by asking passers-by should be treated with grave suspicion; they may have less idea of where they are than you do.

Fixing by horizontal angles As mentioned on page 70, a circular position line can be obtained by measuring the angle between two objects. In practice, such a position line is rarely used on its own; the more common technique is to use two angles, taken at the same time, between three objects. This is known as a *horizontal angle fix*. The angles can be measured by subtracting the compass bearings of the objects, or (more accurately) with a sextant used horizontally.

There are two simple methods of plotting a horizontal angle fix. The first involves the use of tracing paper, or perhaps the surface of a clear protractor (Fig. 1). From a point on the paper (or the centre of the protractor), three lines are drawn such that the angles between them correspond with the measured angles. The paper or protractor is then moved over the surface of the chart until the three lines each pass through the appropriate object on the chart; the vessel is at the point where the lines originate.

24.1 *Horizontal angle fix.*

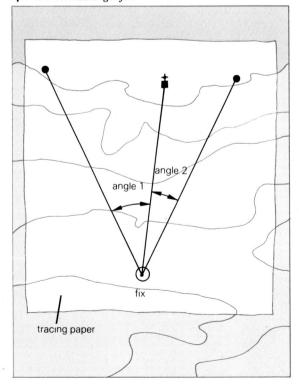

24.2 *A station pointer.*

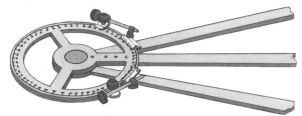

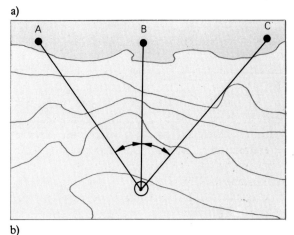

a)

b)

c)

The second method of plotting a horizontal angle fix involves the use of an instrument known as a *station pointer* (Fig. 2). This consists of three arms, mounted on a graduated ring. The centre arm is fixed, whilst the two outer arms can be set to any angle required against the graduations of the ring. In use, the two angles are set up on the arms and the whole instrument is moved about the chart until the ruling edge of each arm passes through the appropriate object. The ship's position is then at the centre of the station pointer. Though more accurate than the tracing paper approach, a station pointer is expensive and cumbersome; they are rarely found in yachts.

Limitations and accuracy Under certain circumstances, a fix by horizontal angles can be ambiguous or inaccurate; to avoid such a situation, the objects chosen for observation should be selected to fulfill one of the following conditions (Fig. 3):

a) All three objects are more or less in line with each other.

b) The middle object is closer to the ship than the outer two.

c) The ship lies inside the triangle formed by joining the three objects.

If one of these three conditions is observed, the accuracy of the resulting fix will be high. If the fix is plotted using the differences between compass bearings as input, the resulting fix will be more accurate than one obtained by plotting the compass bearings themselves, because the systematic errors (variation and deviation) will be eliminated. If a sextant is used for measuring the angles, then the resulting fix is likely to be the most accurate available by visual means; before the advent of precise radio aids, the method was widely used for the very accurate navigation needed in minesweeping. The 95 per cent error of the fix will depend upon the actual geometry of the case, but typical values might be:

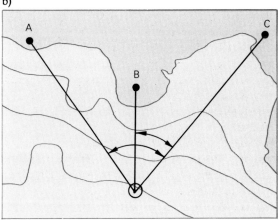

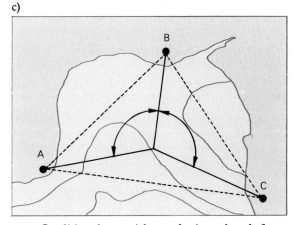

24.3 *Conditions for a satisfactory horizontal angle fix.*

Sextant angles	½ a per cent of mean distance between objects
Angles from compass bearings	2½ per cent of mean distance between objects

Fixing by intersecting position lines By far the most common type of fix in normal navigation is formed by the intersection of two (or more) position lines obtained at the same time. In Figure 4, two position lines, A and B, have been obtained at the same time. From the definition of a position line, it is known that the ship must lie somewhere on the line A; equally, she must also lie somewhere on the line B. The only place where these two facts can both be true is at the point where the position lines intersect; this is a fix. If the position lines did not intersect (i.e., they were parallel), then no fix is possible.

A fix can be obtained from the intersection of any two (or more) position lines, however derived. A transferred position line will serve if it has been transferred to the same time as the other observation(s).

It cannot be emphasized too strongly that a fix can be obtained from two or more position lines of any kind at all; an astronomical position line can cross a sounding, a radar range cross a visual bearing, a visual transit can cross an MFDF bearing. The sole requirements are:
1) The position lines must be taken simultaneously (or transferred to the same time).
2) The position lines must intersect.

Whilst any two intersecting position lines provide a fix, it is obvious that the number of position lines, the accuracy of each and the angle of intersection will all affect the quality of the resulting fix. These aspects are discussed on the facing page.

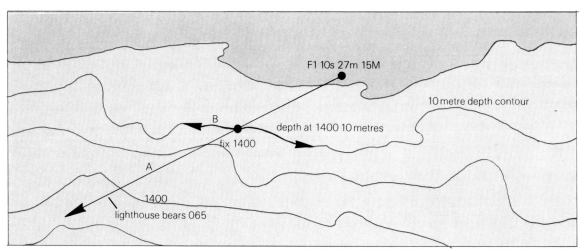

24.4 *Intersecting position line.*

25   Fix accuracy

Having plotted a fix by the intersection of position lines, the navigator needs to assess the quality of the fix and the reliance he can place on it by establishing its 95 per cent error. This will vary from fix to fix, and depends upon a number of factors:

The quality of the individual position lines (Fig. 1) Each position line will have its own 95 per cent error, of which the navigator should be aware. If each position line is regarded as a 'ridge of probability' rather than a line, then the intersection gives rise to a 'heap of probability'. If the 95 per cent errors of the position lines are approximately the same, then the resulting 'heap' will be circular, with a diameter roughly equal to the width of the 'ridges'. The 95 per cent error of the fix can therefore be taken as roughly the same as that of the position lines. If the errors of the position lines are different (Fig. 1b.), then the 'heap' is distorted in shape and the resulting error is greater in one direction than the other (see page 11).

25.1 Effect of individual position line errors: (a) similar errors; (b) differing errors.

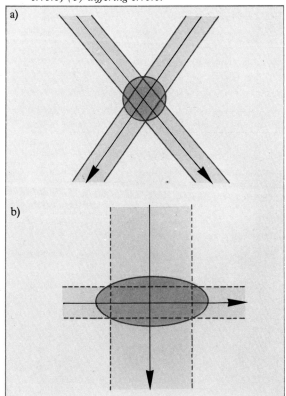

The angle of cut If two position lines of equal error cross at right angles, then the resulting heap is circular and as small as possible. As the angle of cut decreases, the 'heap' becomes more and more elliptical, giving rise to greater error in the fix in one direction. In practical terms, this effect may be ignored as long as the smaller angle of cut is more than 50° (Fig. 2).

Angles of cut less than 50° should be avoided. If their use is essential, then great care must be taken in assessing the resulting errors.

25.2 Effect of angle of cut.

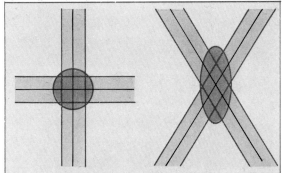

Number of position lines In practice it is wise to plot fixes with at least three position lines whenever possible. From a mathematical point of view, there is little improvement in the resulting error determination, but the plotting of three lines will generally detect any blunders that may have been made in observation or plotting (Figure 3). Three position lines will rarely intersect in a point, as they would if no errors were present. The size of the 'cocked hat' should be compared with the errors of the individual position lines; a blunder is likely if the size of the cocked hat is greater than the position line errors.

25.3 Detecting blunders with three position lines.

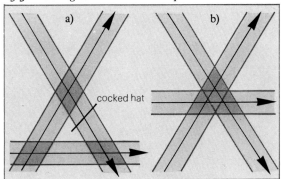

cocked hat

If compass bearings of three objects lying on a common circle are taken, the fix is ambiguous and should be rejected.

Simultaneous observations A fix requires that the position lines result from simultaneous observations. With a single observer, it is impossible to make two observations at once, though the time interval between them may be so short as to be of no significance. However, it may happen that a noticeable interval elapses between observations; in high speed craft in particular, the delay may

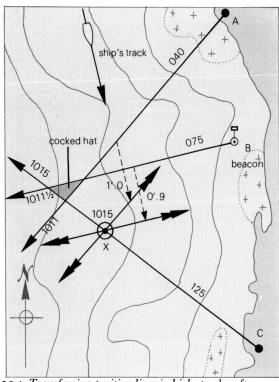

25.4 *Transferring position lines in high speed craft.*

cause inaccuracy. The solution is to transfer the earlier position lines by the distance that the craft has moved in the interval (Fig. 4).

Comparison with DR A fix should be examined for consistency with the dead reckoning position. Whilst the purpose of the fix is to reduce the errors that have accumulated in the reckoning, there should still be consistency between the two. If the 'heap' of the fix is not included within the larger 'heap' of the DR, then one or other must be wrong; a blunder has been detected, and both fix and DR should be re-worked until it has been found.

25.5 *Inconsistency between fix and DR.*

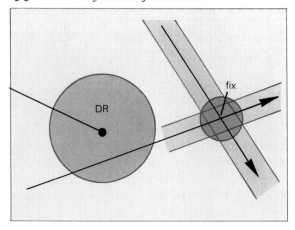

There is a temptation to accept the fix and ignore the (seemingly wrong) DR; it is a potentially dangerous practice to yield to this temptation (Fig. 5).

Practical points

When using the ideas of probability and 95 per cent errors for the first time, it can be helpful to draw the 'ridges' and 'heaps' of probability on the chart, although this may make the chart look messy. As experience is gained with this approach there is no need actually to mark the chart provided that the existence of the errors is never forgotten; the drawing of a shape around a fix, indicating the 95 per cent error, is probably always good practice as it reduces the demand on the navigator's memory and indicates to the rest of the crew what is going on.

There is no need to be over-precise in the assessment of errors; they are only estimations and are subject to random variation. Where 95 per cent errors for different observations are quoted in this book, they are merely suggestions based on the author's experience. Any navigator is entitled to disagree, but should remember that pessimism is generally safer than optimism.

Some navigators may feel that the errors suggested in this book are very large. They should perhaps remember that the figure quoted is the 95 per cent error, not the most likely error (probably half). The 95 per cent error is defined as the error that will only be exceeded on one occasion in twenty. The basis of this idea is discussed in the section on errors (see pages 9–13).

Choosing a position within a 'heap' of probability is influenced by circumstances (Fig. 6). In ordinary circumstances, the middle of the heap will serve as well as any other point; however, it may be wise to choose some other point to build in a margin of safety. It is sensible, for example, to choose the point closest to the nearest danger if it is desired to guarantee that the danger be cleared. In other circumstances it may be wise, in a sailing yacht, to assume a position to the leeward side of the 'heap', so that any errors result in his being to windward and he can be sure of retaining the advantage of the weather gauge. It is always worth avoiding a last-minute beat.

25.6 *Selecting a position within a fix error zone.*

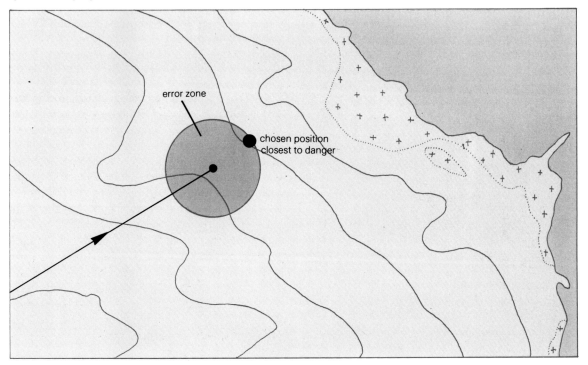

26   Global weather

The atmosphere exerts a pressure on the surface of the earth, but because of the energy input from the sun the atmosphere is warmer in some places (notably around the equator) and cooler in others (around the poles). Warm air is less dense than cold air, so in warmer areas the pressure is less and in cold areas it is greater. There is a tendency for air to move from high-pressure areas to fill low pressure areas, but because of the rotation of the earth such movements, the winds, are deflected to the right in the northern hemisphere and to the left in the southern hemisphere. The result is a pattern of pressure and wind belts across the globe shown in Figure 1.

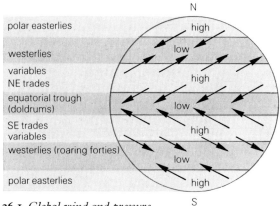

26.1 *Global wind and pressure.*

The effect of the land masses of the earth on this basic pattern is considerable. Not only are the belts of high and low pressure broken up into separate cells over the major oceans; the heating or cooling of large land masses also affects the barometric pressure. Pressure tends to be high over cold ground and low over warm ground. On a continental scale, such effects (known as *monsoons*) exert a major influence on the winds in the oceans that border them. Figures 2 and 3 show the major wind systems of the world for January and July. Note that the systems in tropical and temperate latitudes are shifted bodily north or south, depending on the declination of the sun; note also the influence of the monsoons.

The equatorial trough (doldrums)
This is an area of low pressure situated between the two belts of trade winds, generally north of the equator in the northern summer and south of it in the northern winter. The doldrums vary greatly in width both daily and seasonally, so that one vessel may hardly notice them, whilst another may be stuck for many days with light and baffling winds. Winds are generally light and variable, with occasional squally rain and thunderstorms.

The trade winds
The trade winds are two belts of remarkably steady and persistent winds on either side of the doldrums, and were so named for the very great assistance they gave to trading ships under sail. They blow with an average strength of force four, though the strength varies with the season and can reach force seven at times. The north-east trades blow in the northern hemisphere and the south-east trades in the southern; the trades can be suppressed by the monsoons in certain areas, notably the Indian Ocean, the west Pacific Ocean and the waters off West Africa. They are sometimes interrupted by tropical revolving storms (see pages 92–3).

In the trade winds, the weather is generally fair with an endless procession of small, puffy cumulus clouds across the sky. Rainfall is frequent in the west and visibility, except in the rain, is generally good.

The variables
Between the trade winds and the westerlies there lies a belt of light and variable winds associated with high pressure. In the northern hemisphere, the variables are sometimes called the horse latitudes.

The westerlies
On the poleward side of the variables lie the westerlies, regions where the wind is predominantly from the west, but very variable in character with the passage of a large number of depressions. Gales are frequent, especially in winter. Bad weather is so common in the southern hemisphere that the region is known as the roaring forties (south of 40°S). In the northern hemisphere, fog is common in the west.

The polar regions
Mainly un-navigable by reason of ice, such areas are avoided by all but the most intrepid yachtsmen.

26.2 *World winds – January.*

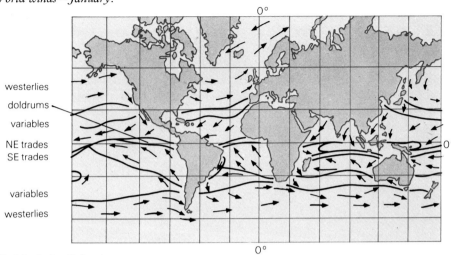

westerlies
doldrums
variables
NE trades
SE trades

variables
westerlies

0°

26.3 *World winds – July.*

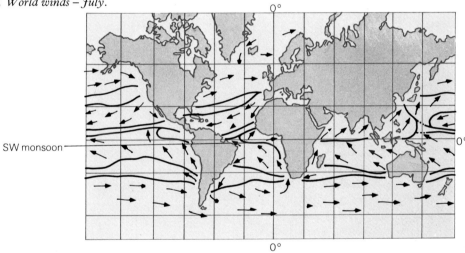

SW monsoon

0°

26.4 *World ocean currents.*

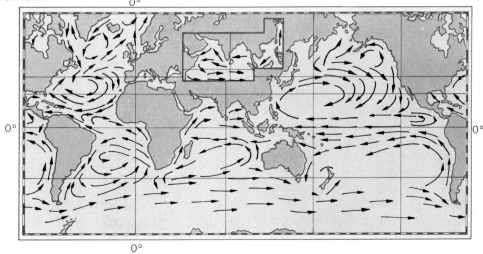

0°

27 Depressions and fronts

Depressions (or *lows*) are areas of low pressure, generally oval in shape which form in middle latitudes and are largely responsible for strong winds and unsettled weather. They can vary greatly in size (from 100 miles to 2,000 miles diameter) and intensity (central pressure 950 mb to 1000 mb). They can move in any direction, but generally tend easterly, and the speed can range from 60 knots for a newly formed vigorous depression to almost zero. The average life of a depression is four to six days, after which they slow down and fill.

Buys Ballot's Law to find the centre of low pressure.

If you face the wind, the centre of low pressure will be between 90° and 135° on your right hand in the northern hemisphere, on your left hand in the southern hemisphere.

A depression has a series of *fronts* associated with it, and Figure 1 shows how both come into being. A front is the boundary between two kinds of air, say polar (cold) air and tropical (warm) air. The front is not stable, and it tends to kink; this causes a circulation of air to build up, with a consequent fall in pressure which forms the depression. As the system gathers momentum, the depression deepens and moves off, carrying the kinked front with it. The leading part of the front, which has cold air in front and warm air behind, is called a *warm front*, and the second front, between the warm air in front and the cold air behind, is called a *cold front*. The cold front tends to travel faster than the warm front, so it will eventually catch up with it to form an *occluded front*. An occluded front can be very vigorous, but it effectively 'pinches off' the kink in the front and the depression will soon start to fill.

The behaviour of fronts and depressions depends on the hemisphere; in the following description, the equivalents in square brackets apply to the southern hemisphere.

In the northern [southern] hemisphere, the winds blow round a depression in an anti-clockwise [clockwise] direction. The wind direction generally follows the isobars, but is inclined inwards to the centre of low pressure by a few degrees; wind strength depends on the pressure

27.1 *The formation of a depression (northern hemisphere).*

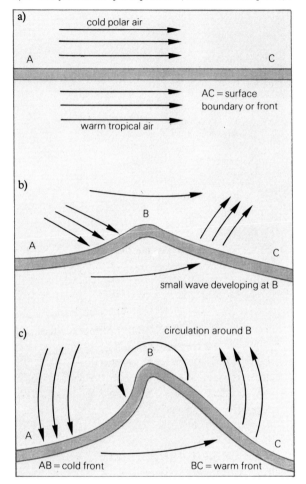

gradient, indicated by the spacing of the isobars (lines of equal pressure). The closer the isobars, the stronger the wind.

The passage of a warm front (Fig. 2) is characterized by the appearance of high, streaky clouds (mares tails) which progressively get lower and thicker, leading at first to drizzle and then rain. At the front itself, the wind will veer [back]. The rain will stop, the temperature will rise and the sky will remain overcast with moderate visibility. The cold front brings squalls, more rain and a fall in temperature. The wind will veer [back] further and the barometer will start to rise. Cold fronts are generally more active than warm fronts, and occluded fronts more active than either.

The pattern of events as a typical depression passes by is as follows:

27.2 *The passage of warm and cold fronts.*

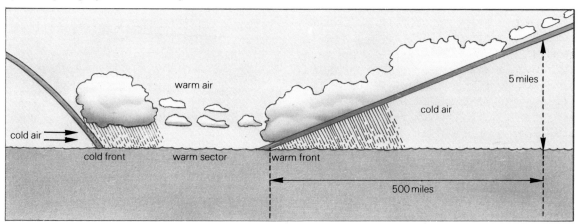

1) If the depression passes north [south] of you, moving from west to east, the first signs are high cirrus clouds and a falling barometer. The winds will shift to SW [NW] or S [N] and freshen as cloud builds up in the west. The clouds will lower until it starts to drizzle and then rain. At the warm front, the wind will veer [back], and the passage of the cold front will cause it to veer [back] even more to W or NW [SW], often with a sharp squall. Behind the depression the weather will be cool, bright and showery, though another depression may well be on its way.

2) If the depression passes south [north] of you, the passage is less eventful, as the fronts do not pass over your position. The barometer will fall, clouds will thicken and the wind will freshen. Prolonged periods of rain and unpleasant weather are possible. The winds in front of the depression will be E, and they will gradually back [veer] through NE [SE] to N [S] or NW [SW]. Sudden changes are unlikely.

Secondary depressions

It is not uncommon for a depression to calve off a secondary depression, which generally forms on the cold front. The secondary usually moves faster than the primary and can be a great deal more vicious, especially on the S [N] side. Secondary depressions can be dangerous, not least because they often come as a surprise to the forecasters as well as the sailors who have to endure them, bringing gales where none were expected (Fig. 3).

27.3 *Secondary depression.*

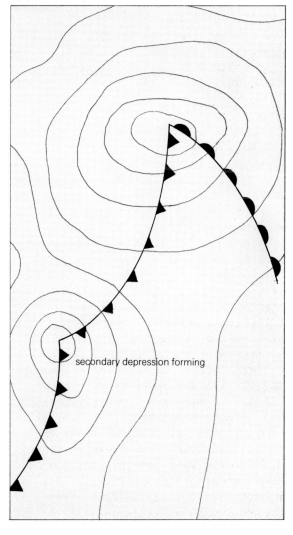

secondary depression forming

28 Tropical revolving storms

(Figures in square brackets refer to the southern hemisphere)

Tropical revolving storms occur in a number of regions, under different names. They resemble a depression in many ways, but are much smaller, more intense and quicker moving. They are intensely dangerous, and must be avoided by yachts if humanly possible, even to the extent of leaving the area or laying the boat up during the dangerous season.

A tropical revolving storm, which may be known as a hurricane, a typhoon, a cyclone or a willy-willy in different areas, is an area of intense

and move off in a WNW [WSW] direction. Sometimes they maintain this course until they strike land and exhaust themselves, but generally they recurve to the NE [SE] in latitude 20° or so. The speed of the storm usually starts at about ten knots, rising to 20–25 knots after recurving, though many go faster.

Generally speaking, when the progress of a storm is erratic, its speed is low. The storm is divided into the *dangerous semicircle* on the pole side of the expected track, and the *navigable semicircle* on the equatorial side. The term 'navigable' should not be taken too literally; it merely means that survival is a little more likely than in the other semicircle.

Area	Local name	Season	Average number per year
West Indies	hurricane	late May–mid Nov	8
		worst months Aug–Oct	
E North Pacific	hurricane	June–October	7–8
		worst months Aug, Sept	
W North Pacific	typhoon	June–November	22
		worst months Aug, Sept	
N Indian Ocean	cyclone	May–Nov	6–8
S Indian Ocean	cyclone	December–April	6
Australia	willy-willy	December–March	1
(Queensland)	hurricane	December–March	2–3
S Pacific	hurricane	December–April	2

winds spiralling in towards an area of low pressure; the rotation is anti-clockwise [clockwise] in the northern [southern] hemisphere. Within 75 miles or so of the centre, gusts of 175 knots have been reported, with mountainous, confused seas and zero visibility because of torrential rain and blown spray. In the eye of the storm, winds are light or moderate and variable, but the earlier passage of the storm has left a huge, confused swell, which will soon be increased by the trailing half of the storm.

Tropical revolving storms can occur at any season, but they are mostly confined to the late summer season of the locality in question. The table above makes this clear.

The general path and progress of a tropical storm is shown in Figure 1, though each storm is highly individual and may vary wildly from the norm. They generally originate in latitude 7°–15°N [S]

Detecting the approach

In these days of weather satellites, the most common warning of tropical storms comes from weather broadcasts; however, if such a warning is not received, the navigator must be able to detect the approach of a storm and decide what to do about it.

Barometer The first warning will usually come from the barometer, which is normally remarkably constant in these regions. For most of the time, only a *diurnal variation*, a change in pressure between night and day, will be seen. If the diurnal variation is suppressed, or if the barometer falls three millibars (0.09 in) or more, trouble is about; if the barometer falls more than five millibars (0.15 in), a tropical storm is in the area.

Swell Even before the barometer begins to fall, a long, low swell from the direction of the storm may be seen.

Weather Sudden changes in wind direction or strength, unusual cloud formations and an unusual 'feel' to the weather can all indicate that something unpleasant is likely to happen.

What to do
The first essential is to decide the direction of the storm centre, its likely path and the relative position occupied by the ship. When the barometer has fallen by five millibars (0.15 in), and the wind has freshened to force six, the storm centre is about 200 miles away. Using Buys Ballot's Law, if you face the wind, the storm centre will be about 110° on your right [left] hand. Two such bearings taken a few hours apart will indicate how the storm is moving. It will rarely be moving towards the equator, and if below 20° latitude it is unlikely to have any east in its movement.

Northern hemisphere
If the wind veers, you are in the dangerous semicircle. Heave to on the starboard tack.

If the wind is steady or backs, you are either directly ahead of the storm or in the navigable semicircle. Run with the wind on the starboard quarter.

Southern hemisphere
If the wind backs, you are in the dangerous semicircle. Heave to on the port tack.

If the wind is steady or veers, you are either directly ahead of the storm or in the navigable semicircle. Run with wind on the port quarter.

In all cases, prepare for heavy weather.

28.1 *Typical storm paths.*

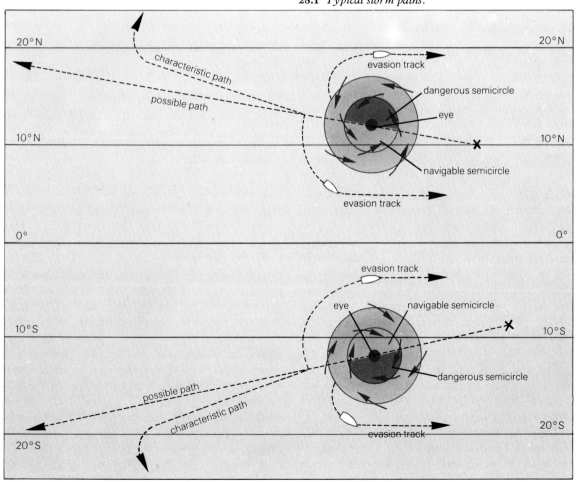

29 Local weather effects

There are a number of local effects which can modify the weather in a particular place.

Fog

Fog is caused by the cooling of the air by the surface with which it comes into contact to the point where the water vapour in the air condenses into droplets. Fog can occur in three main ways:

Advection fog is the most common type of fog found at sea, and is caused by relatively warm air blowing over cold sea; it is most common in late spring and early summer, when the contrast in temperature between sea and air is greatest. This type of fog is often associated with cold currents, such as the Labrador Current, the California Current and the Oya Shio, off Japan. Winds can remain quite strong during advection fog.

Frontal fog is sometimes formed in advance of a warm or occluded front in temperate or high latitudes; it is normally quite narrow in extent.

Radiation fog is formed over the land on clear, cold, still nights (generally when pressure is high); it can drift some ten to fifteen miles offshore. It is thickest during the late night and early morning, but is normally burned off by the sun or dissipated by heat from the relatively warm sea during the forenoon. This type of fog is associated with calms.

Sea breeze

The sea breeze is a local effect, extending no more than ten miles offshore, caused by the heating of the land by the sun until it is much warmer than the sea (Fig. 1). The heated air over the land rises, drawing in cooler air from the sea, to give rise to the onshore wind known as a sea breeze. Sea breezes are most common in tropical and sub-tropical latitudes, though they are found in temperate latitudes (with less force) in the summer. The sea breeze normally sets in during the late forenoon and reaches a peak some two to three hours after local noon; it will die away at about sunset.

The actual effect of the sea breeze will depend on the prevailing wind blowing at the time. A weak prevailing wind can be reduced or even reversed by the sea breeze, or it may merely be deflected towards the shore by the sea breeze effect. Whatever the effect, the sea breeze sets in earlier and lasts longer close inshore, so that is where a yacht wanting to take advantage of it ought to be. A sea breeze uninfluenced by any prevailing wind will average about force four (less in higher latitudes), but may reach force five or six at times.

Land breeze

The land breeze is the complement of the sea breeze; it occurs at night, when the land cools relative to the sea, and cold, dense air moves off the land, giving an off-shore breeze (Fig. 2). The land breeze is generally less marked than the sea breeze. It will set in at about midnight and disappear again at about dawn. As the effect is not as strong as the sea breeze effect, it is easier for a prevailing wind to mask any land breeze that may wish to blow.

Katabatic wind

Katabatic winds are akin to the land breeze, but can happen at any time of day and with considerable force. Where a coast is backed by snow-covered mountains, it is possible for cold air to accumulate (Fig. 3). It then needs only a small trigger for this mass of cold, dense air to slide down the mountain slopes and out to sea. These winds can reach gale force, they can arrive almost without warning and close inshore they can blow down at an angle rather than horizontally. For all these reasons, katabatic winds can be dangerous to small craft.

High coasts and cliffs

An onshore wind which meets high ground will tend to be deflected to blow parallel with the coast; near headlands and around islands, gusts and sudden wind shifts may be expected. If the wind is offshore, a narrow band of fluky wind can be expected in the lee. Squalls can be expected offshore if the air is colder than the sea.

Rivers and straits

A river or strait will tend to funnel the wind along its length, especially if the shore on either side is steep. The wind will increase in strength as the inlet narrows.

29.1 *The sea breeze.*

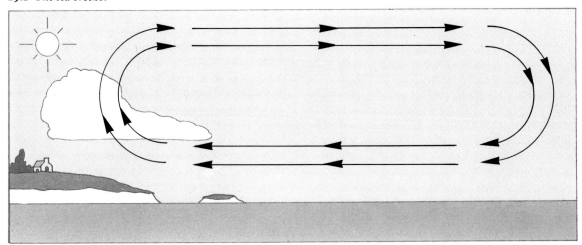

29.2 *The land breeze.*

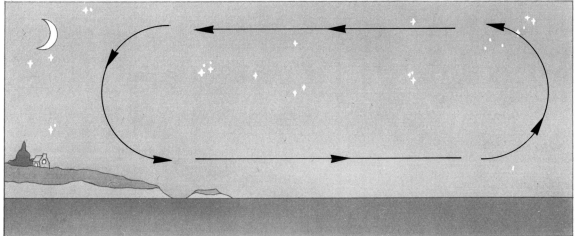

29.3 *Katabatic winds.*

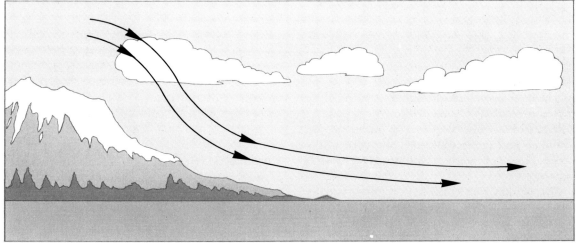

30 Land- and seamarks

For visual fixing, any conspicuous charted object such as a headland, a church, a water tower or a mountain can be used. But such marks are not always in the position where the navigator would like them, and in any case are hard to see at night. From the earliest times, landmarks and seamarks, including lights for night use, have been erected for the mariner.

Landmarks

The landmarks most commonly used for visual navigation by day are *lighthouses* from which lights are exhibited at night. They are located at key positions around the coast, and are painted conspicuously so they can be seen. In harbour approaches, *beacons* are often erected to mark a channel, possibly in pairs to act as leading lines. Beacons are sometimes fitted with a *topmark*, a special shape fitted to the top of the beacon, to distinguish one from another, and they may also carry lights.

A description of the construction and appearance of any landmark carrying a light is given in the *Light List* and the *Pilot* for the area. The *Pilot* also carries a description of any unlit beacon or object of navigational importance.

Seamarks

Seamarks are almost always floating objects moored to the seabed, though occasionally a tower or other construction is built offshore. *Buoys* are widely used to mark channels and as a landfall aid, whilst *lightships* (manned) or *lightfloats* (unmanned) mark more important or dangerous features. All lightships and most buoys carry lights, and lightships may also carry an MF radio beacon transmitter.

Radar reflectors and racons

A buoy is not a particularly large object, and the vast majority are now fitted with a radar reflector to assist in detection by radar; they are sometimes fitted to beacons as well. A *racon* is a device which makes an identifying mark on the radar screen, to label the object to which it is fitted.

Buoyage systems

Buoys are generally established according to an organized system, to help the navigator identify each buoy more easily and find out his position from them. Unfortunately there are several different systems in use around the world, in spite of great efforts from the International Association of Lighthouse Authorities (IALA) to get agreement for a unified system. The IALA system A has now been introduced in most European waters; many countries associated with the British Commonwealth use the Uniform Lateral system, whilst the United States has its own system, which is also found in waters where US influence is strong. Elsewhere, countries will use their own system of buoyage (or none).

A point of particular importance for intending transatlantic voyagers is the difference in American and European systems for lateral marking. In Europe, a buoy to be left to starboard in a channel (when approaching from seaward) is painted green, and a buoy to be left to port is painted red. American practice is the opposite.

A new buoyage scheme for the US, known as IALA system B, has been agreed; it is akin to the system A used in Europe, but maintaining the red-to-starboard principle. Implementation began in Spring 1982 and should be completed about 1988. IALA system A and B are shown on pages 43–4.

When using buoys for navigation, it should not be forgotten that they are moored by chains to the seabed, and can therefore move a little about their charted position. Small buoys used to mark a narrow channel into a yacht haven can be set over the bank they are intended to mark during the flood.

Lights

Lights, whether exhibited from lighthouses, lightships or buoys, are of the utmost value for pilotage at night, and indeed often make a coastline easier to traverse than in daytime.

A navigational light is described by various characteristics:

1) *Character* This describes the behaviour of a light, whether it is fixed, flashes or is coded in some other way. Figure 1 gives the possibilities, with the abbreviation to be found on the chart (older charts may not use the International abbreviations).

30.1 *Light characters.*

Fathoms and Metric Charts			
CLASS OF LIGHT	International abbreviations	Older form (where different)	Illustration Period shown ———————
21 Fixed *(steady light)*	F		
22 **Occulting** *(total duration of light more than dark)*			
22 *Single-occulting*	Oc	Occ	
27 *Group-occulting* *e.g.*	Oc(2)	Gp Occ(2)	
(Ka) *Composite group-occulting* *e.g.*	Oc(2+3)	Gp Occ(2+3)	
23a *Isophase (light and dark equal)*	Iso		
23 **Flashing** *(total duration of light less than dark)*			
23 *Single-flashing*	Fl		
(Kb) *Long-flashing (flash 2s or longer)*	L Fl		
28 *Group-flashing* *e.g.*	Fl(3)	Gp Fl(3)	
(Kc) *Composite group-flashing* *e.g.*	Fl(2+1)	Gp Fl(2+1)	
24 **Quick** *(50 to 79–usually either 50 or 60–flashes per minute)*			
24 *Continuous quick*	Q	Qk Fl	
(Kd) *Group quick* *e.g.*	Q(3)	Qk Fl(3)	
25 *Interrupted quick*	IQ	Int Qk Fl	
(Ke) **Very Quick** *(80 to 159–usually either 100 or 120–flashes per minute)*			
(Ke) *Continuous very quick*	V Q	V Qk Fl	
(Kf) *Group very quick* *e.g.*	V Q(3)	V Qk Fl(3)	
(Kg) *Interrupted very quick*	IV Q	Int V Qk Fl	
(Kh) **Ultra Quick** *(160 or more–usually 240 to 300–flashes per minute)*			
(Kh) *Continuous ultra quick*	UQ		
(Ki) *Interrupted ultra quick*	IUQ		
30a Morse Code *e.g.*	Mo(K)		
29 Fixed and Flashing	F Fl		
26 Alternating *e.g.*	Al.WR	Alt.WR	

COLOUR	International abbreviations	Older form (where different)	RANGE in sea miles	International abbreviations	Older form
67 **White**	W *(may be omitted)*		*Single range* *e.g.*	15M	
66 **Red**	R				
64 **Green**	G		*2 ranges* *e.g.*	14/12M	14,12M
(Kj) **Yellow**	Y				
65 **Orange**	Y	Or	*3 or more ranges* *e.g.*	22-18M	22,20,18M
63 **Blue**	Bu	Bl			
61 **Violet**	Vi				
ELEVATION is given in metres **(m)** or feet **(ft)**			**PERIOD** in seconds *e.g.*	5s	5sec

Reproduced from a portion of BA Chart No. 5011 (1979 ed.) with the sanction of the Controller, HM Stationery Office and of the Hydrographer of the Navy.

2) *Colour* The colour of a light may be white (W) (which may be omitted), red (R), green (G), yellow or orange (Y), blue (Bu) or violet (Vi); the two last are not common. A light may show a single colour over the whole of its arc of visibility, or two or more colours over different arcs. Sometimes a light shows two colours in succession over the same arc, and is known as an alternating light. Al WR, for example, means a light that first shows white and then red.

3) *Period* This is the time in seconds for one complete cycle of the character.

4) *Elevation* The elevation of the light is the height of the lantern above the datum for heights (normally mean high water springs or mean high water). The higher a light, the further it can be seen (if it is bright enough). The geographical range of a light is the same as its dipping distance.

   On a mountainous coast, a light may be set so high that it is often obscured by low cloud.

5) *Nominal range* This is a measure of the brightness of the light; it is the range under which the light will be seen (regardless of elevation) in specified conditions of visibility. A light which exhibits more than one colour may have a different nominal range for each colour.

Fog signals

Fog signals can be of great assistance to the navigator in thick weather, though the behaviour of sound in fog is rather unpredictable, and taking bearings of fog signals 'by ear' may not always work. Buoys are fitted with relatively simple, short-range signals, such as a bell or whistle operated by wave action, or a horn driven by gas. Lighthouses and lightships carry more elaborate apparatus designed to give greater range and clarity.

Diaphone A low-pitched sound, ending in a characteristic 'grunt'

Horn Something like a magnified car horn (or several)

Siren A high-pitched wail

Explosive A bang

A fog signal has a character just like a light, though the period is usually quite long – a minute is typical. Most of the more leisurely 'flashing' rhythms are used, as well as Morse code letters.

When listening for a fog signal that you expect to hear but cannot, bear in mind that the fog which is restricting your visibility may not be present at the lighthouse or lightship, therefore the reason for not hearing the signal could be that it has not been switched on.

31 Tidal theory

Tides are regular and periodic changes in sea level, caused by the gravitational attraction of the sun and moon.

Tidal streams are regular and periodic horizontal movements of water which take place as a consequence of the tides.

According to gravitational theory, any two bodies exert an attraction on each other. The earth attracts the moon, which keeps the moon in its orbit. By the same token, the moon attracts the earth. Most of the earth is rigid, and so responds very little to this force; earth tides do exist, but can only be detected with special instruments. However, the water of the oceans is not rigid, and so is able to respond to the forces exerted by the moon. The way in which this gives rise to a *tide-raising force* is shown in Figure 1. The force of gravity varies with distance; therefore the moon's gravity as seen at a point immediately below it (A) is greater than at places where the moon is on the horizon (B), and water at A will tend to 'pile up' under the moon. Similarly, the moon's gravity at a point diametrically opposite the moon (C) will be *less* than at B′, and the water will tend to lag behind. The net effect is that two humps of water are created, one under the moon and the other opposite it.

31.1 *The tide-raising force.*

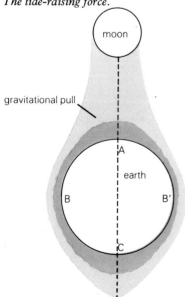

As the earth rotates, this would produce two tides in each lunar day (every 25 hours approximately), and is known as the *semi-diurnal* (i.e., half-daily) tide raising force. However, the moon is constantly changing position in the sky (specifically its declination is changing, page 137), and this also causes a *diurnal* (i.e., daily) force, which combines with the semi-diurnal force to produce the result shown in Figure 2. The relative magnitudes of the semi-diurnal and the diurnal forces can vary very greatly, to the extent that one or the other may disappear altogether.

31.2 *Diurnal and semi-diurnal effects.*

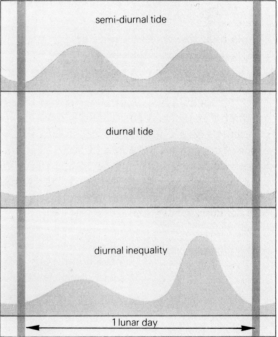

A further complication is the presence of the sun, which also causes tide-raising forces in exactly the same way as the moon. Although the sun is very massive, it is also a very long way away compared with the moon, and the sun's tides are relatively small. Their effect is to modify the tides caused by the moon, in a manner which depends upon their relative positions in the sky (Fig. 3). When the sun, moon and earth are more or less in line (i.e., at full moon and new moon), the tide-raising forces of the sun and the moon add together to produce a bigger tide than the average, a *spring tide*. When the sun and moon are at right

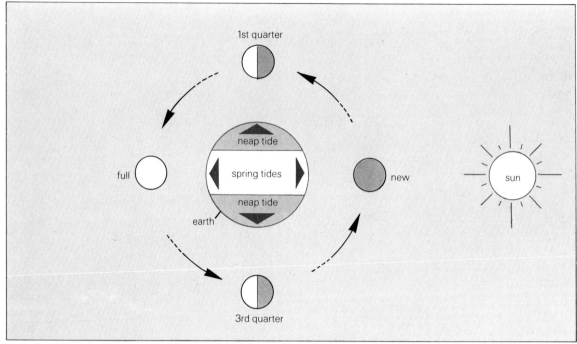

31.3 *Spring and neap tides.*

angles as seen from the earth, their respective tides act in opposition to each other, causing a smaller tide than the average, a *neap tide*. As the sun and moon are roughly in the same relative position every 28 days, there is a regular pattern of spring and neap tides; spring tides happen each fortnight, at new and full moon, while neap tides occur in the alternate weeks, when the moon is in its first or third quarter.

The actual tides as they exist

The foregoing explanation merely describes how the forces that cause the tide are generated. The actual tides are controlled almost entirely by geography. The periodic tide-raising forces set up waves which travel across oceans, alter in height as the depth changes and are reflected from coasts, with the end result that no two places on earth experience exactly the same tides. Some places experience very little tide – the Mediterranean, the Baltic and some Pacific islands have tides which may never exceed 0.6 metres (two feet), whilst places like the Severn estuary (England), Darwin (Australia) and the Bay of Fundy have tides averaging twelve metres (39 feet) or more. In the Atlantic Ocean, the diurnal effect is generally

small, so there are two tides a day of roughly equal height; in the Pacific, the diurnal effect is very much more marked, leading to a pronounced *diurnal inequality* in many places, where one tide of the day is very much bigger than the other. Some places have very complicated tides indeed; Southampton owes its position as a major port to the fact that it has four high tides a day, because of the influence of the Isle of Wight. The shape of the sea bottom also affects the shape of the tidal 'wave' as it approaches the coast. As the water gets shallower, the wave increases in height and gets steeper, so the tide rises more quickly than it falls.

Tidal definitions

The following terms to describe various levels that the water can reach are illustrated in Figure 4:
Lowest astronomical tide (LAT) The lowest level to which the tide can predictably fall. Atmospheric effects can sometimes give rise to a lower level (see below). LAT is frequently used as chart datum to which depths are referred.
Mean low water springs (MLWS) The average height, throughout the year, of two consecutive low waters at spring tides.
Mean low water neaps (MLWN) The average

height, throughout the year, of two consecutive low waters at neap tides.

Mean level (ML) The average level of the sea calculated from a long series of observations.

Mean high water neaps (MHWN) The average height, throughout the year, of two consecutive high waters at neap tides.

Mean high water The average height throughout the year of high water, sometimes used as the reference datum for charted heights.

Mean high water springs (MHWS) The average height, throughout the year, of two consecutive high waters at spring tides. Sometimes called the spring rise. Charted heights of objects on shore are often referred to MHWS.

Highest astronomical tide (HAT) The highest level to which the tide can predictably rise.

Height of the tide The height of the tide at any instant above chart datum.

Range of the tide The difference in height between the levels of successive high and low waters.

Equinoctal tides Spring tides which occur near the equinoxes, when the moon is closest to the earth. These spring tides are greater than average.

Drying height The height of an object covered at MHWS, above chart datum.

Charted sounding The depth of the bottom in a particular position below chart datum.

Meteorological effects

Unusual weather conditions can cause marked variations in the tide:

1) A high barometric pressure reduces the depth of water, and *vice versa*. A change of ten milibars causes an approximate change of 0.1 metre (4 in) in sea level (or a change of 1 in in barometric pressure causes a change of 1 ft in level).

2) A prevailing wind can cause changes in tidal level; an on-shore wind tends to increase levels, and an off-shore wind to depress them.

3) In some areas (e.g., the southern North Sea), a storm surge can occur. Some sudden change in conditions, such as the passage of a vigorous depression, can set up oscillations in sea level; if these oscillations coincide with the tidal wave, tides considerably greater or less than predicted can occur.

31.4 *The definition of tidal levels.*

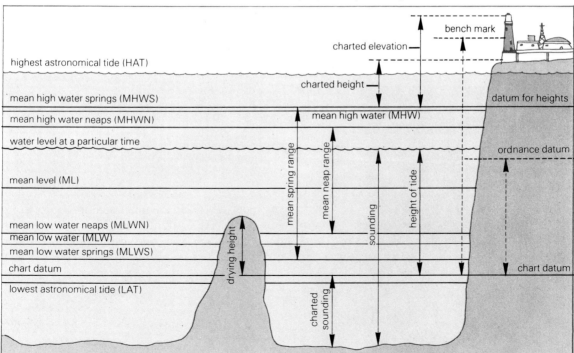

32   Tidal predictions

Tidal heights can be predicted for any time where data is available. The necessary information is published in *Tide Tables*, issued by charting authorities and oceanographical institutes. Many local tide tables are also published by boatyards, yacht equipment suppliers and others; where these are soundly based on the proper predictions they are reliable enough, but they tend to be a mixed bag. Tidal information given in almanacs specially designed for small craft is thoroughly reliable. The *Tide Tables* used for illustration in this book are published by the (British) Hydrographer of the Navy (NP 201). They are issued annually in three volumes to cover the entire world. Tables 1, 2 and 3 are reproductions of parts of the tables in Volume 1, *European Waters*. Tidal publications vary widely in layout around the world, but are easy enough to follow with a little careful study.

In the tables, detailed information of the times and heights of high and low water for each day of the year is given for a series of standard ports (Table 1). A pair of curves is also given for each standard port, showing the way in which the tidal height varies with time at springs and at neaps. These curves are used in predicting the height of the tide at times between high and low water (Table 2). Other ports in the general area of the standard port are known as secondary ports. For these, differences in the time and height of the tide are given, to be applied to those for the standard port (Table 3).

Pacific ports In many Pacific secondary ports, where the tide is largely diurnal in character, the method of time and height differences cannot be used, and an alternative method is needed. Voyagers in these areas should consult the instructions in the *Tide Tables* (Volume 3).

Local time The time zone to which the entries are referred is given at the top of the page (GMT for Dover in Table 1). Many countries operate summer time, and a suitable correction must be applied to obtain local time.

Times and heights of high and low water – standard ports

This information can be read directly from the standard port tables.

For example: High and low waters at Dover on 16 May 1983

HW 0048 6.4 m
LW 0818 0.8 m
HW 1321 6.3 m
LW 2039 0.9 m
Range 6.4–0.8 = 5.6 m (Springs)

Times and heights of high and low water – secondary ports

1) Extract the times of high and low water for the standard port; subtract the height of LW from the height of HW to get the range.
2) From the secondary port table, extract the time correction for high water and for low water; these may require interpolation, according to the actual times of high and low water.
3) Also from the secondary port table, extract the height correction for high and for low water. The figures given are for springs and for neaps, and may require interpolation. The range of the tide obtained in step 1 can be compared with the mean spring and neap ranges given in Table 2 to decide whether it is springs, neaps, or in between.
4) Apply the corrections obtained to find the times and heights of the tides at the secondary port.

For example:
To find the times and heights of the first high and low waters at Deal on 20 May 1983

Dover	HW 0452	5.5 m	LW 1217	1.7 m	range 5.5 – 1.7
					= 3.8 m
Differences	+0018*	−0.3 m	+0009*	0.0 m	
Deal (GMT)	0510	5.2 m	1226	1.7 m	range 3.5 m

* Interpolated figures from Table 3

Intermediate times and heights – standard ports

The problem of finding intermediate times and heights of the tide can take one of two forms:
1) What will be the height of the tide at a particular time?
2) At what time will the height of the tide reach a particular value?

Both of these problems are handled in a similar way, using the tidal curves illustrated in Table 2.

Table 1 *Admiralty* Tide Tables – *standard port.*

ENGLAND, SOUTH COAST - DOVER

LAT 51°07'N   LONG 1°19'E

TIME ZONE **GMT**   TIMES AND HEIGHTS OF HIGH AND LOW WATERS   YEAR **1983**

MAY

Day		Time	M	Time	M	Time	M	Time	M
1	SU	0112	6.4	0833	1.0	1331	6.1	2044	1.2
2	M	0145	6.1	0905	1.2	1406	5.9	2119	1.4
3	TU	0222	5.7	0941	1.6	1447	5.6	2159	1.8
4	W	0310	5.3	1023	1.9	1542	5.3	2247	2.1
5	TH	0420	5.0	1115	2.2	1657	5.1	2350	2.2
6	F	0550	4.8	1224	2.4	1817	5.1		
7	SA	0110	2.2	0702	5.0	1342	2.2	1920	5.3
8	SU	0226	1.9	0755	5.2	1449	1.9	2009	5.6
9	M	0327	1.6	0836	5.6	1545	1.6	2051	6.0
10	TU	0417	1.3	0912	5.9	1635	1.3	2129	6.2
11	W	0505	1.0	0949	6.2	1722	1.1	2206	6.4
12	TH	0549	0.9	1027	6.4	1804	0.9	2244	6.5
13	F	0628	0.8	1106	6.5	1841	0.8	2322	6.6
16	M	0048	6.4	0818	0.8	1321	6.3	2039	0.9
17	TU	0137	6.2	0903	1.0	1413	6.1	2128	1.1
18	W	0234	6.0	0956	1.3	1508	5.9	2224	1.3
19	TH	0339	5.7	1059	1.6	1612	5.7	2333	1.5
20	F	0452	5.5	1217	1.7	1726	5.6		
21	SA	0052	1.5	0624	5.5	1337	1.6	1850	5.7
22	SU	0212	1.3	0738	5.7	1451	1.4	1955	5.9
23	M	0321	1.1	0833	6.0	1555	1.2	2047	6.2
24	TU	0421	0.9	0918	6.1	1649	1.1	2131	6.4
25	W	0513	0.8	1000	6.3	1734	1.0	2213	6.5
26	TH	0556	0.8	1040	6.3	1811	1.0	2255	6.6
27	F	0631	0.9	1120	6.4	1842	1.0	2336	6.5
28	SA	0702	0.9	1200	6.4	1913	1.0		

JUNE

Day		Time	M	Time	M	Time	M	Time	M
1	W	0158	5.8	0917	1.5	1423	5.8	2138	1.6
2	TH	0242	5.5	0956	1.8	1510	5.6	2221	1.8
3	F	0341	5.2	1041	2.0	1609	5.4	2313	2.0
4	SA	0451	5.1	1137	2.2	1716	5.4		
5	SU	0017	2.0	0600	5.1	1242	2.2	1821	5.4
6	M	0126	1.9	0657	5.3	1349	2.0	1917	5.6
7	TU	0230	1.7	0748	5.5	1451	1.8	2005	5.9
8	W	0329	1.4	0834	5.8	1550	1.5	2050	6.1
9	TH	0426	1.2	0918	6.1	1645	1.3	2134	6.3
10	F	0516	1.0	1002	6.3	1736	1.1	2217	6.5
11	SA	0603	0.9	1047	6.5	1822	0.9	2304	6.5
12	SU	0648	0.8	1136	6.6	1907	0.8	2351	6.5
13	M	0730	0.8	1228	6.6	1952	0.8		
16	TH	0236	6.2	1000	1.2	1500	6.2	2227	1.0
17	F	0332	6.0	1059	1.3	1556	6.0	2327	1.2
18	SA	0435	5.8	1204	1.5	1659	5.9		
19	SU	0035	1.3	0549	5.7	1310	1.6	1810	5.8
20	M	0144	1.3	0659	5.7	1418	1.6	1917	5.9
21	TU	0251	1.3	0759	5.8	1521	1.5	2016	6.0
22	W	0352	1.3	0851	5.9	1616	1.4	2107	6.1
23	TH	0442	1.2	0939	6.1	1702	1.4	2153	6.3
24	F	0526	1.2	1023	6.2	1742	1.3	2238	6.3
25	SA	0603	1.2	1104	6.3	1815	1.3	2319	6.3
26	SU	0636	1.2	1143	6.3	1852	1.2	2358	6.3
27	M	0710	1.2	1219	6.3	1928	1.2		
28	TU	0032	6.2	0745	1.2	1252	6.3	2005	1.2

JULY

Day		Time	M	Time	M	Time	M	Time	M
1	F	0218	5.8	0931	1.6	1440	5.9	2156	1.6
2	SA	0305	5.6	1009	1.8	1528	5.8	2238	1.7
3	SU	0402	5.4	1054	1.9	1623	5.6	2329	1.9
4	M	0502	5.3	1147	2.1	1722	5.6		
5	TU	0028	1.9	0601	5.3	1250	2.1	1821	5.6
6	W	0133	1.8	0659	5.5	1358	2.0	1919	5.8
7	TH	0239	1.7	0757	5.7	1507	1.8	2013	5.9
8	F	0346	1.5	0851	5.9	1614	1.5	2107	6.1
9	SA	0448	1.2	0943	6.2	1715	1.2	2200	6.3
10	SU	0546	1.1	1035	6.4	1810	1.0	2252	6.5
11	M	0639	0.9	1127	6.6	1902	0.8	2344	6.6
12	TU	0731	0.8	1217	6.7	1951	0.7		
13	W	0038	6.6	0822	0.8	1306	6.7	2042	0.6
16	SA	0310	6.2	1045	1.2	1529	6.1	2309	1.1
17	SU	0404	6.0	1134	1.5	1624	6.1		
18	M	0003	1.3	0505	5.8	1229	1.7	1729	5.9
19	TU	0104	1.6	0615	5.6	1334	1.9	1839	5.7
20	W	0213	1.7	0726	5.6	1443	1.9	1948	5.7
21	TH	0319	1.7	0827	5.7	1545	1.8	2049	5.8
22	F	0414	1.6	0921	5.9	1637	1.6	2141	6.0
23	SA	0502	1.5	1007	6.1	1720	1.5	2226	6.1
24	SU	0542	1.4	1048	6.2	1800	1.4	2305	6.2
25	M	0618	1.3	1125	6.3	1836	1.3	2340	6.2
26	TU	0655	1.3	1158	6.4	1914	1.2		
27	W	0012	6.2	0730	1.2	1229	6.4	1951	1.2
28	TH	0042	6.2	0804	1.3	1300	6.4	2025	1.2

AUGUST

Day		Time	M	Time	M	Time	M	Time	M
1	M	0308	5.7	1013	1.8	1524	5.9	2244	1.7
2	TU	0402	5.5	1059	2.0	1619	5.7	2336	1.9
3	W	0502	5.4	1157	2.1	1722	5.6		
4	TH	0041	2.0	0608	5.4	1310	2.2	1832	5.5
5	F	0154	1.9	0721	5.5	1430	2.0	1945	5.7
6	SA	0314	1.7	0834	5.8	1552	1.6	2053	5.9
7	SU	0430	1.4	0935	6.1	1659	1.3	2152	6.2
8	M	0533	1.1	1027	6.5	1758	0.9	2244	6.5
9	TU	0634	0.9	1115	6.7	1855	0.7	2333	6.7
10	W	0728	0.7	1200	6.9	1947	0.5		
11	TH	0022	6.8	0818	0.6	1245	6.9	2034	0.4
12	F	0109	6.7	0901	0.7	1330	6.9	2118	0.5
13	SA	0155	6.6	0939	0.9	1413	6.7	2157	0.7
16	TU	0423	5.7	1136	1.9	1649	5.8		
17	W	0015	1.9	0533	5.4	1238	2.2	1805	5.5
18	TH	0127	2.1	0655	5.3	1401	2.2	1926	5.4
19	F	0246	2.1	0806	5.5	1518	2.1	2034	5.5
20	SA	0350	1.9	0905	5.7	1616	1.8	2131	5.7
21	SU	0441	1.7	0952	6.0	1704	1.6	2214	5.9
22	M	0525	1.5	1030	6.2	1746	1.4	2249	6.1
23	TU	0604	1.4	1102	6.4	1824	1.2	2318	6.2
24	W	0639	1.2	1133	6.5	1859	1.1	2346	6.3
25	TH	0712	1.2	1203	6.5	1933	1.1		
26	F	0014	6.3	0742	1.2	1232	6.5	2004	1.1
27	SA	0045	6.3	0809	1.2	1302	6.5	2032	1.1
28	SU	0116	6.2	0836	1.3	1330	6.4	2058	1.2

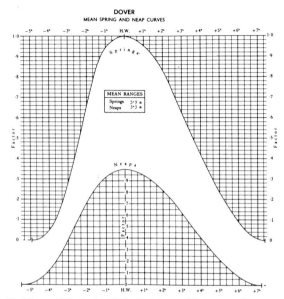

DOVER
MEAN SPRING AND NEAP CURVES

Table 2 *Admiralty* Tide Tables – *tidal curve, Dover*

1) Find the times and heights of the high and low waters either side of the time of interest, as described above. Subtract the LW height from the HW height to get the range of the tide.

2) *Case A* With the desired time as argument (related to the time of HW), find the corresponding factor. Use the spring or neap curve as appropriate, or if necessary use both curves and interpolate.

Multiply the range of the tide (step 1) by the factor thus found, and add the result to the low water height. This is the height of the tide at the time chosen.

3) *Case B* Subtract the height of low water from the desired height, and divide the answer by the range, to establish the factor.

Using this factor as argument, find the time (relative to HW) appropriate to it. There will in fact be two times, one for the rising tide and one for the falling tide. Choose whichever suits the case, and apply the result to the time of HW, to obtain the time required.

Note: If the tide happens to be greater than mean springs (or less than mean neaps), use the spring (or neap) factors.

For example:

Case A What will be the height of the tide at Dover at 1115 GMT on 17 May 1983?

Dover LW 0903 1.0 m HW 1413 6.1 m range 5.1 m (nearly springs)
Time required is 115 GMT = 3 hours before HW Dover
Factor (from Table 2) = 0.28, so rise = 0.28 × 5.1 = 1.4 m
Tidal height at 115 = 1.0 (LW height) + 1.4 = 2.4 m

Case B On 6th June 1983, at what time will the height of tide first rise to 3.5 metres at Dover?

Dover LW 0126 1.9 m HW 0657 5.3 m range 3.4 m (neaps)
Height required = 3.5 m, so rise = 3.5 − 1.9 = 1.6 m
Factor = rise ÷ range = 1.6 ÷ 1.9 = 0.47 m
Interval (from Table 2) = 2 h 45 m before HW = 0412 GMT

Note: If this problem had specified a falling tide, this would have occurred 3 h 40 m after HW, or at 1037 GMT.

Intermediate times and heights – secondary ports
These are handled in exactly the same way as standard ports, but it is necessary to begin with tidal times, heights and range worked out for the secondary port. The tidal curve for the standard port is used to establish the factor.

Accuracy of tidal predictions
Whilst the basic predictions in the *Tide Tables* (particularly for standard ports) are generally very accurate, the effect of weather conditions can introduce considerable errors. Tidal figures should therefore not be regarded as particularly accurate, and a 95 per cent error of fifteen minutes (in time) and 0.5 m (1.6 feet) (in height) should not be thought unlikely. For smaller secondary ports, and in areas where the tide behaves curiously, the errors may be greater.

Reduction to soundings
When a sounding is taken, the depth actually measured will differ from the charted depth by the height of the tide; in order to compare the two, the sounding must be *reduced*. For this to be done, the height of the tide must be established at some point offshore. The range of the tide is smaller offshore

ENGLAND, SOUTH AND EAST COASTS

No.	PLACE	Lat. N.	Long. W.	High Water		Low Water (Zone G.M.T.)		MHWS	MHWN	MLWN	MLWS	M.L. Z₀ m.	
81	**SHOREHAM** (see page 18)			0500 and 1700	1000 and 2200	0000 and 1200	0600 and 1800	**6·2**	**5·0**	**1·9**	**0·7**		
75	Worthing	50 48	0 22	+0015	0000	+0010	−0005	−0·1	−0·2	0·0	0·0	⊙	
81	**SHOREHAM**	50 50	0 15	STANDARD PORT				See Table V				3·36	
82	Brighton	50 49	0 08	−0010	−0005	−0005	−0005	+0·3	+0·1	0·0	−0·1	3·49	
		N.	**E.**										
83	Newhaven	50 47	0 04	−0015	−0010	0000	0000	+0·4	+0·2	0·0	−0·2	3·61	
84	Eastbourne	50 46	0 17	−0010	−0005	+0015	+0020	+1·1	+0·6	+0·2	+0·1	3·77	
89	**DOVER** (see page 22)			0000 and 1200	0600 and 1800	0100 and 1300	0700 and 1900	**6·7**	**5·3**	**2·0**	**0·8**		
85	Hastings	50 51	0 35	0000	−0010	−0030	−0030	+0·8	+0·5	+0·1	−0·1	3·85	
86	Rye (Approaches)	50 55	0 47	+0005	−0010	⊙	⊙	+1·0	+0·7	⊙	⊙	⊙	
86a	Rye (Harbour)	50 56	0 46	+0005	−0010	⊙	⊙	−1·4	−1·7	⊙	⊙	1·97	
87	Dungeness	50 54	0 58	−0010	−0015	−0020	−0010	+1·0	+0·5	+0·2	−0·1	4·03	
88	Folkestone	51 05	1 12	−0020	−0005	−0010	−0010	+0·4	+0·4	0·0	−0·1	3·74	
89	**DOVER**	51 07	1 19	STANDARD PORT				See Table V				3·70	
98	Deal	51 13	1 25	+0010	+0020	+0010	+0005	−0·6	−0·3	0·0	0·0	3·13	x
99	Richborough	51 18	1 21	+0015	+0015	+0030	+0030	−3·4	−2·6	−1·7	−0·7	1·42	c
102	Ramsgate	51 20	1 25	+0020	+0020	−0007	−0007	−1·8	−1·5	−0·8	−0·4	2·56	
103	**MARGATE** (see page 26)			0100 and 1300	0700 and 1900	0100 and 1300	0700 and 1900	**4·8**	**3·9**	**1·4**	**0·5**		
102a	Broadstairs	51 21	1 27	−0020	−0008	+0007	+0010	−0·2	−0·2	−0·1	−0·1	⊙	
103	**MARGATE**	51 24	1 23	STANDARD PORT				See Table V				2·67	
104	Herne Bay	51 23	1 07	+0034	+0022	+0015	+0032	+0·4	+0·4	0·0	0·0	2·73	
105	Whitstable Approaches	51 22	1 02	+0042	+0029	+0025	+0050	+0·6	+0·6	+0·1	0·0	⊙	
108	**SHEERNESS** (see page 30)			0200 and 1400	0800 and 2000	0200 and 1400	0700 and 1900	**5·7**	**4·8**	**1·5**	**0·6**		
	River Swale												
106	Grovehurst Jetty	51 22	0 46	−0007	0000	0000	+0016	0·0	0·0	0·0	−0·1	⊙	

Table 3 *Admiralty* Tide Tables – *secondary port differences.*

than it is on the coast, and to reduce soundings accurately a co-tidal chart is needed. For a rough rule of thumb, use three-quarters of the range within a few miles of the shore, and half the range further out. The *rule of twelfths* may be used to estimate heights between high and low water. This states that the tide will rise (or fall):

Range × one twelfth in the first hour

Range × two twelfths in the second hour

Range × three twelfths in the third and fourth hours

Range × two twelfths in the fifth hour

Range × one twelfth in the sixth hour.

Do not rely too heavily on the results.

33 Tidal streams

Associated with the vertical rise and fall of the tides are horizontal movements of the water, known as *tidal streams*. Like the tides, they are of no significance in the deep oceans and become more significant as the coast is approached. Their strength depends very much upon the geography of the area, and in a few places can reach speeds of eight knots or more. They can also give rise to races, overfalls and bores (see below), and no craft, however large and powerful, can afford to ignore their effects.

Tidal streams, like the tides which give rise to them, are cyclic in nature; the water moves to and fro, but there is no net movement. Over a complete tide, the tidal streams cancel themselves out. Tidal streams take one of two main forms:

1) *Rectilinear*, in which the water flows in one direction for half the tide, and then reverses to flow in the opposite direction for the remaining half of the tide. The moment when the tidal stream stops and changes direction is known as *slack water*.

2) *Rotary*, in which the tidal stream constantly changes direction around the compass, often with no period of slack water.

Of these two types, rectilinear motion is most often found in narrow channels, estuaries, rivers and straits; rotary motion is generally to be found in open seas and wide bays.

Tidal streams are greatly affected by the detailed geography of the area, including the sea bed. In their turn, tidal streams can also affect the sea state; when wind and tide oppose each other, the sea becomes shorter, higher and more confused than it would otherwise be, and may be dangerous to small craft. The major tidal stream effects that the navigator should look for, to use to his advantage or to avoid, are:

1) A tidal stream flowing parallel to an indented coast can often be worked to advantage. The tidal stream runs more strongly past headlands, and less strongly within bays (Fig. 1). The tidal stream tends to set into and out of a bay, and there may be a back eddy in the tidal lee of a headland.

2) An irregular bottom or a shoal or shelf can deflect a tidal stream upwards, causing an area of disturbed seas, known as an *overfall*. In strong wind-against-tide situations, these areas can be dangerous (Fig. 2).

3) If a tidal stream is forced through a narrow channel, its speed increases dramatically, leading to a *race* (Fig. 3). If a race can be carried in calm weather, it can give a boat a very useful lift; passage against the tidal stream may be literally impossible. Because of the difficult seas caused by a race, they should be avoided, whichever way they are running, in bad weather.

4) In some rivers with narrow channels, the new flood in the lower reaches can fight with the old ebb still running further up. Eventually the flood wins, and sends a wave, known as a *bore*, surging up the river; this can be dangerous. The River Severn has perhaps the best-known example of a bore.

5) When a tidal stream flows through a channel fringed by wide, flat mud- or sand-banks, there is a tendency for the water to set onto the banks at the flood, and off the banks on the ebb (Fig. 4). This can be important for a yacht going out against the flood; if it hugs one bank to keep in shallow water (and hence less tidal stream), it might be set onto the bank and aground.

6) Areas where tidal streams converge or diverge (as at the junctions of rivers or estuaries) can lead to unpredictable tidal streams and confused seas.

Predicting tidal streams

In most parts of the world, tidal streams can be related to the tide at a nearby standard port. Slack water will be related to high water at the port, though generally the two times will not be the same; tidal streams tend to run a little longer (up to three hours) after the time of high water on the adjacent coast. For most areas it is possible to produce chartlets or tables of tidal streams, related to high water at a suitable standard port, and this is the method most often adopted. There are a few areas where this is not possible (for example, the Straits of Malacca), and special arrangements have to be made.

33.1 *Tidal streams along a coast.*

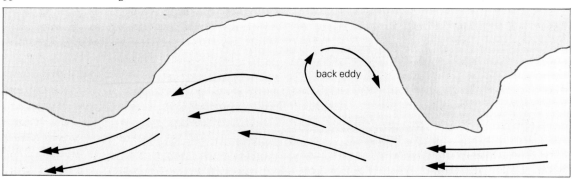

33.2 *Overfalls.*

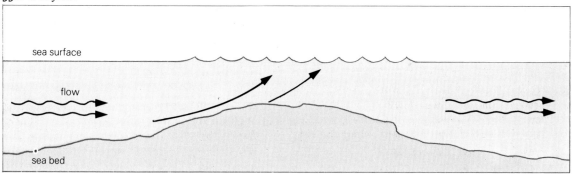

33.3 *A race.*

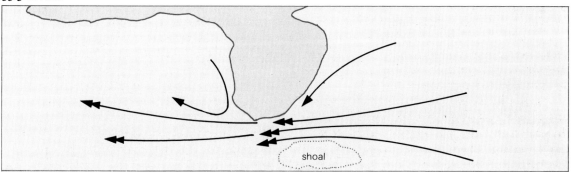

33.4 *Tidal streams setting across banks: (a) on the flood; (b) on the ebb.*

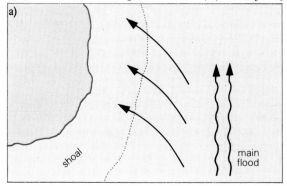 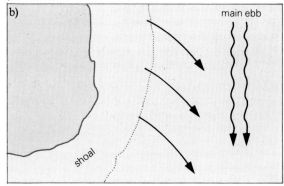

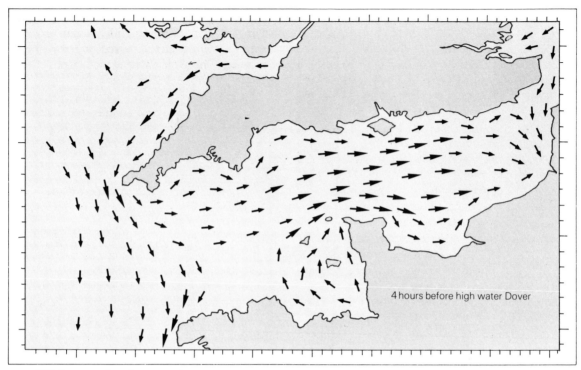

4 hours before high water Dover

33.5 *Tidal stream chart from an atlas.*

Table 1 *Extract from NOS Tidal Current Tables.*

TABLE 2. – CURRENT DIFFERENCES AND OTHER CONSTANTS, 1983

NO.	PLACE	METER DEPTH (ft)	Lat. (° ' N)	Long. (° ' W)	Min. before Flood (h.m.)	Flood (h.m.)	Min. before Ebb (h.m.)	Ebb (h.m.)	Flood ratio	Ebb ratio	Minimum before Flood (knots deg.)	Maximum Flood (knots deg.)	Minimum before Ebb (knots deg.)	Maximum Ebb (knots deg.)
	LONG ISLAND SOUND Time meridian, 75°W				on THE RACE, p.34									
	Connecticut River													
2551	Lynde Point, channel east of........		41 16	72 20	+0 42	+0 50	+0 18	+0 29	0.3	0.2	0.0 --	0.9 344	0.0 --	0.7 161
2556	Saybrook Point, 0.2 mile northeast of..		41 17.02	72 20.87	+0 35	+0 51	+0 47	+0˙30	0.5	0.4	0.0 --	1.5 355	0.0 --	1.5 160
2561	Railroad drawbridge..............	15	41 19.00	72 20.77	+0 27	-0 26	+0 54	+1 06	0.4	0.3	0.0 --	1.0 360	0.0 --	1.0 198
						+0 35			0.2			0.6 359		
							+1 31		0.3			0.9 356		
2566	Eustasia Island, 0.6 mile ESE of.....		41 23.30	72 24.23	+1 53	+1 38	+1 23	+1 26	0.4	0.4	0.0 --	1.1 290	0.0 --	1.4 070
2571	Eddy Rock Shoal, west of.............	15	41 26.57	72 27.78	+1 41	+2 16	+2 01	+1 20	0.3	0.2	0.0 --	0.8 350	0.0 --	0.6 155
2576	Higganum Creek, 0.5 mile ESE of......		41 30.02	72 32.62	+3 06	+2 52	+2 35	+3 01	0.3	0.3	0.0 --	0.8 270	0.0 --	1.0 080
2581	Wilcox Island Park, east of..........		41 34.33	72 38.88	+4 06	+3 36	+3 07	+3 35	0.3	0.3	0.0 --	0.9 355	0.0 --	1.0 160
2586	Rocky Hill........................	9	41 39.82	72 37.73	+4 41	+3 37	+3 21	+3 30	0.2	0.2	0.0 --	0.6 335	0.0 --	0.8 135
2591	Hartford Jetty <42>..........	9	41 45.07	72 39.02	+5 45	+4 39	+3 22	+4 29	0.2	0.2	0.0 --	0.1 290	0.0 --	0.7 095
2596	Saybrook Breakwater, 1.5 miles SE of..		41 14.78	72 19.05	-1 30	-1 11	-0 55	-1 57	0.7	0.6	0.0 --	1.9 260	0.0 --	2.0 070
2601	Mulford Point, 3.1 miles northwest of..	15	41 12.00	72 19.08	-0 06	-1 05	-0 05	-0 24	0.7	0.6	0.0 --	1.9 269	0.0 --	2.3 066
2606	Orient Point, 1 mile WNW of...........		41 10.02	72 15.11	-1 09	-2 02	-0 33	-1 15	0.5	0.9	0.0 --	1.4 245	0.0 --	3.1 055
						-0 59			0.3			0.8 255		
						-0 09			0.7			2.1 245		
2611	Rocky Point, 0.3 mile north of.......	15	41 08.63	72 21.42	-0 27	-1 02	-1 01	-0 28	0.6	0.6	0.0 --	1.8 279	0.0 --	2.1 041
2616	Cornfield Point, 3 miles south of.....	7	41 12.9	72 22.4	-0 56	-0 17	-0 03	-0 20	0.6	0.4	0.0 --	2.0 256	0.0 --	1.7 094
2621	Cornfield Point, 1.1 miles south of..	15	41 14.65	72 23.40	-1 01	-1 34	-1 02	-2 03	0.5	0.5	0.0 --	1.4 293	0.0 --	1.6 108
2626	Kesley Point, 2.1 miles southeast of..		41 14.10	72 27.93	-0 35	-1 02	-0 54	-1 00	0.5	0.5	0.0 --	1.5 260	0.0 --	1.8 070
2631	Six Mile Reef, 1.5 miles north of.....		41 12.66	72 28.87	-0 17	-0 12	-0 23	-0 41	0.3	0.4	0.0 --	1.0 290	0.0 --	1.3 095
2636	Six Mile Reef, 2 miles east of........		41 10.83	72 26.90	-0 36	-0 12	-0 07	-0 35	0.6	0.6	0.0 --	1.6 235	0.0 --	2.1 040
2641	Horton Point, 1.4 miles NNW of........		41 06.30	72 27.40	+0 04	+0 08	-0 03	-0 18	0.5	0.6	0.0 --	1.4 260	0.0 --	2.0 040
2646	Kelsey Point, 1 mile south of.........		41 14	72 30	-1 32	-1 00	-1 03	-1 51	0.6	0.3	0.0 --	2.0 249	0.0 --	1.5 118
2651	Hammonasset Point, 1.2 miles SW of....	15	41 14.22	72 34.00	-0 59	-1 15	-0 44	-1 31	0.3	0.3	0.0 --	1.0 287	0.0 --	1.0 106
2656	Hammonasset Point, 5 miles south of...	15	41 09.80	72 34.17	-0 03	-0 03	-0 24	-0 06	0.5	0.4	0.0 --	1.4 284	0.0 --	1.5 090
2661	Mattituck Inlet, 1 mile northwest of..	15	41 01.68	72 34.22	-0 21	-0 15	-0 08	-0 26	0.3	0.3	0.0 --	0.9 241	0.0 --	1.0 053
2666	Sachem Head, 1 mile SSE of............		41 13.65	72 42.30	-0 38	-0 36	-0 35	-1 02	0.3	0.4	0.0 --	1.1 255	0.0 --	1.0 065
2671	Sachem Head, 6.2 miles south of.......	15	41 08.73	72 42.30	+0 29	+0 24	-0 12	-0 04	0.2	0.3	0.0 --	0.6 260	0.0 --	0.9 065
2676	Roanoke Point, 5.6 miles north of.....		41 04.37	72 42.53	-0 02	-0 02	-0 15	-0 24	0.2	0.3	0.0 --	0.7 255	0.0 --	0.9 050
2681	Roanoke Point, 2.3 miles NNW of.......		41 00.92	72 42.97	-1 19	-0 22	-0 10	-0 29	0.3	0.2	0.0 --	0.9 270	0.0 --	0.7 070
2686	Sachem Head, 1 mile south of..........		41 14	72 43	-0 46	+0 03	-0 33	-0 38	0.3	0.3	0.0 --	0.9 278	0.0 --	1.2 084
2691	Herod Point, 2.8 miles north of.......	15	41 00.97	72 49.93	-0 29	-0 17	-0 27	-0 06	0.2	0.2	0.1 020	0.4 290	0.1 020	0.6 090
2696	Herod Point, 6.5 miles north of.......	15	41 04.65	72 49.80	-0 27	+0 06	+0 12	-0 07	0.3	0.2	0.0 --	0.9 254	0.0 --	0.7 070
2701	New Haven Harbor entrance <12>.......		41 14	72 55	-1 11	-1 34	-0 37	-1 15	0.4	0.2	0.0 --	1.4 319	0.0 --	0.9 152
2706	City Point, 1.3 miles northeast of....		41 17.83	72 54.42	+0 11	+0 30	+0 33	+0 08	0.1	0.1	0.0 --	0.3 015	0.0 --	0.3 060
2711	Oyster River Pt., 1.3 miles SSE of <1>..		41 12.87	72 58.00	- --	-0 15	- --	-0 47	0.1	0.1	0.0 --	0.3 255	0.0 --	0.3 060
2716	Pond Point, 4.2 miles SSE of..........		41 08.60	72 58.08	-0 20	+0 04	-0 04	-0 14	0.2	0.2	0.0 --	0.6 265	0.0 --	0.6 065
2721	Stratford Shoal, 6 miles east of......		41 04.52	72 58.43	+0 01	-0 02	-0 07	-0 09	0.2	0.2	0.0 --	0.9 265	0.0 --	0.6 060
2726	Sound Beach, 2.2 miles south of.......		41 00.33	72 58.45	-0 03	-0 06	-0 15	-0 29	0.3	0.3	0.0 --	0.9 270	0.0 --	0.9 075
2731	Charles Island, 0.8 mile SSE of.......		41 10.77	73 02.63	-0 51	-0 36	-0 30	-0 54	0.1	0.1	0.0 --	0.4 250	0.0 --	0.4 070
	Housatonic River													
2736	Milford Point, 0.2 mile west of.......	10	41 10.35	73 06.82	-0 06	+0 01	+0 15	-0 55	0.4	0.3	0.0 --	1.2 330	0.0 --	1.2 135
2741	Railroad drawbridge, above............	5	41 12.53	73 06.67	+0 34	+0 13	+0 29	-0 55	0.4	0.4	0.0 --	1.0 350	0.0 --	1.3 185
2746	Fowler Island, 0.1 mile NNW of........	5	41 14.40	73 06.23	+0 48	+0 10	+0 30	+0 48	0.4	0.3	0.0 --	1.1 040	0.0 --	1.1 270

Endnotes can be found at the end of Table 2.

Having established the time of high water at the appropriate standard port, there are two ways of finding the tidal stream at any location:

1) By using a *Tidal Stream Atlas*, which gives a chartlet for each hour of the tide, with arrows showing the direction and numbers giving the spring and neap rate of the tidal stream (Fig. 5). Similar chartlets are printed in many yachting almanacs.

2) The chart of the area may also carry tidal stream information, either in the form of a table giving rates and directions for certain positions, or by means of feathered arrows (on older charts). When using a table, the navigator should not forget that the directions given refer to the true compass (not the magnetic). Two rates are given, for springs and neaps, and interpolation should be used if required.

3) Some charting authorities publish tidal stream or tidal current tables, rather than atlases.

Tidal stream estimates from any source should be made as carefully as possible, interpolating if required.

Accuracy of tidal stream predictions

However carefully tidal stream predictions are made, the only thing that can be said about them with confidence is that they will be wrong. In tidal waters, errors in estimating tidal stream are without doubt the dominant source of error in dead reckoning. There are three main reasons for the poor quality of the predictions:

1) The information upon which the predictions are based is very much more sparse than the information used for *Tide Tables*. It generally relates to one short period of time which may not be typical.

2) The predictions are only accurate (!) for the exact position in which they were made; a position only a few metres away may experience a different tidal stream.

3) Tidal streams appear to be more affected by meteorological effects than the actual tide itself.

The navigator should always be aware that his tidal stream estimates may be grossly in error, and he should always try to check them. Passing close to a navigational buoy, an anchored fishing boat or a fishing float can give a valuable clue; on a cross-tide leg, a back bearing of the mark just left can show if the tidal stream is being under- or over-estimated (it seems a fact of life that under-estimation is much more common); or a careful comparison of a fix with the estimated position may show that something is wrong.

RADIO AIDS TO NAVIGATION

34 Medium frequency direction finding

Medium frequency direction finding (MFDF) is by far the most important radio aid to navigation for the yachtsman. Although the accuracy is generally poor, the equipment required can be relatively cheap and easy to use, and there are generally enough radio beacons in well-travelled areas to provide useful position lines.

MFDF is used in two principal ways; as the radio waves employed follow the curvature of the earth, they can be received at a considerable distance (200 miles or more in some circumstances), and so form a useful landfall aid. Secondly, as radio waves are relatively little affected by the weather they can provide positional information in poor visibility.

Principles

MFDF equipment consists of a suitable receiver in the ship, connected to an antenna with directional properties. The principle of such an antenna is shown in Figure 1; when the antenna (which often consists of a coil of wire wound around a ferrite rod) is pointing directly towards the transmitter, the signal received is at a minimum, and when the antenna is rotated through a right angle, the received signal is at a maximum. A bearing of the transmitter is taken by rotating the antenna until a minimum (a null) is found, and noting the direction in which the antenna is pointing. As the antenna has a directional response resembling a figure-eight, the bearing obtained is ambiguous; to put it simply, the simple MFDF antenna does not tell you if the transmitter is in front of you or behind you. This 180° ambiguity is known as the *sense ambiguity*. In most circumstances it will cause the navigator no difficulty, but various means are available for its resolution (see below).

34.1 *A directional antenna.*

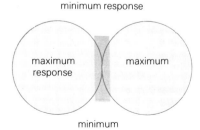

minimum response

maximum response

maximum

minimum

Most MFDF antennae for the yacht market are of this simple type, generally with a magnetic compass attached to allow the direct reading of magnetic bearings (Fig. 2). More expensive equipment can offer improved facilities. A sense antenna may be fitted to provide a way of resolving the sense ambiguity described above, and an array of two loops at right angles to each other can be used to indicate bearings automatically, with the sense ambiguity resolved; such an automatic direction finder (ADF) can offer a very much improved performance, but with a substantial cost and space penalty.

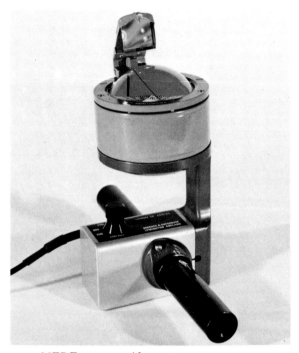

34.2 *MFDF antenna with compass.*

Receivers for use with MFDF antennae must be properly designed for the purpose; they must be fitted with quick and accurate means of tuning to the frequency of the desired beacon; they must have good selectivity and sensitivity to pick out a weak beacon signal in the presence of interference; and certain types of radio beacon require the use of a device within the receiver known as a beat frequency oscillator (BFO).

The actual procedure for taking radio bearings will vary according to the equipment in use. The manufacturers instructions should be followed carefully; the successful use of MFDF equipment depends very much upon experience, and every opportunity should be taken to practice.

Radio beacons

In principle, radio bearings can be taken of any radio transmission that the MFDF set is capable of receiving; in practice, almost all radio bearings are taken of specially established transmitters known as radiobeacons. It is sometimes also possible to take bearings of broadcast transmitters carrying entertainment programmes.

Marine radiobeacons

Marine radiobeacons are established by lighthouse authorities around the coast, especially for use by mariners. They are generally established at lighthouses, on lightships or at other positions of navigational importance. The details of each beacon are listed in the appropriate *List of Radio Signals* (*Light List* in the USA). It is common practice to group together a number of beacons in the same area onto a common frequency; each beacon in the group will transmit at a different time, to allow several bearings of different beacons to be obtained without having to re-tune the receiver. Marine radio-beacons generally operate on a six-minute cycle, with each beacon occupying one minute of the cycle. The *sequence number* of the beacon indicates which slot it occupies in each cycle; Table 1 translates the sequence number into the actual time (minutes past each hour) that each beacon transmits. Some modern MFDF sets incorporate a clock which keeps track of the current sequence number, but this should never be used as the sole means of identification; the Morse identification transmitted by the beacon should always be checked before using a bearing.

Aero radiobeacons

Radiobeacons are widely used by aircraft, and suitably sited aero radiobeacons can be useful at sea; details of such beacons are given in the *List of Radio Signals* (*Light List* in the USA). Aero beacons are generally powerful, and each one operates continuously on its own frequency.

Aeromarine radiobeacons

Aeromarine beacons are established in areas where radio aids tend to be few and far between, and are designed to suit the needs both of the seaman and the aviator. They generally have similar characteristics to aero radiobeacons.

Broadcast transmitters

It is sometimes possible to use broadcast transmitters for radio bearings, but there are difficulties. One of these is the problem of finding out exactly where the transmitter is sited; this information is not easy to obtain and transmitters can be sited at some distance from the studios which originate the broadcast.

34.3 *Synchronized broadcast transmitters.*

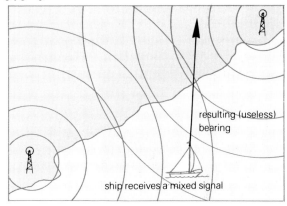

A more fundamental difficulty arises with the growing practice of synchronizing transmitters to improve the coverage of broadcast stations. This means that two or more transmitters carry the same programme on the same frequency. If any attempt is made to take a bearing, then part of the signal may come from one transmitter and part from another; the resulting bearing will be seriously in error (Fig. 3). However, the powerful signal from a broadcast transmitter can be very useful if it is known not to be synchronized (e.g., when situated on an island or in some other remote area of population).

Table 1 *Sequence numbers and times of marine radiobeacons*

Sequence	Time (minutes past the hour)									
1	00	06	12	18	24	30	36	42	48	54
2	01	07	13	19	25	31	37	43	49	55
3	02	08	14	20	26	32	38	44	50	56
4	03	09	15	21	27	33	39	45	51	57
5	04	10	16	22	28	34	40	46	52	58
6	05	11	17	23	29	35	41	47	53	59

35 Taking MFDF bearings

The actual process of taking MFDF bearings will vary according to the equipment being used; however, the following sequence illustrates the process for the most common type of equipment – the hand-held antenna with magnetic compass attached.

1) From the chart, identify suitable radio-beacons in the vicinity of the DR position.
2) From the *List of Radio Signals* (or other suitable document), extract the following information (Table 1):
   a) The frequency of the beacon
   b) The Morse identification code
   c) The sequence number
   d) The maximum range
   e) The mode of emission (A1, A2, A2★ etc).
3) When possible, choose beacons which are close to your position; in any event, do not use beacons beyond their listed maximum range.
4) Tune the receiver (and, if necessary, the antenna) to the given frequency, and adjust the set in accordance with the mode of emission. The maker's handbook will explain how to do this.
5) Listen for the beacon at the time indicated by its sequence number; move the antenna about and adjust the tuning if necessary to get a clear signal.
6) Make a positive identification of the beacon by reading the Morse identity code transmitted several times at the beginning of its sequence.
7) When the beacon transmits a long dash, turn the antenna until the signal goes through a minimum (a null). This null is best detected by ear, but some sets provide a meter indication and/or a dimming light as well.
8) Move the antenna through the null several times, and observe the compass reading of the minimum signal. If the null is diffuse or difficult to detect, the resulting bearing should be used with caution.
9) Re-check the identification at the end of the sequence.
10) Plot the resulting position line; if taking bearings at long range, apply the half-convergency correction (see below). This is not necessary for bearings of beacons within 50 miles.

Sense ambiguity

With simple equipment, there is no way of resolving the sense ambiguity within the set itself, so that bearings may be wrong by 180°. In most situations, no ambiguity exists; for a beacon on the coast, the reciprocal bearing probably lies inland, for example. However, where doubt exists, as in Figure 1, two steps may be taken to resolve it:

1) An unambiguous bearing of another radio-beacon may indicate which of the two reciprocal bearings is correct.
2) Otherwise, a second bearing of the original beacon should be taken after sufficient time for the bearing to have made a noticeable change. The sense in which the bearing has changed, clockwise or anticlockwise, will always allow you to decide on which side of the beacon you lie.

Automatic direction finding

ADF equipment will automatically swing to the bearing of the beacon, with sense ambiguities resolved, as soon as the beacon begins to transmit (the reading may be unsteady during the Morse identification). ADF sets are normally very easy to use, but two cautions should be observed:

1) As with all MFDF bearings, it is vital to identify the beacon by means of its Morse identification.
2) An ADF will indicate a bearing of the beacon relative to the ship's head. This relative bearing must be added to or subtracted from the magnetic ship's head to obtain a magnetic bearing to plot on the chart.

Errors in MFDF

Whilst MFDF is an invaluable aid for yachts, it is subject to numerous (and sometimes large) errors. These errors must be properly understood if MFDF is to become a trusted tool in the navigator's box of tricks.

Systematic errors

1) *DF compass deviations.* If the MFDF set has a magnetic compass attached, this can suffer from deviations, like any other compass. In wood, glass fibre or aluminium boats, it should be possible to find, by experiment, locations where the DF compass is not deviated; look out

RADIOBEACONS AND RADIO DIRECTION-FINDING STATIONS

(Atlantic Coast) UNITED STATES

RC	Highland Lt, Cape Cod[1]					42°02′23″N	70°03′43″W	**5849**	
		286	A2*						

No	Name	Ident	Range	Seq	Fog	Clear
5849	Highland Lt	**HI**	100	1	Cont	Cont
5841	Nantucket Sh	**NS**	100	2	Cont	Cont
5779	Montauk Pt	**Y**	20	3	Cont	Cont
5747	Ambrose	**T**	125	4	Cont	Cont
5893	Great Duck I	**GD**	50	5	Cont	Cont
5885	Manana I	**MI**	100	6	Cont	Cont

1) Located 352° 52m from the Lt

RC	**Cape Cod Canal Breakwater**[1]					41°46′29″N	70°29′51″W	**5853**
	U	318	A2*	20 n miles	H24			

1) Located 224° 815 m from Lt J0372

RC Marker	**Scituate Harbour** **SH**	295	A2*	10 n miles		42°12′00″N	70°43′12″W	**5855**

RC	**Boston Lt Buoy B** **BH**	304	A2*	30 n miles	H24	42°22′40″N	70°47′00″W	**5857**

Aero RC	**Lynnfield** **SEW**	382	A2*	100 n miles	H24	42°27′08″N	70°57′50″W	**5861**

RC	**Eastern Point Lt, Gloucester Harbour** **EP**	325	A2*	10 n miles	H24	42°34′49″N	70°39′54″W	**5865**

RC	**Portland Lt Buoy P** **PH**	301	A2*	30 n miles	H24	43°31′36″N	70°05′30″W	**5869**

RC	**Halfway Rock Lt** **HR**	291	A2*	10 n miles	H24	43°39′20″N	70°02′15″W	**5877**

RC Marker	**The Cuckolds Lt** **CU**	320	A2*	10 n miles	H24	43°46′46″N	69°39′02″W	**5881**

RC	**Manana Island Fog Signal Station** **MI**—Grouped with 5849		43°45′48″N	69°19′38″W	**5885**

RC	**Matinicus Rock Lt** **MR**	314	A2*	20 n miles	H24	43°47′00″N	68°51′22″W	**5889**

Table 1 *Extract from* List of Radio Signals (Light List).

for instruments, radios, cameras or other magnetic equipment. The hand-held type of MFDF equipment can only be used with difficulty in steel or concrete boats; the crossed-loop type of set is much more satisfactory.

2) *Siting error.* A relatively small error may be introduced by the actual siting of the aerial within the vessel. This error is generally unimportant, and can be minimized by placing the aerial on the centreline of the ship.

3) *Quadrantal error.* This is the most important of the systematic errors of MFDF, and arises because some of the structure of the boat itself can act as an aerial, causing a distortion of the incoming signal from the beacon. It is called quadrantal error, because it does not affect signals coming from the bow or the stern, or from either beam. The error is at a maximum for signals on either bow or either quarter (Fig. 2). Quadrantal error can be minimized by making sure there are no continuous loops of metal around the boat; guardrails are the most common offenders, and the loop should be broken by insulators or a rope lanyard in at least two places.

Simple hand-held equipment does not permit the correction of these systematic errors. They should be minimized by careful siting of the set,

35.1 *Resolving sense ambiguity.*

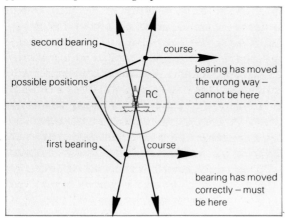

second bearing

course

bearing has moved the wrong way – cannot be here

possible positions

RC

first bearing

course

bearing has moved correctly – must be here

and the errors measured by 'swinging' the MFDF; this involves comparing MFDF bearings of a suitable beacon with visual bearings taken at the same time. A correction table can then be drawn up.

Random errors

1) *Night effect* Radio waves from a beacon may reach the receiving antenna by two paths – the ground wave which follows the surface of the earth, or the sky wave which is reflected from the ionosphere. The reception of sky wave signals can cause substantial errors in MFDF bearings. The effect of sky waves on MFDF are most marked at night, and especially within two hours of sunset or sunrise. Sky wave effects can often be detected by erratic and fluttering signals and a poor null. Such bearings should be used cautiously (if at all), and bearings close to sunrise or sunset should be avoided altogether.

2) *Land effect* The velocity of a radio wave depends to some extent on the nature of the surface over which it travels. This has the effect of causing the wave to be refracted where it passes from land to sea (Fig. 3). The angle of refraction is zero for a wave that crosses the coast at right angles, and can be six or seven degrees for a wave crossing at a grazing angle (the refraction is always towards the land). Marine radiobeacons are normally sited in such a way that land effects are unimportant, but aero or aero-marine beacons may not be. Similar effects may

be seen with radio waves that have to cross mountains between the transmitter and the receiver.

Random errors in MFDF can be very large – six or seven degrees for land effect and tens of degrees for night effect. Land effect can usually be avoided by choosing beacons which do not have to cross land on their way to your antenna; night effect can almost always be detected by the poor quality of the null. This is why it is better to detect the null by ear rather than by a meter or lamp.

The 95 per cent error of a properly installed and calibrated MFDF set will probably be of the order of 5° in good conditions, 10° in moderate conditions and 15° (or more) in bad conditions.

35.2 *Quadrantal error.*

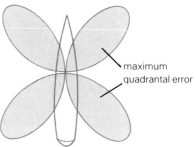

maximum quadrantal error

Half convergency

Radio waves follow a great circle path, and as is shown on page 15, a great circle and a rhumb line (line of constant bearing) do not in general coincide. To obtain the compass bearing of a distant MFDF station, a correction must be applied to the measured bearing; this correction is called the *half convergency*. It can be computed with a calculator by using the equation ($\frac{1}{2}$d. long sin [mid lat]), or the table on page 191 may be used. Half convergency is always applied towards the equator. It need not be applied for beacons less than 50 miles away, or for a beacon which lies almost due north or south.

35.3 *Coastal refraction.*

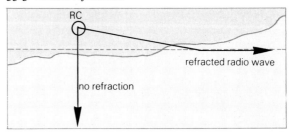

RC

refracted radio wave

no refraction

36   The principles of radar

Radar is a method of using radio waves to detect distant objects and displaying their position relative to the radar-equipped vessel on a display screen. It will work equally well by day or by night, in clear weather or in fog, but large seas or heavy rain or snow may affect its performance. In merchant ships, radar has become an indispensable aid to navigation and collision avoidance; the less elaborate sets suitable for fitting in yachts offer a much reduced, but still useful, performance.

A radar set works by transmitting short, powerful pulses of radio energy from a directional antenna. When these pulses, moving away at the speed of light, strike a solid object, part of the energy is reflected back towards the transmitter. A receiving antenna detects the very small returning signal, called for obvious reasons an 'echo'. The range of the reflecting object can be calculated by the time interval between the transmitted pulse and the returning echo, using the fact that radio waves travels at about 162,000 nautical miles a second; the direction of the reflecting object is given by the direction in which the transmitting and receiving antennae are pointing. These antennae (which may be combined in one antenna) are caused to rotate (Fig. 1).

36.1 *Principles of radar.*

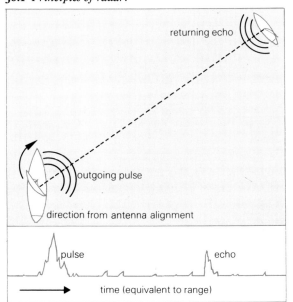

returning echo

outgoing pulse

direction from antenna alignment

pulse   echo

time (equivalent to range)

A typical small radar set will operate at 10,000 MHz, which corresponds to a wavelength of three centimetres (one and a quarter inches). The transmitted pulse will have a power of between three and ten kW, but will last for less than a microsecond (one millionth of a second); the pulses will be repeated about 1,000 or 2,000 times a second. At the same time, the antenna array rotates at twenty or thirty revolutions per minute. The maximum range of the set will be sixteen miles or more, but the range at which any particular object will be detected depends upon its size, the material from which it is made and its height above sea level; the height of the radar antenna is also an important factor in detection range.

The received echoes are displayed on a screen known as a plan position indicator (PPI). A radial line, known as a trace, rotates around the screen in synchronism with the antennae; a returning echo causes the trace to brighten at a distance from the centre which is proportional to the range of the object, causing a bright mark (or 'paint') on the screen. As the aerials (and the trace) sweep round, a picture of detectable objects is built up, rather like a map centred on the ship's position.

The bearing of an object can be measured by means of a radial cursor and a scale around the edge of the PPI; range can either be estimated using fixed 'range rings' at known increments of range, or measured more exactly by means of a unit which produces a variable range ring under the operator's control. When the range ring is moved to coincide with an object, its range can be read on a display attached to the unit.

Adjustment of a radar set

Each make or model of radar has its own procedures for switching on and adjustment, and these will be described in detail in the maker's handbook. For best results, you should follow the maker's instructions carefully; however, the following general points may be of some help in getting a good picture.

1) *Brightness* As its name suggests, this controls the brightness of the picture; it should be set so that the picture is clear, but without any tendency to smear across the screen.
2) *Gain* This controls the sensitivity of the receiver. If it is set too low, echoes will be lost

because the receiver misses them; if set too high, echoes can be obscured or lost in excessive 'noise' (a speckled effect on the screen). A suitable setting of the gain control is one which just leaves faint speckling on the screen.

3) *Tuning* Like any other receiver, the radar receiver must be tuned to the correct frequency. If it is not, echoes may be lost. The tuning control should be varied until maximum response is apparent on the PPI.

4) *Sea clutter* This control is designed to minimize the effect of waves close to the ship, which 'clutter' the centre of the screen with a host of unwanted echoes. The sea clutter control reduces the gain of the receiver at short ranges, without affecting the gain at longer ranges. It should only be used when necessary, and even then it should be used with care; too much control can cause small echoes nearby, such as navigational buoys and other yachts, to be lost.

5) *Rain clutter* Heavy rain, snow or hail, and sometimes storm clouds, can show up on the PPI as blotches with soft edges, rather like cotton wool in appearance. The rain clutter control can be used to help reveal small echoes which might otherwise be obscured. It should be adjusted to give best results, and turned off when not in use

Factors affecting radar detection range

The range at which any particular object will be detected by a radar set depends upon a number of factors:

1) *Antenna height* As radar waves travel in straight lines, a high antenna has a more distant radar horizon than one low down; when installing a set, the antenna should be mounted as high as topweight and other considerations permit.

2) *Transmitter power* Greater power in the transmitted pulse will lead to stronger echoes and hence longer detection ranges, but the power of most radars is adequate for the purpose for which they are intended.

3) *Receiver sensitivity* The inherent sensitivity of any radar receiver is adequate, but will only be achieved if the various controls, especially gain and tuning, are properly adjusted.

4) *Target height* A high target, such as a cliff, will

be picked up at a longer range than a low one, because the radar energy can see it further round the curvature of the earth (Fig. 2).

5) *Target size* A big target will reflect more energy than a small one, and hence will be detected at a greater range.

6) *Target material* Some materials reflect radar energy better than others; steel and stone reflect well, wood, fibreglass and sand reflect badly. It is possible to enhance the echo of an object by fitting a *radar reflector* (Fig. 3); this is often done to navigational buoys, and a radar reflector is an essential piece of safety equipment for the small yacht, especially if made of wood or fibreglass.

7) *Atmospheric conditions* Heavy rain and high seas can both cause clutter on the screen which obscures echoes; the proper adjustment of the clutter controls will reduce this problem, but not cure it entirely. Another atmospheric effect which can occur (though very rarely) is anomalous propagation, in which the radar waves travel very much further round the curvature of the earth than normal, leading to unusually

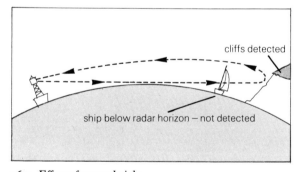

36.2 *Effect of target height.*

long range detection of large targets such as land.

All these various factors are combined into Table 1, which gives typical figures of performance for a yacht radar in proper adjustment and under good conditions. These figures are only representative, and wide variations may be found in practice; however, they may serve as a guide as to what to expect.

Caution When sailing in thick and heavy weather, it is not safe to assume that commercial shipping will detect you on their radar, even if you have

36.3 Radar reflector.

taken the seamanlike precaution of rigging a good radar reflector. Quite apart from questions of good or bad watchkeeping, the echo of a yacht will be small, and can very easily be lost in sea clutter. A radar reflector helps, but if the sea clutter on the other ship's radar is extensive, it may reach beyond the detection range of your yacht, even with a radar reflector. In these circumstances, you are very unlikely to be picked up on radar.

Table 1 *Typical detection ranges for a yacht radar (antenna height ten metres, 3kW transmitter power)*

	miles
Bold, high land	25
Large ships	11
Medium ships	8
Fishing vessels	3
Yachts with radar reflector	$2\frac{1}{2}$–3
Yachts without radar reflector	1
Navigational buoys with reflectors	$2\frac{1}{2}$
Dinghy (wood or fibreglass)	$\frac{1}{2}$
Withy (thin wooden channel marker)	$\frac{1}{2}$**

**Withies show up remarkably well on radar, and can be very useful when navigating in fog.

37 Using radar

A radar set in a yacht can be used in any one of four ways, and it is possible to switch rapidly from one to another if the circumstances require. The four main tasks are:

1) Landfall – detecting land at long range.
2) Coastal navigation, either in fog or as a supplement to visual navigation.
3) Lookout – the detection of approaching shipping
4) Collision avoidance in thick weather.

1) *Landfall* Radar can be a very valuable landfall aid, as the set can often pick up land which is well beyond visual range, even in relatively clear conditions. However, the actual detection range will depend upon the antenna height of the set and the nature of the coast. A mountainous coastline with high cliffs may well be detected at the maximum range of which the set is capable, while low-lying, sandy coasts may not appear on the PPI until quite close.

Another factor in making a landfall is the nature of the coastline; at long range, a low-lying coast may be below the radar horizon, whilst high ground in the hinterland may be above it, and hence be detected. The identification of a feature on the radar may not be easy, though examination of the height contours on the chart can indicate which areas are likely to be detected first.

2) *Coastal navigation* Radar is a very useful aid to coastal navigation in all conditions. In fog, it may be the most accurate and reliable aid available, but even in good visibility radar can help the navigator a great deal. When used to supplement visual navigation, radar's biggest contribution is its ability to provide range information. If an object is conspicuous both to the eye and the radar, a simultaneous radar range and visual bearing can be taken to provide a reliable fix.

In poor visibility, radar becomes the primary navigational aid. The most important thing to remember is that radar provides accurate ranges, but very inaccurate bearings (see below). When collecting position lines to form a fix, it is very much better to use two or three ranges of radar-conspicuous objects than to use radar bearings (Fig. 1).

A radar picture is not easy to interpret correctly, and every opportunity should be taken to practise blind pilotage when conditions are good, to build up skill and confidence for the occasion when the visibility closes in. It is best to avoid the temptation to conn the ship by eye off the radar screen; rather, use the radar to fix the ship at frequent intervals, and make careful allowance for such factors as tidal stream. If at all possible, a blind passage should be meticulously planned in advance.

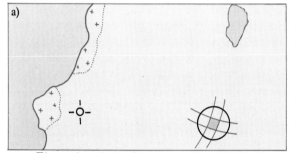

37.1 *Fixes using: (a) radar ranges; (b) radar bearings.*

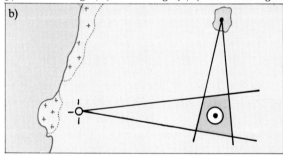

The identification of navigational marks is not always easy. If a coastline is at some little distance, parts of it may paint on the screen, while other lower-lying regions do not appear at all. And, whilst the display on the PPI may look like a map, it is formed from the view as seen by the radar antennae; a nearby bluff, for example, may obscure part of the coastline behind, so that the appearance of the coast alters as the ship moves past it (Fig. 2). It can also be hard to pick out navigational buoys on the screen from small craft nearby, or to distinguish the echo of a light vessel from merchant ships. Some important marks carry a

37.2 *Effect of a change of viewpoint on radar pictures.*

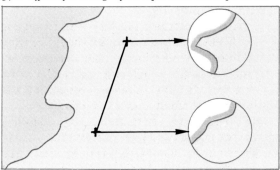

Racon, a radar transponder which 'labels' an echo so that it can be identified. These can be very helpful where they exist, but it is good practice to fix the ship on the chart frequently, and use the fix to identify new radar objects as they come into range. This process also helps to avoid the momentary confusion which often occurs when the ship alters course; as the radar picture is related to the ship's head (in the 12 o'clock position), it revolves as the ship turns and changes appearance radically.

3) *Lookout* For detecting the presence of nearby ships, radar is at its most valuable in poor conditions – in fog obviously, but also when high seas or blown spray make a visual lookout difficult. However, radar should only be regarded as an aid to lookout; echoes may be lost if the set wanders off tune or if the clutter controls are not used properly. Never rely exclusively on a radar lookout, but use it rather to supplement and extend the visual lookout being kept by the watch on deck.

4) *Collision Avoidance* **The use of a small, yacht-type radar for collision avoidance at close quarters is extremely dangerous, and should be avoided if at all possible.**
Commercial shipping uses radar for collision avoidance as a routine measure, but with equipment and skills denied to the average yachtsman. Even so, in spite of special training, north-stabilized and true-motion radar, plotting aids and computer-controlled collision avoidance systems, so-called 'radar-assisted collisions' still occur. The relatively primitive radar typically fitted in a yacht is totally unsuited for this task and the operator is most unlikely to have the training or experience to make safe decisions on the basis of the information he sees. The main reason for this situation is the fact that the radar picture is related to ship's head – i.e. the bow of the ship is always represented at the 12 o'clock position. Even on autopilot, yachts are not steered perfectly and in a seaway they can yaw considerably. Thus the relative bearing of the target ship on the radar can change from sweep to sweep, making it very difficult to estimate its actual bearing; allied to the poor bearing accuracy inherent in the radar to begin with, it is clear that it is almost impossible to decide if the bearing of the target is constant or not, which defines the risk of collision. The difficulties are at their most apparent when the two ships are end-on (or nearly so) to each other, which is the most dangerous situation to be in. It is only too easy to misinterpret the radar picture and alter course the wrong way – towards the ship you are trying to avoid.
Never assume that the other ship can see you on his radar, just because you can see him on yours.
If you are forced into the position of having to use radar for collision avoidance, take steps to keep clear as early as possible. Try to prevent other ships coming within a mile of you – two miles is better. Have the best radar watchkeeper on board at the set, and keep the deck watch informed about what is happening; if a mistake is made, it will be they who have to get you out of it.

Radar errors

Radar is most accurate in measuring ranges, especially if a variable range marker unit is fitted. Bearings are very much less accurate, partly because of the beam width of the antenna (typically 3°) and partly because of the tendency for small craft to yaw. The 95 per cent errors might typically be:

Range	
with range rings	2 per cent of range in use
with variable range marker	1 per cent of range in use

Bearing	
good conditions	± 6°
bad conditions	± 15°

38 Hyperbolic radio aids to navigation

Following their initial introduction in the Second World War, a number of radio aids to navigation are available which use a common principle of measuring the difference in range between a number of transmitting stations. In general, the cost and complexity of these navigation systems put them beyond the reach of the average yachtsman, but they may sometimes be found in larger craft. Modern developments in electronics may reduce the cost of some systems, especially Loran C, to the point where they come into much wider use in yachts, though the present coverage of Loran C is inadequate in Europe.

These navigation systems are known as *hyperbolic* aids because the position lines that the equipment produces take the form of a series of hyperbolae. The principle of these aids is shown in Figure 1. Two radio transmitters are arranged to send out a short pulse of energy at exactly the same moment, and these pulses are picked up by a receiver in the craft; because the speed of light (and radio waves) is constant, the difference in the time that the two pulses are received in the craft gives the difference in the range (or distance) of the two transmitters. If the pulses arrive together, then the two transmitters are equi-distant and the craft must lie somewhere on the perpendicular bisector of the base-line (the line joining the two transmitters). In all other cases, it can be shown that the craft lies on a hyperbolic position line with the nearer transmitter as its focus. In practice, a number of transmitters are grouped in such a way as to provide a number of hyperbolic position lines which intersect to provide a fix. A special chart with an overprinted 'lattice' is used for plotting fixes (Fig. 2) The three hyperbolic systems available for general navigation are Loran C, Decca and Omega, all of which require special receivers and signal processing equipment; the earlier Loran A system is now obsolescent.

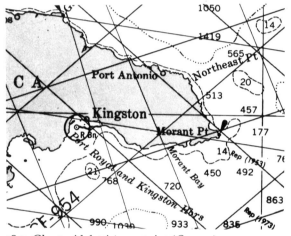

38.2 *Chart with lattice overprint (Omega).*

Loran C

One of the first hyperbolic aids to be developed was called Loran (LOng RAnge Navigation), and Loran C is an improved version of this original system. It operates on LF (low frequency) and has a maximum range of about 1500 nautical miles at night, and rather less by day. Receiver operation is automatic, and time differences can be read directly from a numerical display for plotting on a Loran C lattice chart. Modern receivers sometimes incorporate a microprocessor which can translate time differences into latitude and longitude; this is an obvious advantage, as it eliminates the need to carry the special lattice charts otherwise needed for plotting position lines.

The accuracy of a Loran C position line depends upon a number of factors, including the position of the craft within the lattice and the ionospheric conditions which can affect the transmission of the radio signals. In favourable circum-

38.1 *Principle of hyperbolic radio aids.*

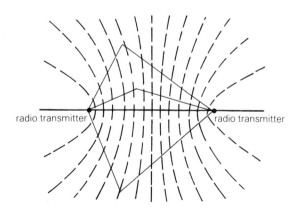

radio transmitter   radio transmitter

stances at short range, the 95 per cent accuracy can be less than a quarter of a mile; the error increases with distance to perhaps one or two miles at a range of 1000 miles from the baseline.

The major drawback of Loran C, which is in many ways an excellent aid, is that it has been installed for military rather than civil use; hence the coverage of the world by Loran C shows gaps which are annoying from the yachtsman's point of view (Fig. 3). The most notable omission is the area south of the Dover Strait, which excludes the

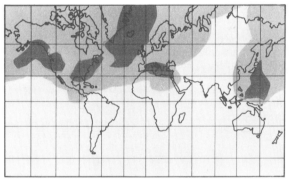

38.3 *Loran C coverage (1981).*

most important yachting areas of England and France.

Decca
Decca is a short-range, high accuracy hyperbolic system working in the low frequency band, which is widely used by commercial and military users both at sea and in the air. Decca equipment was only available on hire from the Decca Navigator Company, but they have recently (1982) introduced a yacht version for sale. Some 'pirate' Decca receivers have been put on the market, but these should be viewed with caution.

Decca is not quite as easy to use as Loran C because it is necessary to guard against an ambiguity known as 'lane slippage'; but with a careful study of the handbook and a little practice, it will provide fixes of the highest quality. The maximum range of a particular Decca chain is about 250

miles from the master station (less at night), and chains are generally arranged to provide an overlap of coverage.

The accuracy of Decca is very high; close to the base line, the 95 per cent error may be less than 100 yards (90 metres), and at 100 miles it will be between a half and one mile, depending upon the position of the craft within the lattice. At long ranges ionospheric effects can become important and errors may be as much as ten times greater at times, particularly during winter nights. Because of these effects and also the need for lane identification, great care should be taken when entering the Decca coverage, especially at night, to make quite sure that the Decca receiver is properly set up and telling the truth.

The accuracy of Decca has caused problems in the past; fishing vessels use the system a great deal to find their grounds, and have developed a habit of running to and from the grounds along a particular Decca line as shown on their equipment. There have been a number of stem-to-stem collisions between boats travelling in opposite directions along the same Decca line!

Omega
Omega is a VLF (very low frequency) hyperbolic system recently introduced by the United States Navy. Eight stations, operating on a basic frequency of 10.2 kilohertz, provide between them a virtually world-wide coverage.

To offset the advantage of global coverage, Omega is not particularly accurate; a 95 per cent accuracy of one mile by day and two miles by night is as much as one can expect, though various ways of providing automatic corrections for varying conditions have been tried. One approach is for a fixed Omega receiver to detect variations in the received signal, which are then broadcast as corrections for Omega users in the vicinity.

Another drawback with Omega is that it cannot recover the position of the vessel after the equipment has been switched off. Whilst operating, the Omega receiver will provide position lines continuously, but if switched off (or after a breakdown) it must be told by the navigator exactly where it is within the lattice.

39 Other radio aids

There are several other radio aids which can be used by yachts although for various reasons they are limited in their scope. They are all designed to give a vessel the bearing of the transmitting beacon without using the directional type of antenna needed for MFDF.

Consol

Consol is a system originally developed in Germany during the Second World War under the title *Elektra Sonne*; it is now obsolescent and many of the stations have been closed down. A similar system, called Consolan, was installed on the eastern seaboard of the United States but this, too, is now closed down.

Consol is described technically as a collapsed hyperbolic system, and the effect is to produce a radial fan of signals from the transmitter, rather like the spokes of a wheel (Fig. 1). The only equipment required by the ship is a beacon-band receiver fitted with a BFO (beat frequency oscillator).

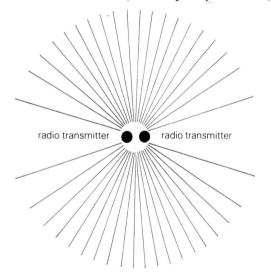

radio transmitter   radio transmitter

39.1 *Consol collapsed lattice.*

After tuning the receiver to the correct frequency, the operator will hear the identification of the station in Morse, followed by a series of 60 Morse symbols (dots or dashes). The sequence will begin with a series of either dots or dashes; at some point the signal will fade out, and then re-appear with the opposite symbol. For example, the sequence

may begin with dots, fade out and then return as dashes (or *vice versa*). The operator counts the number of symbols he can hear before the fade-out (known as the equisignal), and then the number of symbols that he hears after the equisignal. It is normal for a number of symbols to be lost in the equisignal, so the operator must then work out his final count, making use of the knowledge that there were 60 symbols altogether in the sequence.

For example:

Before equisignal	20 dots	5 dashes
After equisignal	36 dashes	50 dots
Total heard	56	55
Missed in equisignal	4	5
Correction (half)	2	$2\frac{1}{2}$
Final count	22 dots	$7\frac{1}{2}$ dashes

The final count is expressed as the number of symbols heard *before* the equisignal; it is also necessary to note which symbol this was, a dot or a dash, as this affects the position line. Having established the count, the position line can then be plotted on a special chart with a printed overlay of the Consol counts. Alternatively, tables have been published which convert the count into true bearings, which can be plotted on a normal chart; when working at long range, it may be necessary to correct these bearings for half convergency (see page 191). As the pattern repeats itself a number of times around the horizon, a reliable dead reckoning position may be needed to resolve any ambiguity in the bearing.

Consol is delightfully simple to use, and can be effective over 1000 miles or more; a major advantage is that no special equipment is needed, though best results require practice. However, the accuracy is not particularly good; a 95 per cent error of 1° to 2° can be expected by day, and double this at night. Bearings at about 400 miles (where the ground wave and the first sky wave of the signal mix together) may be considerably more in error.

Radio lighthouse

The radio lighthouse is a system, still in the experimental stage, which offers the prospect of a radio aid thoroughly suitable for yachts and small craft in coastal waters. It is in principle very much like Consol, but operates in the international marine mobile band on VHF (very high frequency). As with Consol, it is only necessary to tune the vessel's own VHF receiver to the correct channel, identify the radio lighthouse by its callsign, and then count the symbols that follow (the signal differs in detail from the Consol signal). The resulting count can then be translated into a true bearing of the transmitter by means of special tables.

Unlike Consol, the radio lighthouse is intended to be a short-range aid – of the order to twenty miles, depending on the heights of the transmitting and receiving antennae. The suggestion is that it should be sited with important lighthouses or lightships to provide adequate cover of coastal waters, with sufficient beacons within range to allow for reliable fixing. If expectations are met and the radio lighthouse is put into service, it would offer yachts a far more suitable aid in coastal waters than MFDF. In 1982, there were a number of experimental installations in European waters.

The accuracy of the radio lighthouse is probably better than 2° on 95 per cent of occasions, and the system is much less subject to propagation errors because of the short ranges involved and the high frequency of the transmissions. Like Consol, it has the advantage that no special equipment is needed, though it seems likely that special receivers which make the process quicker and easier by automatic tuning and counting will appear on the market.

VOR
VOR (vhf omni-range) is a radio aid widely used by aircraft. If VOR beacons are suitably sited, they can also be used by small craft within VHF range of the shore. The VOR set carried in the vessel picks up the signal from the beacon, and translates this automatically into a continuous reading of the magnetic bearing of the station from the craft; by switching channels, another VOR beacon within range can be used to provide a fix.

It is only in certain areas where VOR beacons happen to be suitably sited for marine use that yachts can use the system; it is most popular in the waters of the United States. The range of these beacons is limited by low antenna height in small craft.

ASTRONOMICAL NAVIGATION

40 The principles of astronomical navigation

Many navigators, even some with considerable experience, are under the impression that astronomical navigation is difficult. On the contrary, finding one's position by observation of heavenly bodies is no more difficult and time-consuming than (for example) the use of MF direction finding. To be sure, a special instrument (a sextant) is needed with associated books of tables, and good results will need practice; but the end result is a system for observing position lines of very high quality anywhere on the surface of the earth, provided only that the sky is not totally obscured. Unless the trans-oceanic navigator is prepared to invest in one of the modern electronic systems, then astronomical navigation is the only method available; in any case, the 'electronic navigator' would need a back-up system. It is not always appreciated that astronomical navigation can be just as useful for coastal work. It may be, for example, that a distant headland is in sight, so the navigator has one position line from its compass bearing; if the sun is shining, he may be able to get another position line to give him his distance off.

The principle of astronomical navigation is extremely straightforward; it can even be thought of as a special case of obtaining a position line by vertical sextant angle (see page 71), extended to cover the case of an object of infinite height. By measuring the height of the object, i.e. the angle between the object and the horizon, it is possible to calculate a distance, and hence obtain a position line.

The first step is to associate some point on the surface of the earth with the position of the heavenly body in the sky. This can be done by joining the centre of the earth with the body in question; the position where this imaginary line meets the surface of the earth is known as the *geographical position* (GP) of the body (Fig. 1). It is the point where the body would be seen vertically overhead (in the zenith, as astronomers say). As the earth rotates on its axis and revolves around the sun, the geographical position is constantly moving (at speeds of up to 900 n miles an hour), but it can be established for any second during the year by using the tables in the *Nautical Almanac* (see page 137).

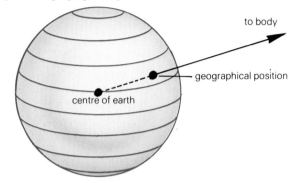

40.1 *The geographical position.*

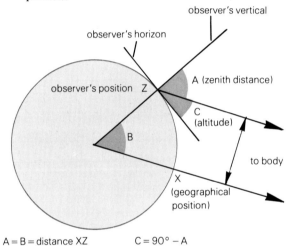

40.2 *The relationship between altitude and geographical position.*

A = B = distance XZ   C = 90° − A

The whole basis of astronomical navigation is that the angle of a heavenly body above the horizon is directly related to the distance of the geographical position (Fig. 2). Because the body is a very long way away from the earth (the sun is 93,000,000 miles away), it can be assumed that rays of light reaching the earth are parallel. The argument then runs as follows:

1) By simple geometry, the angle A, between the observer's zenith (the point directly above his head) and the object, is equal to the angle B, the angle at the centre of the earth between the observers position and the geographical position of the body.

2) By definition, the angle B is equivalent to the distance on the surface of the earth between X (the GP of the body) and Z (the position of the observer) (see page 15).

40.3 *Plotting the position line at high altitudes.*

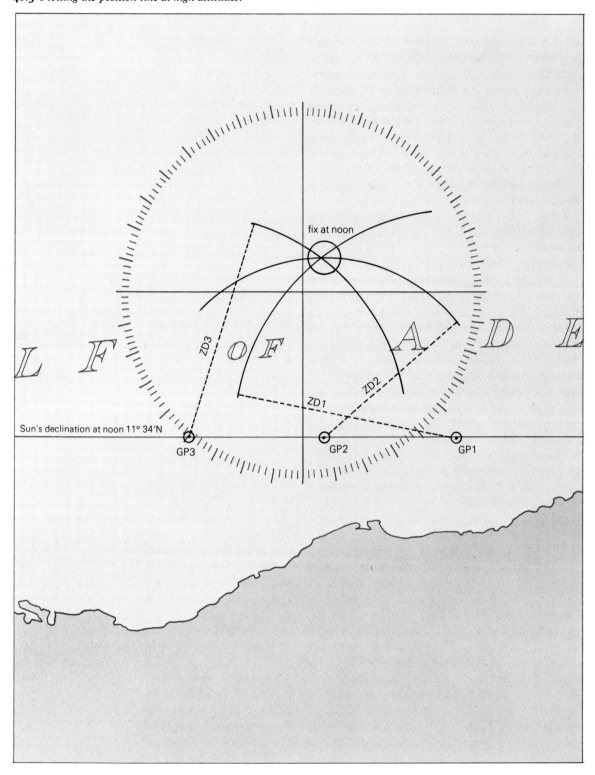

3) Therefore, the angle A, measured in minutes of arc, is equal to the distance between X and Z in nautical miles.

4) In a small craft, there is no practical way of measuring the angle A directly; however it is easy to observe the angle C, the angle between the body and the horizon directly below it.

5) The angles A and C must add together to give 90°, the total angle between the horizon and the zenith; therefore the angle C equals 90° minus angle A.

The angle A is known as the *zenith distance* of the body, and the angle C is known as the *altitude*.

A simple numerical example may help to make the theory clear; assume that the altitude of a body is measured as 30°:

Altitude (angle C)   30°
Zenith distance (angle A) 90° − 30° = 60°
Therefore distance X to Z 60° × 60 = 3600 n
                                          miles

Provided that the GP (from the *Nautical Almanac*) can be plotted on the same chart as the observer's DR position, then the position line can easily be drawn by setting a pair of compasses to the zenith distance and striking an arc from the GP; however, this is not always practicable, because as the example above shows, the distance involved can be considerable. The lowest altitude at which a body can reliably be observed is about 15°, which implies a zenith distance of 4500 nautical miles; even if it were possible to plot such a position line on a chart, the pencil line would be several miles thick (at the scale of the chart), and the potential accuracy of the method would be totally lost. This difficulty is overcome by the *intercept method*, described on pages 147–9.

There are certain rare occasions when the GP of the body and the position lines can be drawn directly. These occasions arise when the body (almost always the sun) passes close overhead, i.e. near noon in tropical latitudes. In such circumstances, the GP of the sun will be close to the ship and can be plotted. Having established the zenith distance, the position circle can be plotted directly (Fig. 3). If the process is repeated a few minutes later, when the sun's GP has moved sufficiently, a second position circle can be drawn; the intersection of these two circles gives a fix. A possible ambiguity exists, because two circles intersect in two points, but knowledge of the DR position should be able to resolve this difficulty. Otherwise, a third observation will settle the matter definitely.

An astronomical position line of this kind is not easy to observe, as the altitude is very great (85° or more).

41 Taking sextant altitudes

Astronomical navigation involves the measurement of the altitude of a heavenly body by means of a sextant. The principle and construction of this remarkable instrument are described on pages 45–7; this section deals with its use in measuring altitudes. At first, the beginner is likely to find this quite difficult, but the technique can soon be mastered with a little practice. It is rather like learning to ride a bicycle – hard at first, but it soon becomes almost second nature.

The basic idea is simple enough (Fig. 1). Holding the sextant vertically, the navigator looks at the horizon directly below the body through the plain (unsilvered) section of the horizon glass; he then adjusts the index arm until the reflected image of the body is co-incident with the horizon. When the object and the horizon are exactly in line (with the sextant held truly vertical), the graduated scale and micrometer show the sextant altitude of the body. For most sights, the navigator needs to record the exact time, so the geographical position of the body can be established from the *Nautical Almanac*.

Preparation Remove the sextant carefully from its box and check that it does not seem to have suffered accidental damage since it was last used, and that the mirrors, shades, lenses and scales are clean. Every sextant should be fitted with a lanyard; put the lanyard round your neck immediately to protect it from dropping. If the sextant is supplied with a choice of telescopes, then ship the star telescope (bell shaped); this telescope, which gives an upright image and a wide field of view, is the most generally suitable for use in a yacht.

The index error of the sextant should be checked every time the instrument is used. The easiest way is to look at the horizon with the arm set to zero. The micrometer should then be adjusted until the direct and the reflected images of the horizon form a continuous unbroken line (Fig. 2). The reading of the sextant is then the index error. The error may be *on the arc* (Fig. 3a), in which case it has to be *subtracted* from the measured angle; if the error is *off the* arc (Fig. 3b), it must be *added*.

41.1 *Taking sextant altitudes. (below left)*

41.2 *Checking the index error. (below)*

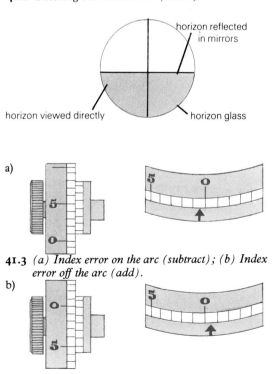

41.3 *(a) Index error on the arc (subtract); (b) Index error off the arc (add).*

Position To take an observation, the navigator must find a position where he has a clear view of both the object and the horizon (not always easy in a sailing yacht). He must also make sure that he is safe; he needs both hands to operate the sextant, and must make sure that there is no risk of being thrown off balance. Apart from the risk of personal injury or damage to the sextant, it is not unknown for navigators to be lost overboard whilst taking sights. A safety harness is a seamanlike precaution.

Apart from getting a clear view of the body and the horizon, the navigator should choose a position according to the state of the horizon. If it appears to be hazy, then a low position brings the sea horizon closer and makes it look sharper. In a seaway, a high position should be chosen to take the eye (if possible) above the tops of nearby waves, which obscure the true horizon.

Having found a safe and suitable position, the navigator should try to 'lock' his legs and the lower part of his body to the boat, leaving the head, arms and upper body free to move to compensate for the motion of the boat; it is often helpful to brace the body against the safety line. If the motion is so violent that the use of the sextant is difficult, it may be possible to improve conditions by altering course or, if necessary, heaving to.

Finding the object It can be quite difficult to find the object in the sextant's field of view, particularly if the object is faint, like a star. There are three ways of tackling the problem:

1) Set the sextant to zero, and look directly at the object. *Caution*: when looking at the sun, adjust the shades to reduce the light and prevent damage to the eyes. Then bring the sextant slowly down to the horizontal, at the same time moving the index arm so as to keep the object in the silvered part of the horizon glass (Fig. 4).

2) An alternative method, which some navigators find easier for faint objects, is to use the sextant upside down (Fig. 5). This time, the object is kept in the *clear* part of the horizon glass, and the arm is adjusted until the horizon appears in the silvered part. The sextant can now be reversed and used normally.

3) Stars and planets are almost always observed at dawn and dusk, when there is sufficient light to give a clear horizon; this means that the sky is

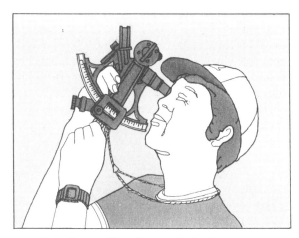

41.4 *Bringing an object down to the horizon.*

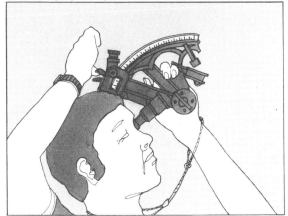

41.5 *Bringing the horizon up to the object.*

still bright and faint stars may only be visible through the sextant telescope. The only way to find such objects is to predict their position in the sky from the DR position; the sextant is set to the predicted altitude and swept across the appropriate bearing until the object is seen. The way of predicting the position of a star is given on page 159.

Use of shades Both the horizon and the index glasses are fitted with shades or filters to cut down the light of the sun. Both should be used when finding the sun; thereafter the horizon glass need only be shaded if the sun is low and the horizon bright. The shades on the index glass should always be used unless the sun is veiled by thin cloud. They should be adjusted to give a clear image which can be viewed without strain; it is a mistake to have too bright an image of the sun.

Measuring the altitude Having found the object in the field of view, it is now possible to take the exact altitude by lining the object up with the horizon. The altitude will be correct only if the sextant is vertical. This can be ensured by rocking the sextant slightly from side to side (Fig. 6). The object will swing from side to side like the bob of a pendulum. The sextant is vertical when the 'bob' is at its lowest point.

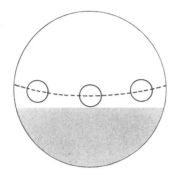

41.6 *Rocking the sextant to ensure that it is vertical.*

It is generally better not to chase the altitude of the body by continual adjustment of the index arm, but rather to set the sextant to an altitude and let the body move. If the body is in the eastern half of the sky, it is rising. Set an altitude a little greater than the actual position and wait until the body rises to the altitude you have set. If the body is in the western sky, it is sinking so the sextant should be set to a lower altitude. Then watch the body as it approaches the horizon and note the time when they are in line.

Stars and planets are effectively points of light, and the altitude is taken by putting this point onto the horizon (Fig. 7a). The sun and the moon both have sensible diameters, and the sextant altitude is taken on the top or the bottom edge – known as the *upper* and *lower limbs*. For the sun, it is conventional to take the lower limb, though the upper can be used if desired (Fig. 7b). With the moon, it is necessary to use whichever limb is visible, depending on the phase (Fig. 7c).

Recording the results When taking sights, it is almost always necessary to record the exact time on the ship's chronometer or master watch. This is most conveniently done by recruiting another crew member as 'scribe', to record the watch times and matching sextant altitudes. The single-

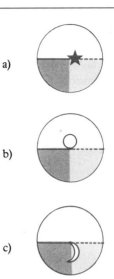

41.7 *Bringing (a) a star (b) the sun and (c) the moon to the horizon.*

handed navigator must devise some suitable alternative, such as a stopwatch or digital wristwatch to carry his time around with him.

It is not wise to rely on a single observation of a body; a series should be taken and averaged, to reduce the errors that may arise. A useful technique is to take either three or five observations at equal intervals of altitude (say, five minutes of arc). It is then only necessary to average the times, as the average altitude is equal to the middle value of the set. It is also possible to examine the time intervals between the observations; if these are equal, it tends to indicate that the observations are good.

For example:

Altitude	Time	Interval
34°20′.0	10 h 14 m 02 s	
34°25′.0	10 h 14 m 34 s	32 seconds
34°30′.0	10 h 15 m 03 s	29 seconds
Average 34°25′.0	10 h 14 m 33 s	

In this example, the intervals between the observations (32 and 29 seconds) are more or less equal, so the set of observations is probably acceptable.

Of course, conditions may be such that only one hurried sight is possible, as the sun peeps momentarily through overcast. Any sight is better than no sight at all, but it must be remembered that a single observation is not as reliable as the average of a consistent set.

42 Sextant altitude corrections

The angle actually measured on the sextant is known as the *sextant altitude* of the body; a number of corrections must be applied to this angle to get the *observed altitude* (Ho), which is the basis of the position line to be derived.

Index error The index error of a sextant is the zero error of the instrument, caused by the two mirrors not being exactly parallel. It should be checked every time the sextant is used, as described on the previous page.

The index error is applied to the sextant altitude; index error on the arc is subtracted, and index error off the arc is added (see examples below).

Dip The angle measured by a sextant is that between the body and the sea horizon; however, as Figure 1 shows, the sea horizon is always below the true horizontal, by an amount which depends on the height of eye of the observer. The correction for *dip* is given in the *Nautical Almanac* (Table 1), using height of eye as an argument. This table, like other altitude correction tables, is arranged as a *critical entry* table; the correction given applies to all values of height of eye between the two values immediately above and below the correction. For example, a dip correction of $-4'.2$ applies to any height of eye from 5.5 metres up to (but not including) 5.8 metres. The dip correction is *always subtracted* to give the *apparent altitude*.

42.1 *Dip of the sea horizon.*

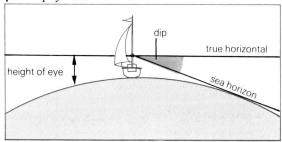

Refraction As the rays of light from the body observed pass through the various layers of atmosphere, they are bent or refracted, by an amount which depends mainly on the altitude of the body (Fig. 2). This correction, which is always negative, is incorporated in the various correction tables with other corrections.

42.2 *Refraction.*

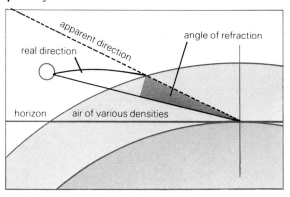

Semidiameter Semidiameter is the somewhat curious name given by astronomers to the radius of the sun or the moon. A correction must be applied to the measured altitude to allow for the fact that the observation was made on either the upper or lower limb of the sun or moon, whereas the altitude required is of its centre. Semidiameter depends on the size of the body and its distance from the earth. For lower limb observations, semidiameter is added, for upper limb observations it is subtracted. This correction is incorporated in the sun and moon correction tables (Tables 1 and 2).

Parallax This correction is only of importance for observations of the moon, and it arises because the moon is relatively close to the earth – close enough for the diameter of the earth to affect the observations (Fig. 3). It depends upon various factors, chiefly the altitude and the distance of the moon. A special correction is given in the moon correction tables (Table 2), which require a quantity called horizontal parallax (HP) as argument.

42.3 *Parallax.*

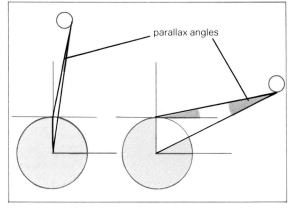

Table 1 *Sun, star and planet corrections.*

A2 ALTITUDE CORRECTION TABLES 10°–90°—SUN, STARS, PLANETS

OCT.—MAR. SUN APR.—SEPT.						STARS AND PLANETS				DIP				
App. Alt.	Lower Limb	Upper Limb	App. Alt.	Lower Limb	Upper Limb	App. Alt.	Corrⁿ	App. Alt.	Additional Corrⁿ	Ht. of Eye	Corrⁿ	Ht. of Eye	Ht. of Eye	Corrⁿ

SUN OCT.—MAR. (App. Alt. / +Lower Limb −Upper Limb):

| 9 34 +10·8 −21·5 | 9 45 +10·9 −21·4 | 9 56 +11·0 −21·3 | 10 08 +11·1 −21·2 | 10 21 +11·2 −21·1 | 10 34 +11·3 −21·0 | 10 47 +11·4 −20·9 | 11 01 +11·5 −20·8 | 11 15 +11·6 −20·7 | 11 30 +11·7 −20·6 | 11 46 +11·8 −20·5 | 12 02 +11·9 −20·4 | 12 19 +12·0 −20·3 | 12 37 +12·1 −20·2 | 12 55 +12·2 −20·1 | 13 14 +12·3 −20·0 | 13 35 +12·4 −19·9 | 13 56 +12·5 −19·8 | 14 18 +12·6 −19·7 | 14 42 +12·7 −19·6 | 15 06 +12·8 −19·5 | 15 32 +12·9 −19·4 | 15 59 +13·0 −19·3 | 16 28 +13·1 −19·2 | 16 59 +13·2 −19·1 | 17 32 +13·3 −19·0 | 18 06 +13·4 −18·9 | 18 42 +13·5 −18·8 | 19 21 +13·6 −18·7 | 20 03 +13·7 −18·6 | 20 48 +13·8 −18·5 | 21 35 +13·9 −18·4 | 22 26 +14·0 −18·3 | 23 22 +14·1 −18·2 | 24 21 +14·2 −18·1 | 25 26 +14·3 −18·0 | 26 36 +14·4 −17·9 | 27 52 +14·5 −17·8 | 29 15 +14·6 −17·7 | 30 46 +14·7 −17·6 | 32 26 +14·8 −17·5 | 34 17 +14·9 −17·4 | 36 20 +15·0 −17·3 | 38 36 +15·1 −17·2 | 41 08 +15·2 −17·1 | 43 59 +15·3 −17·0 | 47 10 +15·4 −16·9 | 50 46 +15·5 −16·8 | 54 49 +15·6 −16·7 | 59 23 +15·7 −16·6 | 64 30 +15·8 −16·5 | 70 12 +15·9 −16·4 | 76 26 +16·0 −16·3 | 83 05 +16·1 −16·2 | 90 00 |

SUN APR.—SEPT. (App. Alt. / +Lower Limb −Upper Limb):

| 9 39 +10·6 −21·2 | 9 51 +10·7 −21·1 | 10 03 +10·8 −21·0 | 10 15 +10·9 −20·9 | 10 27 +11·0 −20·8 | 10 40 +11·1 −20·7 | 10 54 +11·2 −20·6 | 11 08 +11·3 −20·5 | 11 23 +11·4 −20·4 | 11 38 +11·5 −20·3 | 11 54 +11·6 −20·2 | 12 10 +11·7 −20·1 | 12 28 +11·8 −20·0 | 12 46 +11·9 −19·9 | 13 05 +12·0 −19·8 | 13 24 +12·1 −19·7 | 13 45 +12·2 −19·6 | 14 07 +12·3 −19·5 | 14 30 +12·4 −19·4 | 14 54 +12·5 −19·3 | 15 19 +12·6 −19·2 | 15 46 +12·7 −19·1 | 16 14 +12·8 −19·0 | 16 44 +12·9 −18·9 | 17 15 +13·0 −18·8 | 17 48 +13·1 −18·7 | 18 24 +13·2 −18·6 | 19 01 +13·3 −18·5 | 19 42 +13·4 −18·4 | 20 25 +13·5 −18·3 | 21 11 +13·6 −18·2 | 22 00 +13·7 −18·1 | 22 54 +13·8 −18·0 | 23 51 +13·9 −17·9 | 24 53 +14·0 −17·8 | 26 00 +14·1 −17·7 | 27 13 +14·2 −17·6 | 28 33 +14·3 −17·5 | 30 00 +14·4 −17·4 | 31 35 +14·5 −17·3 | 33 20 +14·6 −17·2 | 35 17 +14·7 −17·1 | 37 26 +14·8 −17·0 | 39 50 +14·9 −16·9 | 42 31 +15·0 −16·8 | 45 31 +15·1 −16·7 | 48 55 +15·2 −16·6 | 52 44 +15·3 −16·5 | 57 02 +15·4 −16·4 | 61 51 +15·5 −16·3 | 67 17 +15·6 −16·2 | 73 16 +15·7 −16·1 | 79 43 +15·8 −16·0 | 86 32 +15·9 −15·9 | 90 00 |

STARS AND PLANETS (App. Alt. / Corrⁿ):

| 9 56 −5·3 | 10 08 −5·2 | 10 20 −5·1 | 10 33 −5·0 | 10 46 −4·9 | 11 00 −4·8 | 11 14 −4·7 | 11 29 −4·6 | 11 45 −4·5 | 12 01 −4·4 | 12 18 −4·3 | 12 35 −4·2 | 12 54 −4·1 | 13 13 −4·0 | 13 33 −3·9 | 13 54 −3·8 | 14 16 −3·7 | 14 40 −3·6 | 15 04 −3·5 | 15 30 −3·4 | 15 57 −3·3 | 16 26 −3·2 | 16 56 −3·1 | 17 28 −3·0 | 18 02 −2·9 | 18 38 −2·8 | 19 17 −2·7 | 19 58 −2·6 | 20 42 −2·5 | 21 28 −2·4 | 22 19 −2·3 | 23 13 −2·2 | 24 11 −2·1 | 25 14 −2·0 | 26 22 −1·9 | 27 36 −1·8 | 28 56 −1·7 | 30 24 −1·6 | 32 00 −1·5 | 33 45 −1·4 | 35 40 −1·3 | 37 48 −1·2 | 40 08 −1·1 | 42 44 −1·0 | 45 36 −0·9 | 48 47 −0·8 | 52 18 −0·7 | 56 11 −0·6 | 60 28 −0·5 | 65 08 −0·4 | 70 11 −0·3 | 75 34 −0·2 | 81 13 −0·1 | 87 03 0·0 | 90 00 |

Additional Corrⁿ — 1980

VENUS

Jan. 1-Feb. 26
42 +0′1

Feb. 27-Apr. 13
47 +0′2

Apr. 14-May 9
46 +0′3

May 10-May 25
11 +0′4
41 +0′5

May 26-June 3
6 +0′5
20 +0′6
31 +0′7

June 4-June 26
4 +0′6
12 +0′7
22 +0′8

June 27-July 6
6 +0′5
20 +0′6
31 +0′7

July 7-July 21
11 +0′4
41 +0′5

July 22-Aug. 17
46 +0′3

Aug. 18-Oct. 2
47 +0′2

Oct. 3-Dec. 31
42 +0′1

MARS

Jan. 1-Apr. 28
41 +0′2
75 +0′1

Apr. 29-Dec. 31
60 +0′1

DIP (Ht. of Eye m / Corrⁿ / Ht. of Eye ft):

| 2·4 −2·8 8·0 | 2·6 −2·9 8·6 | 2·8 9·2 | 3·0 −3·0 9·8 | 3·2 −3·1 10·5 | 3·4 −3·2 11·2 | 3·6 −3·3 11·9 | 3·8 −3·4 12·6 | 4·0 −3·5 13·3 | 4·3 −3·6 14·1 | 4·5 −3·7 14·9 | 4·7 −3·8 15·7 | 5·0 −3·9 16·5 | 5·2 −4·0 17·4 | 5·5 −4·1 18·3 | 5·8 −4·2 19·1 | 6·1 −4·3 20·1 | 6·3 −4·4 21·0 | 6·6 −4·5 22·0 | 6·9 −4·6 22·9 | 7·2 −4·7 23·9 | 7·5 −4·8 24·9 | 7·9 −4·9 26·0 | 8·2 −5·0 27·1 | 8·5 −5·1 28·1 | 8·8 −5·2 29·2 | 9·2 −5·3 30·4 | 9·5 −5·4 31·5 | 9·9 −5·5 32·7 | 10·3 −5·6 33·9 | 10·6 −5·7 35·1 | 11·0 −5·8 36·3 | 11·4 −5·9 37·6 | 11·8 −6·0 38·9 | 12·2 −6·1 40·1 | 12·6 −6·2 41·5 | 13·0 −6·3 42·8 | 13·4 −6·4 44·2 | 13·8 −6·5 45·5 | 14·2 −6·6 46·9 | 14·7 −6·7 48·4 | 15·1 −6·8 49·8 | 15·5 −6·9 51·3 | 16·0 −7·0 52·8 | 16·5 −7·1 54·3 | 16·9 −7·2 55·8 | 17·4 −7·3 57·4 | 17·9 −7·4 58·9 | 18·4 −7·5 60·5 | 18·8 −7·6 62·1 | 19·3 −7·7 63·8 | 19·8 −7·8 65·4 | 20·4 −7·9 67·1 | 20·9 −8·0 68·8 | 21·4 −8·1 70·5 |

DIP (Ht. of Eye / Corrⁿ):

m:
1·0 − 1·8
1·5 − 2·2
2·0 − 2·5
2·5 − 2·8
3·0 − 3·0
See table
←

m:
20 − 7·9
22 − 8·3
24 − 8·6
26 − 9·0
28 − 9·3
30 − 9·6
32 −10·0
34 −10·3
36 −10·6
38 −10·8
40 −11·1
42 −11·4
44 −11·7
46 −11·9
48 −12·2

ft.:
2 − 1·4
4 − 1·9
6 − 2·4
8 − 2·7
10 − 3·1
See table
←

ft.:
70 − 8·1
75 − 8·4
80 − 8·7
85 − 8·9
90 − 9·2
95 − 9·5
100 − 9·7
105 − 9·9
110 −10·2
115 −10·4
120 −10·6
125 −10·8
130 −11·1
135 −11·3
140 −11·5
145 −11·7
150 −11·9
155 −12·1

This quantity is given in the daily pages of the almanac for each hour of the year; it is extracted from the tables at the same time as the other ephemeral data (see page 156).

A number of other factors also affect the correction of apparent altitude to true altitude, but these are included in the various correction tables and need not concern the navigator.

Refraction, semidiameter, parallax and various other factors are combined as appropriate into tables for correcting apparent altitude (i.e., sextant altitude corrected for index error and dip) into *observed altitude*. Samples of these tables are given in Tables 1 and 2; the originals are given in the *Nautical Almanac* (NP 314). Other almanacs and books of nautical tables may include altitude correction tables on a different basis; if using these, the instructions given should be studied and followed carefully.

Stars and planets (Table 1)
The correction for stars and planets is solely for refraction, and is always negative. It is the sole correction for all stars and the planets Jupiter and Saturn. For Venus and Mars, there are small additional corrections depending on the date, caused by parallax and phase. The Venus correction can be almost 1', but the Mars correction can safely be ignored by all except the very precise navigator.

The sun (Table 1)
The sun correction table is somewhat more complicated, because of the need to include corrections for semidiameter and parallax. The table is in two parts, for October to March and for April to September; in each section the total correction is given for the lower limb (always positive) and the upper limb (always negative).

The moon (Table 2)
Because the moon is so close to the earth, the correction table for the moon is the most complicated of all – though still not difficult to use; if in doubt, the instructions are printed beside the table in the almanac.

The table is in two parts. The first correction is taken from the upper part, using the apparent altitude as argument. First find the appropriate column (each one appropriate to a 5° 'band' of altitudes), and then find the correction in the column according to the exact altitude (to the nearest 10' of arc). Then, follow *the same column* down to the lower part of the table, and find the second correction using the horizontal parallax as argument and the sub-columns L or U, depending on whether the lower or upper limb was observed. Both corrections are always *added* to apparent altitude, but 30' must be subtracted from the result if the upper limb was observed.

Additional correction tables
The tables illustrated cover apparent altitudes between 10° and 90°; in practice, because of the variable nature of refraction, it is not wise to take altitudes below about 15° if they can be avoided. However, if there is no choice but to use a low altitude sight, then special correction tables are supplied in the almanac. Particularly at low altitudes, it may also be necessary to correct for temperature and barometric pressure (both affecting refraction). A special table is supplied for this purpose, though it can be ignored for almost all normal sights; only if the temperature is very different from 10°C (50°F), or the barometric pressure very different from 1010 millibars (29.8 inches), is the correction liable to amount to much. Above altitudes of 25°, the correction is insignificant anyway.

Accuracy of true altitude
The accuracy of the measured altitude (corrected as described) is the dominant factor in assessing astronomical position lines; all other sources of error are insignificant by comparison. Typical 95 per cent errors for a practised observer using a good sextant might be:

Good conditions	1 mile (1 minute of arc)
Moderate conditions	2 miles (2 minutes of arc)
Poor conditions	10 miles (10 minutes of arc)

The novice should not expect to do so well, but accuracy will come with practice.

Table 2 *Moon corrections.*

ALTITUDE CORRECTION TABLES 0°–35°—MOON

App. Alt.	0°–4° Corrⁿ	5°–9° Corrⁿ	10°–14° Corrⁿ	15°–19° Corrⁿ	20°–24° Corrⁿ	25°–29° Corrⁿ	30°–34° Corrⁿ	App. Alt.
00	0 33.8	5 58.2	10 62.1	15 62.8	20 62.2	25 60.8	30 58.9	00
10	35.9	58.5	62.2	62.8	62.1	60.8	58.8	10
20	37.8	58.7	62.2	62.8	62.1	60.7	58.8	20
30	39.6	58.9	62.3	62.8	62.1	60.7	58.7	30
40	41.2	59.1	62.3	62.8	62.0	60.6	58.6	40
50	42.6	59.3	62.4	62.7	62.0	60.6	58.5	50
00	1 44.0	6 59.5	11 62.4	16 62.7	21 62.0	26 60.5	31 58.5	00
10	45.2	59.7	62.4	62.7	61.9	60.4	58.4	10
20	46.3	59.9	62.5	62.7	61.9	60.4	58.3	20
30	47.3	60.0	62.5	62.7	61.9	60.3	58.2	30
40	48.3	60.2	62.5	62.7	61.8	60.3	58.2	40
50	49.2	60.3	62.6	62.7	61.8	60.2	58.1	50
00	2 50.0	7 60.5	12 62.6	17 62.7	22 61.7	27 60.1	32 58.0	00
10	50.8	60.6	62.6	62.6	61.7	60.1	57.9	10
20	51.4	60.7	62.6	62.6	61.6	60.0	57.8	20
30	52.1	60.9	62.7	62.6	61.6	59.9	57.8	30
40	52.7	61.0	62.7	62.6	61.5	59.9	57.7	40
50	53.3	61.1	62.7	62.6	61.5	59.8	57.6	50
00	3 53.8	8 61.2	13 62.7	18 62.5	23 61.5	28 59.7	33 57.5	00
10	54.3	61.3	62.7	62.5	61.4	59.7	57.4	10
20	54.8	61.4	62.7	62.5	61.4	59.6	57.4	20
30	55.2	61.5	62.8	62.5	61.3	59.6	57.3	30
40	55.6	61.6	62.8	62.4	61.3	59.5	57.2	40
50	56.0	61.6	62.8	62.4	61.2	59.4	57.1	50
00	4 56.4	9 61.7	14 62.8	19 62.4	24 61.2	29 59.3	34 57.0	00
10	56.7	61.8	62.8	62.3	61.1	59.3	56.9	10
20	57.1	61.9	62.8	62.3	61.1	59.2	56.9	20
30	57.4	61.9	62.8	62.3	61.0	59.1	56.8	30
40	57.7	62.0	62.8	62.2	60.9	59.1	56.7	40
50	57.9	62.1	62.8	62.2	60.9	59.0	56.6	50

H.P.	L	U	L	U	L	U	L	U	L	U	L	U	L	U	H.P.
54.0	0.3	0.9	0.3	0.9	0.4	1.0	0.5	1.1	0.6	1.2	0.7	1.3	0.9	1.5	54.0
54.3	0.7	1.1	0.7	1.2	0.7	1.2	0.8	1.3	0.9	1.4	1.1	1.5	1.2	1.7	54.3
54.6	1.1	1.4	1.1	1.4	1.1	1.4	1.2	1.5	1.3	1.6	1.4	1.7	1.5	1.8	54.6
54.9	1.4	1.6	1.5	1.6	1.5	1.6	1.6	1.7	1.6	1.8	1.8	1.9	1.9	2.0	54.9
55.2	1.8	1.8	1.8	1.8	1.9	1.9	1.9	1.9	2.0	2.0	2.1	2.1	2.2	2.2	55.2
55.5	2.2	2.0	2.2	2.0	2.3	2.1	2.3	2.1	2.4	2.2	2.4	2.3	2.5	2.4	55.5
55.8	2.6	2.2	2.6	2.2	2.6	2.3	2.7	2.3	2.7	2.4	2.8	2.4	2.9	2.5	55.8
56.1	3.0	2.4	3.0	2.5	3.0	2.5	3.0	2.5	3.1	2.6	3.1	2.6	3.2	2.7	56.1
56.4	3.4	2.7	3.4	2.7	3.4	2.7	3.4	2.7	3.4	2.8	3.5	2.8	3.5	2.9	56.4
56.7	3.7	2.9	3.7	2.9	3.8	2.9	3.8	2.9	3.8	3.0	3.8	3.0	3.9	3.0	56.7
57.0	4.1	3.1	4.1	3.1	4.1	3.1	4.1	3.1	4.2	3.1	4.2	3.2	4.2	3.2	57.0
57.3	4.5	3.3	4.5	3.3	4.5	3.3	4.5	3.3	4.5	3.4	4.5	3.4	4.6	3.4	57.3
57.6	4.9	3.5	4.9	3.5	4.9	3.5	4.9	3.5	4.9	3.5	4.9	3.6	4.9	3.6	57.6
57.9	5.3	3.8	5.3	3.8	5.2	3.8	5.2	3.7	5.2	3.7	5.2	3.7	5.2	3.7	57.9
58.2	5.6	4.0	5.6	4.0	5.6	4.0	5.6	4.0	5.6	3.9	5.6	3.9	5.6	3.9	58.2
58.5	6.0	4.2	6.0	4.2	6.0	4.2	6.0	4.2	6.0	4.1	5.9	4.1	5.9	4.1	58.5
58.8	6.4	4.4	6.4	4.4	6.4	4.4	6.3	4.4	6.3	4.3	6.3	4.3	6.2	4.2	58.8
59.1	6.8	4.6	6.8	4.6	6.7	4.6	6.7	4.6	6.7	4.5	6.6	4.5	6.6	4.4	59.1
59.4	7.2	4.8	7.1	4.8	7.1	4.8	7.1	4.8	7.0	4.7	7.0	4.7	6.9	4.6	59.4
59.7	7.5	5.1	7.5	5.0	7.5	5.0	7.5	5.0	7.4	4.9	7.3	4.8	7.2	4.7	59.7
60.0	7.9	5.3	7.9	5.3	7.9	5.2	7.8	5.2	7.8	5.1	7.7	5.0	7.6	4.9	60.0
60.3	8.3	5.5	8.3	5.5	8.2	5.4	8.2	5.4	8.1	5.3	8.0	5.2	7.9	5.1	60.3
60.6	8.7	5.7	8.7	5.7	8.6	5.7	8.6	5.6	8.5	5.5	8.4	5.4	8.2	5.3	60.6
60.9	9.1	5.9	9.0	5.9	9.0	5.9	8.9	5.8	8.8	5.7	8.7	5.6	8.6	5.4	60.9
61.2	9.5	6.2	9.4	6.1	9.4	6.1	9.3	6.0	9.2	5.9	9.1	5.8	8.9	5.6	61.2
61.5	9.8	6.4	9.8	6.3	9.7	6.3	9.7	6.2	9.5	6.1	9.4	5.9	9.2	5.8	61.5

DIP

Ht. of Eye (m)	Ht. of Eye (ft)	Corrⁿ	Ht. of Eye (m)	Ht. of Eye (ft)	Corrⁿ
2.4	8.0	−2.8	9.5	31.5	−5.5
2.6	8.6	−2.9	9.9	32.7	−5.6
2.8	9.2	−3.0	10.3	33.9	−5.7
3.0	9.8	−3.1	10.6	35.1	−5.8
3.2	10.5	−3.2	11.0	36.3	−5.9
3.4	11.2	−3.3	11.4	37.6	−6.0
3.6	11.9	−3.4	11.8	38.9	−6.1
3.8	12.6	−3.5	12.2	40.1	−6.2
4.0	13.3	−3.6	12.6	41.5	−6.3
4.3	14.1	−3.7	13.0	42.8	−6.4
4.5	14.9	−3.8	13.4	44.2	−6.5
4.7	15.7	−3.9	13.8	45.5	−6.6
5.0	16.5	−4.0	14.2	46.9	−6.7
5.2	17.4	−4.1	14.7	48.4	−6.8
5.5	18.3	−4.2	15.1	49.8	−6.9
5.8	19.1	−4.3	15.5	51.3	−7.0
6.1	20.1	−4.4	16.0	52.8	−7.1
6.3	21.0	−4.5	16.5	54.3	−7.2
6.6	22.0	−4.6	16.9	55.8	−7.3
6.9	22.9	−4.7	17.4	57.4	−7.4
7.2	23.9	−4.8	17.9	58.9	−7.5
7.5	24.9	−4.9	18.4	60.5	−7.6
7.9	26.0	−5.0	18.8	62.1	−7.7
8.2	27.1	−5.1	19.3	63.8	−7.8
8.5	28.1	−5.2	19.8	65.4	−7.9
8.8	29.2	−5.3	20.4	67.1	−8.0
9.2	30.4	−5.4	20.9	68.8	−8.1
9.5	31.5		21.4	70.5	

MOON CORRECTION TABLE

The correction is in two parts; the first correction is taken from the upper part of the table with argument apparent altitude, and the second from the lower part, with argument H.P., in the same column as that from which the first correction was taken. Separate corrections are given in the lower part for lower (L) and upper (U) limbs. All corrections are to be **added** to apparent altitude, *but 30′ is to be subtracted from the altitude of the upper limb.*

For corrections for pressure and temperature see page A4.

For bubble sextant observations ignore dip, take the mean of upper and lower limb corrections and subtract 15′ from the altitude.

App. Alt. = Apparent altitude = Sextant altitude corrected for index error and dip.

43 Time, longitude and hour angle

As explained earlier, one of the fundamental pieces of information needed in astronomical navigation is the geographical position of the heavenly body being observed – this is the position on the surface of the earth from which the body appears to be vertically overhead. Because the earth itself is both rotating on its axis and moving in an orbit around the sun, the geographical position moves very quickly. By using the *Nautical Almanac*, the geographical position of the body can be established for any particular time throughout the year, but to make proper use of this information it is necessary to understand the somewhat unfamiliar relationship between time, longitude and the related quantity known as hour angle.

Figure I shows the earth, viewed from a point in space directly above the south pole. The sun is shining from what can be considered a fixed direction, while the earth is rotating clockwise. If we imagine a gigantic clock face, graduated into 24 one-hour divisions, fixed to the sun, and also imagine an hour hand attached to the earth, then this hour hand will sweep through the 24 hours of the day as the earth rotates on its axis. The time thus measured is *solar time*, the time that would be shown (in daylight) on a sundial.

Figure I also shows that the time of day, measured by the sun, depends upon the longitude of the observer. The datum for measuring time is the same as the datum for measuring longitude, the Greenwich meridian. If an observer is west of the Greenwich meridian, his time is *earlier* than that at Greenwich; if he is east of the Greenwich meridian his time is *later*. There is an exact relationship between time and longitude. As the earth rotates through 360° in 24 hours (or 15° in one hour), a time difference of one hour is the same as a longitude difference of 15°.

The situation is complicated by the fact that the earth also travels in an orbit around the sun, with a period of one year. The earth moves faster in some parts of its orbit than in others, and this makes the sun an irregular timepiece; each day, from noon to noon or midnight to midnight, has a slightly different length. To overcome this difficulty, the astronomers have invented the *mean sun*, an imaginary body which clocks off a regular day of 24 hours exactly (Fig. 2). At different times of the year, the true sun can be up to a quarter of an hour fast or slow on the mean sun – a quantity known as the *equation of time*. This quantity is not often used in astronomical navigation, but is given on the daily pages of the *Nautical Almanac* if needed.

In Figure 2, the imaginary clock face has now been fixed with relationship to the mean sun, and the hour hand at the Greenwich meridian now sweeps out *Greenwich mean time*. The hour hand of an observer in a different longitude shows his *local mean time*, which is, of course, related to Greenwich mean time by his longitude, at the rate of one hour of time for 15° of longitude. For example:

GMT 12 h 00 m 00 s longitude 30°W LMT 10 h 00 m 00 s
17 h 30 m 00 s 〃 75°E 〃 22 h 30 m 00 s

43.1 *Time and longitude.*

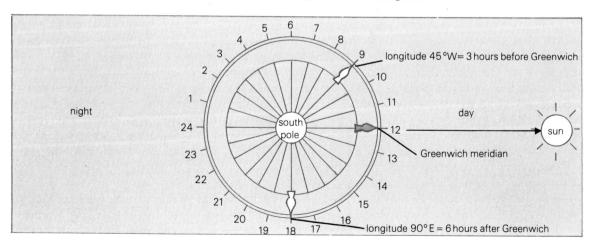

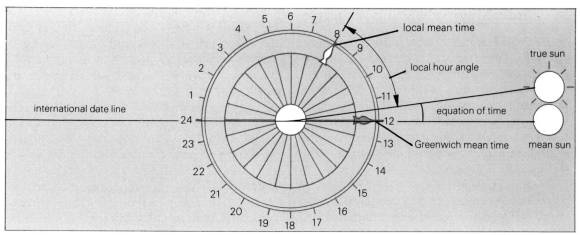

43.2 *The mean sun and hour angle.*

It may happen that the combination of Greenwich mean time and the observer's longitude puts him on the opposite side of the midnight mark of the clock face, which means that the date changes. For example:

GMT 01 h 00 m 00 s longitude 45°W LMT 22 h 00 m 00 s
 5 May   *the previous day*
                                           4 May
   17 h 30 m 00 s   150°E   03 h 30 m 00 s
   12 August   *the next day*
                                      13 August

One curious effect of the relationship between time and longitude is that, if nothing were done, a traveller who went round the world would find that the date on his calendar would be different from the date being kept at his starting point – he would apparently have gained or lost a day, depending on which way round the world he went. To correct for this, the *international date line* has been established, running more or less along the meridian of 180° east or west (with diversions to keep island groups on the same side). The date on the eastern side of the line is one day behind the date on the western side (as is the day of the week). A vessel crossing the date line has to adjust its calendar appropriately; crossing from east to west, add a day – from west to east, subtract a day.

Local mean time depends upon the longitude, but it would be very inconvenient if every place within a country kept a different time. National governments therefore establish a *civil time*, which is the official time to be kept in that country (big countries like Australia or the United States need several civil times as they span a lot of longitude). Civil time is generally (but not always) an exact number of hours ahead of or behind GMT; details are given in the *Nautical Almanac*. Many countries also keep some form of daylight saving time in summer – generally one hour ahead of the normal civil time. This is called *summer time*.

For convenience, a similar scheme is adopted by ships at sea. The world is divided up into 24 zones, each 15° wide in longitude, centred on the Greenwich meridian; the time kept in each zone is an appropriate number of hours ahead or behind Greenwich (Fig. 3). Thus, between 7½°W and 7½°E, GMT is kept, between 7½°W and 22½°W, zone + 1 is kept, and so on. The sign given to the zone indicates how many hours must be added to or subtracted from the local zone time to get back to GMT.

It is very often necessary to convert from civil time or zone time to GMT, as all entries in the *Nautical Almanac* are referred to GMT. In making this conversion, the navigator must always be alert to the possibility of the date at Greenwich being different from the date he is keeping; this could result in his looking up data in the almanac for the wrong day. Each such conversion should contain a check of the *Greenwich date*. For example:

Zone date and time   24 May 04 h 45 m
Zone kept   −6 hours
Greenwich date and time   23 May 22 h 45 m

43.3 *Time zones.*

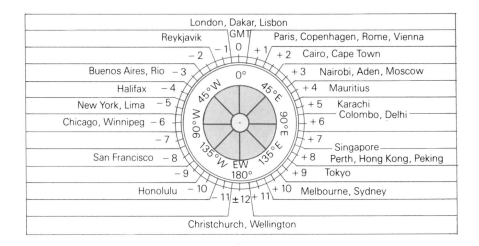

Hour angle

As can be seen in Figure 2, the true sun is not in line with the mean sun – the difference between them being the equation of time. Another way of considering this is to say that the sun has a longitude which changes continually as the earth rotates; the same thing can be said of any heavenly body. For convenience, the longitude of heavenly bodies is not used in navigation; it is replaced by a very similar quantity known as *Greenwich hour angle*. The Greenwich hour angle of a body is the angle, measured westwards, between the meridian of Greenwich and the meridian over which the body stands. Unlike longitude, the Greenwich hour angle starts at 0° when the body is on the Greenwich meridian, and increases throughout (roughly) 24 hours to 360°, when it is once more on the Greenwich meridian. The Greenwich hour angle of important heavenly bodies is tabulated for each hour in the daily pages of the *Nautical Almanac*.

The navigator generally is more interested in the angle between his own meridian and the body, rather than the Greenwich meridian. He can obtain this angle, known as the *local hour angle*, by combining the GHA from the nautical almanac with his longitude, using the rule:

GHA to LHA – add easterly longitude
　　　　　　 subtract westerly longitude.

For example:

GHA　　 27°15′.9
Long E　14°11′.5　(E long, so add)
LHA　　 41°27′.4

GHA　　 331°11′.2
Long W　72°54′.0　(W long, so subtract)
LHA　　 258°17′.2

If the combination of GHA and longitude results in a negative number, add 360°; if the result exceeds 360°, then subtract 360° from the answer.

For example:

GHA　　 345°
Long E　44°
LHA　　 389° − 360° = 29°

GHA　　 35°
Long W　102°
LHA　　 −67° + 360° = 353°

Keeping GMT

To establish the GP of a body, GMT must be known. A modern quartz timepiece, with a periodic check from a radio time signal, will suit admirably but it is wise to have a back-up timepiece as well. A quartz wristwatch will be quite suitable, even if it belongs to another member of the crew. This, too, should be checked regularly against time signals.

44 The geographical position – declination and Greenwich hour angle

The geographical position of any body of navigational importance can be established for any second of GMT throughout the year by using the *Nautical Almanac*. Various almanacs exist, mostly published by the national authorities of various countries. The *Nautical Almanac* used in this book is the one published jointly by the British Nautical Alamanac Office and the United States Naval Observatory; the British publication is known as N.P. 314. Almanacs are normally published at least a year in advance, to cope with the needs of vessels making extended passages.

The data from this almanac is now used by a dozen other countries, with necessary changes for language and so on.

The *Nautical Almanac* defines the geographical positions of bodies by using two quantities which correspond closely with latitude and longitude – *declination* and *Greenwich hour angle* respectively.

The declination of a body is exactly equivalent to the latitude of the geographical position; it is expressed in degrees, minutes and decimals either north or south of the equator.

The longitude of the geographical position is expressed as its Greenwich hour angle (GHA). The only real difference between them is that longitude is given either east or west of the Greenwich meridian; GHA is given in degrees, minutes and decimals *west* of the Greenwich meridian. It is possible (though not often necessary) to convert GHA to longitude by the following process:

GHA between 0° and 180° – longitude west = GHA

GHA between 180° and 360° – longitude east = 360° − GHA

Both the declination and the Greenwich hour angle for the navigationally important objects are given for each hour throughout the year on the daily pages of the *Nautical Almanac* (Table 1). Each page opening gives the data needed by a navigator for three days, with the hours of GMT down the left-hand side of each page. The daily pages contain much information apart from declination and GHA; these items will be described as they are needed.

Finding the declination

Declination is the easier of the two quantities to obtain, as it changes relatively slowly.

Stars The declination of the 57 most commonly used stars is given in the right-hand column of the left page (Table 1). This value can be used without correction at any time during the three days to which the daily page refers.

Sun, Venus, Mars, Jupiter, Saturn Each of these bodies has its own column for both GHA and declination. Using the correct day and the hour of GMT, extract the value of declination for the hour, not forgetting to note whether it is north or south. Also, glance down the column to see if the declination is increasing in magnitude or decreasing; this is needed for the correction of declination for minutes of GMT described below. Then record the value *d*, given at the foot of the column; if the declination is increasing in magnitude, give *d* a + sign, otherwise call it −. *d* gives the rate of change of declination in one hour.

Moon The declination of the moon is obtained in the same way as that of the sun and planets, except that *d* is given for each hour rather than a three-day period.

Correcting declination The declination is constantly changing, as expressed by the value of *d*; the value given in the *Nautical Almanac* is only correct at the exact hour of GMT, so a correction must be applied for the minutes past the hour of the observation. In the case of the sun and the planets, *d* is small and a mental interpolation is quite accurate enough – for 15 minutes past the hour, use $\frac{1}{4}d$, 30 minutes past $\frac{1}{2}d$, 45 minutes past $\frac{3}{4}d$ and so on. For the moon, *d* can be quite large (up to 10′ per hour) and a more accurate interpolation is needed. A table of increments and corrections is provided at the back of the almanac, for correcting both GHA and declination. To obtain the *d* correction, find the section of the table corresponding to the minutes of GMT (Table 2). In the columns headed '*v* or *d*', search for the appropriate value of *d* (small type). The correction to apply is given beside it in larger type.

Whether *d* is interpolated by eye or by means of the increments and corrections table, the value found should be added or subtracted from the declination found in the daily pages, according to the sign given to *d* earlier.

Table 1 Almanac *daily page.*

1980 MAY 3, 4, 5 (SAT., SUN., MON.)

G.M.T.	ARIES G.H.A.	VENUS −4.2 G.H.A.	Dec.	MARS +0.4 G.H.A.	Dec.	JUPITER −1.8 G.H.A.	Dec.	SATURN +1.0 G.H.A.	Dec.	STARS Name	S.H.A.	Dec.
3 00	221 02.7	136 57.5 N27	38.3	68 30.5 N13	28.6	68 13.2 N12	30.5	48 49.7 N 5	55.3	Acamar	315 37.9	S40 23.2
01	236 05.2	151 58.2	38.4	83 32.4	28.3	83 15.6	30.4	63 52.2	55.3	Achernar	335 46.1	S57 20.2
02	251 07.7	166 58.8	38.4	98 34.3	28.0	98 18.1	30.4	78 54.8	55.4	Acrux	173 36.9	S62 59.6
03	266 10.1	181 59.5 ··	38.5	113 36.1 ··	27.7	113 20.5 ··	30.4	93 57.3 ··	55.4	Adhara	255 32.5	S28 57.0
04	281 12.6	197 00.2	38.6	128 38.0	27.4	128 22.9	30.4	108 59.9	55.4	Aldebaran	291 18.6	N16 28.0
05	296 15.1	212 00.8	38.6	143 39.8	27.0	143 25.3	30.3	124 02.4	55.4			
06	311 17.5	227 01.5 N27	38.7	158 41.7 N13	26.7	158 27.7 N12	30.3	139 04.9 N 5	55.5	Alioth	166 42.3	N56 04.2
07	326 20.0	242 02.2	38.7	173 43.5	26.4	173 30.1	30.3	154 07.5	55.5	Alkaid	153 18.3	N49 24.8
S 08	341 22.5	257 02.9	38.8	188 45.4	26.1	188 32.6	30.3	169 10.0	55.5	Al Na'ir	28 15.5	S47 03.3
A 09	356 24.9	272 03.5 ··	38.9	203 47.2 ··	25.8	203 35.0 ··	30.2	184 12.6 ··	55.6	Alnilam	276 12.2	S 1 13.0
T 10	11 27.4	287 04.2	38.9	218 49.1	25.5	218 37.4	30.2	199 15.1	55.6	Alphard	218 20.8	S 8 34.5
U 11	26 29.8	302 04.9	39.0	233 50.9	25.2	233 39.8	30.2	214 17.6	55.6			
R 12	41 32.3	317 05.6 N27	39.0	248 52.8 N13	24.8	248 42.2 N12	30.2	229 20.2 N 5	55.6	Alphecca	126 32.0	N26 46.9
D 13	56 34.8	332 06.3	39.1	263 54.6	24.5	263 44.6	30.1	244 22.7	55.7	Alpheratz	358 09.9	N28 58.6
A 14	71 37.2	347 07.0	39.1	278 56.4	24.2	278 47.1	30.1	259 25.3	55.7	Altair	62 32.7	N 8 48.9
Y 15	86 39.7	2 07.7 ··	39.2	293 58.3 ··	23.9	293 49.5 ··	30.1	274 27.8 ··	55.7	Ankaa	353 40.9	S42 24.8
16	101 42.2	17 08.4	39.2	309 00.1	23.6	308 51.9	30.1	289 30.4	55.7	Antares	112 56.9	S26 23.3
17	116 44.6	32 09.1	39.3	324 02.0	23.3	323 54.3	30.0	304 32.9	55.8			
18	131 47.1	47 09.8 N27	39.3	339 03.8 N13	22.9	338 56.7 N12	30.0	319 35.4 N 5	55.8	Arcturus	146 18.4	N19 17.1
19	146 49.6	62 10.5	39.4	354 05.7	22.6	353 59.1	30.0	334 38.0	55.8	Atria	108 20.9	S68 59.4
20	161 52.0	77 11.2	39.4	9 07.5	22.3	9 01.5	30.0	349 40.5	55.8	Avior	234 28.4	S59 27.1
21	176 54.5	92 11.9 ··	39.5	24 09.3 ··	22.0	24 03.9 ··	29.9	4 43.0 ··	55.9	Bellatrix	278 59.3	N 6 19.8
22	191 57.0	107 12.6	39.5	39 11.2	21.7	39 06.4	29.9	19 45.6	55.9	Betelgeuse	271 28.8	N 7 24.1
23	206 59.4	122 13.3	39.6	54 13.0	21.3	54 08.8	29.9	34 48.1	55.9			
4 00	222 01.9	137 14.0 N27	39.6	69 14.8 N13	21.0	69 11.2 N12	29.9	49 50.7 N 5	55.9	Canopus	264 07.7	S52 41.4
01	237 04.3	152 14.7	39.7	84 16.7	20.7	84 13.6	29.8	64 53.2	56.0	Capella	281 12.1	N45 58.7
02	252 06.8	167 15.4	39.7	99 18.5	20.4	99 16.0	29.8	79 55.7	56.0	Deneb	49 48.6	N45 12.3
03	267 09.3	182 16.2 ··	39.7	114 20.4 ··	20.1	114 18.4 ··	29.8	94 58.3 ··	56.0	Denebola	182 59.1	N14 41.0
04	282 11.7	197 16.9	39.8	129 22.2	19.7	129 20.8	29.7	110 00.8	56.0	Diphda	349 21.5	S18 05.8
05	297 14.2	212 17.6	39.8	144 24.0	19.4	144 23.2	29.7	125 03.4	56.0			
06	312 16.7	227 18.3 N27	39.8	159 25.9 N13	19.1	159 25.6 N12	29.7	140 05.9 N 5	56.1	Dubhe	194 22.2	N61 51.7
07	327 19.1	242 19.1	39.9	174 27.7	18.8	174 28.0	29.7	155 08.4	56.1	Elnath	278 44.8	N28 35.4
08	342 21.6	257 19.8	39.9	189 29.5	18.5	189 30.5	29.6	170 11.0	56.1	Eltanin	90 57.5	N51 29.3
S 09	357 24.1	272 20.5 ··	40.0	204 31.4 ··	18.1	204 32.9 ··	29.6	185 13.5 ··	56.1	Enif	34 11.9	N 9 46.9
U 10	12 26.5	287 21.3	40.0	219 33.2	17.8	219 35.3	29.6	200 16.0	56.2	Fomalhaut	15 51.9	S29 43.6
N 11	27 29.0	302 22.0	40.0	234 35.0	17.5	234 37.7	29.6	215 18.6	56.2			
D 12	42 31.5	317 22.8 N27	40.1	249 36.8 N13	17.2	249 40.1 N12	29.5	230 21.1 N 5	56.2	Gacrux	172 28.5	S57 00.3
A 13	57 33.9	332 23.5	40.1	264 38.7	16.9	264 42.5	29.5	245 23.7	56.2	Gienah	176 18.0	S17 26.0
Y 14	72 36.4	347 24.2	40.2	279 40.5	16.5	279 44.9	29.5	260 26.2	56.3	Hadar	149 23.1	S60 16.7
15	87 38.8	2 25.0 ··	40.2	294 42.3 ··	16.2	294 47.3 ··	29.4	275 28.7 ··	56.3	Hamal	328 29.6	N23 22.0
16	102 41.3	17 25.7	40.2	309 44.1	15.9	309 49.7	29.4	290 31.3	56.3	Kaus Aust.	84 17.0	S34 23.5
17	117 43.8	32 26.5	40.2	324 46.0	15.6	324 52.1	29.4	305 33.8	56.3			
18	132 46.2	47 27.3 N27	40.3	339 47.8 N13	15.2	339 54.5 N12	29.3	320 36.3 N 5	56.4	Kochab	137 17.9	N74 14.3
19	147 48.7	62 28.0	40.3	354 49.6	14.9	354 56.9	29.3	335 38.9	56.4	Markab	14 03.6	N15 05.7
20	162 51.2	77 28.8	40.3	9 51.4	14.6	9 59.3	29.3	350 41.4	56.4	Menkar	314 41.8	N 4 00.6
21	177 53.6	92 29.5 ··	40.4	24 53.3 ··	14.3	25 01.7 ··	29.3	5 43.9 ··	56.4	Menkent	148 36.9	S36 16.4
22	192 56.1	107 30.3	40.4	39 55.1	13.9	40 04.1	29.2	20 46.5	56.4	Miaplacidus	221 44.9	S69 38.5
23	207 58.6	122 31.1	40.4	54 56.9	13.6	55 06.5	29.2	35 49.0	56.5			
5 00	223 01.0	137 31.8 N27	40.4	69 58.8 N13	13.3	70 08.9 N12	29.2	50 51.6 N 5	56.5	Mirfak	309 17.0	N49 47.4
01	238 03.5	152 32.6	40.5	85 00.5	13.0	85 11.4	29.1	65 54.1	56.5	Nunki	76 29.3	S26 19.2
02	253 05.9	167 33.4	40.5	100 02.4	12.6	100 13.8	29.1	80 56.6	56.5	Peacock	53 58.8	S56 47.7
03	268 08.4	182 34.2 ··	40.5	115 04.2 ··	12.3	115 16.2 ··	29.1	95 59.2 ··	56.6	Pollux	243 58.7	N28 04.6
04	283 10.9	197 35.0	40.6	130 06.0	12.0	130 18.6	29.1	111 01.7	56.6	Procyon	245 26.2	N 5 16.4
05	298 13.3	212 35.7	40.6	145 07.8	11.7	145 21.0	29.0	126 04.2	56.6			
06	313 15.8	227 36.5 N27	40.6	160 09.6 N13	11.3	160 23.4 N12	29.0	141 06.8 N 5	56.6	Rasalhague	96 29.6	N12 34.4
07	328 18.3	242 37.3	40.6	175 11.5	11.0	175 25.8	29.0	156 09.3	56.7	Regulus	208 10.2	N12 03.8
08	343 20.7	257 38.1	40.6	190 13.3	10.7	190 28.2	28.9	171 11.8	56.7	Rigel	281 36.6	S 8 13.7
M 09	358 23.2	272 38.9 ··	40.6	205 15.1 ··	10.3	205 30.6 ··	28.9	186 14.4 ··	56.7	Rigil Kent.	140 25.5	S60 45.2
O 10	13 25.7	287 39.7	40.6	220 16.9	10.0	220 33.0 ·	28.9	201 16.9	56.7	Sabik	102 41.2	S15 42.0
N 11	28 28.1	302 40.5	40.7	235 18.7	09.7	235 35.4	28.8	216 19.4	56.7			
D 12	43 30.6	317 41.3 N27	40.7	250 20.5 N13	09.4	250 37.8 N12	28.8	231 22.0 N 5	56.8	Schedar	350 09.7	N56 25.5
A 13	58 33.1	332 42.1	40.7	265 22.3	09.0	265 40.2	28.8	246 24.5	56.8	Shaula	96 55.8	S37 05.3
Y 14	73 35.5	347 42.9	40.7	280 24.1	08.7	280 42.6	28.8	261 27.0	56.8	Sirius	258 56.2	S16 41.6
15	88 38.0	2 43.7 ··	40.7	295 25.9 ··	08.4	295 45.0 ··	28.7	276 29.6 ··	56.8	Spica	158 57.5	S11 03.6
16	103 40.4	17 44.5	40.7	310 27.8	08.0	310 47.4	28.7	291 32.1	56.8	Suhail	223 11.0	S43 21.5
17	118 42.9	32 45.3	40.8	325 29.6	07.7	325 49.8	28.7	306 34.6	56.9			
18	133 45.4	47 46.2 N27	40.8	340 31.4 N13	07.4	340 52.2 N12	28.6	321 37.2 N 5	56.9	Vega	80 55.8	N38 45.8
19	148 47.8	62 47.0	40.8	355 33.2	07.1	355 54.6	28.6	336 39.7	56.9	Zuben'ubi	137 33.0	S15 57.6
20	163 50.3	77 47.8	40.8	10 35.0	06.7	10 57.0	28.6	351 42.2	56.9			
21	178 52.8	92 48.6 ··	40.8	25 36.8 ··	06.4	25 59.4 ··	28.5	6 44.8 ··	57.0			
22	193 55.2	107 49.4	40.8	40 38.6	06.1	41 01.8	28.5	21 47.3	57.0			
23	208 57.7	122 50.3	40.8	55 40.4	05.7	56 04.2	28.5	36 49.8	57.0			

										Name	S.H.A.	Mer. Pass.
										Venus	275 12.1	14 50
										Mars	207 13.0	19 21
										Jupiter	207 09.3	19 20
Mer. Pass. 9 10.4		v 0.7 d 0.0		v 1.8 d 0.3		v 2.4 d 0.0		v 2.5 d 0.0		Saturn	187 48.8	20 37

1980 MAY 3, 4, 5 (SAT., SUN., MON.) 93

G.M.T.	SUN G.H.A.	SUN Dec.	MOON G.H.A.	v	Dec.	d	H.P.
d h	° '	° '	° '	'	° '	'	'
3 00	180 47.1	N15 39.2	328 25.9	10.8	S17 39.5	4.5	55.7
01	195 47.1	39.9	342 55.7	10.7	17 44.0	4.5	55.8
02	210 47.2	40.7	357 25.4	10.6	17 48.5	4.3	55.8
03	225 47.3 ··	41.4	11 55.0	10.6	17 52.8	4.3	55.8
04	240 47.3	42.1	26 24.6	10.6	17 57.1	4.2	55.8
05	255 47.4	42.9	40 54.2	10.5	18 01.3	4.1	55.8
06	270 47.5	N15 43.6	55 23.7	10.4	S18 05.4	4.0	55.9
07	285 47.5	44.3	69 53.1	10.4	18 09.4	3.9	55.9
S 08	300 47.6	45.1	84 22.5	10.4	18 13.3	3.8	55.9
A 09	315 47.7 ··	45.8	98 51.9	10.3	18 17.1	3.8	55.9
T 10	330 47.7	46.5	113 21.2	10.3	18 20.9	3.6	55.9
U 11	345 47.8	47.3	127 50.5	10.2	18 24.5	3.5	56.0
R 12	0 47.8	N15 48.0	142 19.7	10.2	S18 28.0	3.5	56.0
D 13	15 47.9	48.7	156 48.9	10.2	18 31.5	3.4	56.0
A 14	30 48.0	49.5	171 18.1	10.1	18 34.9	3.2	56.0
Y 15	45 48.0 ··	50.2	185 47.2	10.0	18 38.1	3.2	56.0
16	60 48.1	50.9	200 16.2	10.0	18 41.3	3.1	56.1
17	75 48.2	51.6	214 45.2	10.0	18 44.4	2.9	56.1
18	90 48.2	N15 52.4	229 14.2	9.9	S18 47.3	2.9	56.1
19	105 48.3	53.1	243 43.1	9.9	18 50.2	2.8	56.1
20	120 48.3	53.8	258 12.0	9.9	18 53.0	2.7	56.1
21	135 48.4 ··	54.6	272 40.9	9.8	18 55.7	2.5	56.2
22	150 48.5	55.3	287 09.7	9.7	18 58.2	2.5	56.2
23	165 48.5	56.0	301 38.4	9.7	19 00.7	2.4	56.2
4 00	180 48.6	N15 56.7	316 07.1	9.7	S19 03.1	2.3	56.2
01	195 48.6	57.5	330 35.8	9.7	19 05.4	2.2	56.3
02	210 48.7	58.2	345 04.5	9.6	19 07.6	2.1	56.3
03	225 48.8 ··	58.9	359 33.1	9.5	19 09.7	1.9	56.3
04	240 48.8	15 59.6	14 01.6	9.6	19 11.6	1.9	56.3
05	255 48.9	16 00.3	28 30.2	9.5	19 13.5	1.8	56.3
06	270 48.9	N16 01.1	42 58.7	9.4	S19 15.3	1.6	56.4
07	285 49.0	01.8	57 27.1	9.4	19 16.9	1.6	56.4
S 08	300 49.1	02.5	71 55.5	9.4	19 18.5	1.5	56.4
U 09	315 49.1 ··	03.2	86 23.9	9.4	19 20.0	1.3	56.4
N 10	330 49.2	04.0	100 52.3	9.3	19 21.3	1.3	56.5
11	345 49.2	04.7	115 20.6	9.3	19 22.6	1.1	56.5
D 12	0 49.3	N16 05.4	129 48.9	9.2	S19 23.7	1.1	56.5
A 13	15 49.4	06.1	144 17.1	9.3	19 24.8	0.9	56.5
Y 14	30 49.4	06.8	158 45.4	9.2	19 25.7	0.8	56.5
15	45 49.5 ··	07.5	173 13.6	9.1	19 26.5	0.8	56.6
16	60 49.5	08.3	187 41.7	9.1	19 27.3	0.6	56.6
17	75 49.6	09.0	202 09.8	9.1	19 27.9	0.5	56.6
18	90 49.6	N16 09.7	216 37.9	9.1	S19 28.4	0.3	56.7
19	105 49.7	10.4	231 06.0	9.1	19 28.8	0.3	56.7
20	120 49.7	11.1	245 34.1	9.0	19 29.1	0.2	56.7
21	135 49.8 ··	11.8	260 02.1	9.0	19 29.3	0.1	56.7
22	150 49.9	12.6	274 30.1	8.9	19 29.4	0.1	56.7
23	165 49.9	13.3	288 58.0	8.9	19 29.3	0.1	56.8
5 00	180 50.0	N16 14.0	303 25.9	8.9	S19 29.2	0.3	56.8
01	195 50.0	14.7	317 53.9	8.8	19 28.9	0.3	56.8
02	210 50.1	15.4	332 21.7	8.9	19 28.6	0.5	56.8
03	225 50.1 ··	16.1	346 49.6	8.8	19 28.1	0.6	56.9
04	240 50.2	16.8	1 17.4	8.9	19 27.5	0.6	56.9
05	255 50.2	17.6	15 45.3	8.7	19 26.9	0.8	56.9
06	270 50.3	N16 18.3	30 13.0	8.8	S19 26.1	0.9	56.9
07	285 50.3	19.0	44 40.8	8.8	19 25.2	1.1	57.0
08	300 50.4	19.7	59 08.6	8.7	19 24.1	1.1	57.0
M 09	315 50.4 ··	20.4	73 36.3	8.7	19 23.0	1.2	57.0
O 10	330 50.5	21.1	88 04.0	8.7	19 21.8	1.4	57.0
N 11	345 50.5	21.8	102 31.7	8.7	19 20.4	1.4	57.0
D 12	0 50.6	N16 22.5	116 59.4	8.6	S19 19.0	1.6	57.1
A 13	15 50.7	23.2	131 27.0	8.7	19 17.4	1.7	57.1
Y 14	30 50.7	23.9	145 54.7	8.6	19 15.7	1.8	57.1
15	45 50.8 ··	24.6	160 22.3	8.6	19 13.9	1.9	57.1
16	60 50.8	25.4	174 49.9	8.6	19 12.0	2.0	57.2
17	75 50.9	26.1	189 17.5	8.6	19 10.0	2.1	57.2
18	90 50.9	N16 26.8	203 45.1	8.6	S19 07.9	2.2	57.2
19	105 51.0	27.5	218 12.7	8.5	19 05.7	2.4	57.2
20	120 51.0	28.2	232 40.2	8.6	19 03.3	2.5	57.3
21	135 51.1 ··	28.9	247 07.8	8.5	19 00.8	2.5	57.3
22	150 51.1	29.6	261 35.3	8.5	18 58.3	2.7	57.3
23	165 51.1	30.3	276 02.8	8.5	18 55.6	2.8	57.4
	S.D. 15.9	d 0.7	S.D. 15.3		15.4		15.6

Twilight / Sunrise / Moonrise

Lat.	Naut.	Civil	Sunrise	Moonrise 3	4	5	6
°	h m	h m	h m	h m	h m	h m	h m
N 72	////	////	01 23	01 45	■	■	■
N 70	////	////	02 12	00 14	01 53	03 05	03 24
68	////	00 13	02 43	24 56	00 56	01 58	02 35
66	////	01 35	03 05	24 22	00 22	01 22	02 04
64	////	02 10	03 23	23 57	24 56	00 56	01 40
62	00 11	02 35	03 37	23 38	24 36	00 36	01 22
60	01 24	02 55	03 50	23 22	24 19	00 19	01 07
N 58	01 57	03 10	04 00	23 09	24 06	00 06	00 53
56	02 20	03 24	04 09	22 57	23 54	24 42	00 42
54	02 38	03 35	04 17	22 47	23 43	24 32	00 32
52	02 53	03 45	04 25	22 38	23 34	24 24	00 24
50	03 06	03 54	04 31	22 30	23 26	24 16	00 16
45	03 31	04 12	04 45	22 13	23 08	23 59	24 44
N 40	03 51	04 27	04 56	21 59	22 54	23 45	24 32
35	04 06	04 39	05 06	21 47	22 42	23 33	24 22
30	04 19	04 49	05 15	21 37	22 31	23 23	24 12
20	04 39	05 06	05 29	21 19	22 13	23 05	23 56
N 10	04 54	05 20	05 42	21 04	21 57	22 50	23 43
0	05 07	05 32	05 53	20 49	21 42	22 35	23 31
S 10	05 18	05 43	06 05	20 35	21 27	22 21	23 16
20	05 28	05 54	06 17	20 20	21 11	22 06	23 03
30	05 37	06 06	06 31	20 02	20 53	21 48	22 47
35	05 42	06 12	06 39	19 52	20 42	21 38	22 37
40	05 47	06 19	06 48	19 41	20 30	21 26	22 27
45	05 52	06 27	06 58	19 27	20 16	21 12	22 14
S 50	05 58	06 37	07 11	19 10	19 59	20 55	21 59
52	06 00	06 41	07 17	19 03	19 51	20 47	21 52
54	06 03	06 45	07 24	18 54	19 41	20 38	21 44
56	06 06	06 50	07 31	18 44	19 31	20 28	21 35
58	06 08	06 56	07 39	18 33	19 20	20 17	21 25
S 60	06 12	07 02	07 48	18 20	19 06	20 04	21 13

Sunset / Twilight / Moonset

Lat.	Sunset	Civil	Naut.	Moonset 3	4	5	6
°	h m	h m	h m	h m	h m	h m	h m
N 72	22 40	////	////	02 28	■	■	■
N 70	21 46	////	////	04 00	04 07	04 46	06 19
68	21 14	////	////	04 40	05 05	05 53	07 07
66	20 51	22 25	////	05 07	05 39	06 28	07 38
64	20 33	21 47	////	05 28	06 04	06 54	08 01
62	20 18	21 21	////	05 45	06 23	07 14	08 19
60	20 06	21 01	22 35	05 59	06 39	07 31	08 34
N 58	19 55	20 45	22 00	06 12	06 53	07 44	08 47
56	19 46	20 31	21 36	06 22	07 04	07 56	08 58
54	19 37	20 20	21 17	06 31	07 15	08 07	09 08
52	19 30	20 10	21 02	06 40	07 24	08 16	09 17
50	19 23	20 01	20 49	06 47	07 32	08 24	09 24
45	19 09	19 42	20 23	07 03	07 49	08 42	09 41
N 40	18 58	19 27	20 04	07 16	08 03	08 56	09 54
35	18 48	19 15	19 48	07 28	08 15	09 08	10 06
30	18 39	19 05	19 35	07 37	08 26	09 19	10 16
20	18 25	18 48	19 15	07 54	08 44	09 37	10 33
N 10	18 12	18 34	19 00	08 09	09 00	09 53	10 47
0	18 00	18 22	18 47	08 23	09 14	10 07	11 01
S 10	17 49	18 10	18 36	08 37	09 29	10 22	11 15
20	17 36	17 59	18 25	08 51	09 45	10 38	11 30
30	17 22	17 47	18 16	09 08	10 03	10 56	11 47
35	17 14	17 41	18 11	09 18	10 13	11 06	11 56
40	17 05	17 34	18 06	09 29	10 25	11 18	12 07
45	16 54	17 25	18 00	09 43	10 39	11 32	12 20
S 50	16 42	17 14	17 55	09 57	10 57	11 50	12 36
52	16 36	17 12	17 52	10 06	11 05	11 58	12 44
54	16 29	17 07	17 50	10 15	11 14	12 07	12 52
56	16 22	17 02	17 47	10 24	11 24	12 17	13 01
58	16 14	16 57	17 44	10 35	11 36	12 28	13 11
S 60	16 04	16 51	17 41	10 48	11 49	12 42	13 23

Day	SUN Eqn. of Time 00h	12h	Mer. Pass.	MOON Mer. Pass. Upper	Lower	Age	Phase
	m s	m s	h m	h m	h m	d	
3	03 08	03 11	11 57	02 11	14 36	18	
4	03 14	03 17	11 57	03 02	15 28	19	
5	03 20	03 22	11 57	03 55	16 21	20	◖

Finding the Greenwich hour angle The GHA of a body changes very much more quickly than the declination, so the correction is a little more involved. The GHA is normally made up of three components:

The value for the exact hour from the daily tables.

An increment for minutes and seconds past the hour.

A further small (v) correction for irregularity.

Sun The GHA for the exact hour is given on the daily page. The increment for minutes and seconds is found in the table of increments and corrections (Table 2). In the 'box' appropriate to the minutes, find the seconds in the left-hand column; the increment is then found in the column headed 'Sun, Planets'. This should always be *added* to the GHA found in the daily pages. There is no v correction for the sun.

Planets The GHA for the hour is found in the appropriate column of the daily page and the increment for minutes and seconds is given in the table of increments and corrections, exactly as for the sun. However, a v correction must also be applied, using the value of v to be found at the foot of the column. If v is small, the correction may be interpolated mentally, otherwise the table of increments and corrections may be used. The procedure is exactly the same as for the d correction of declination. NOTE The v correction for Venus is sometimes negative.

Moon The procedure is the same as for the planets, except that v is given for each hour, and the increment is given in a separate column of the table of increments and corrections.

Stars The *Nautical Almanac* gives details of 173 stars (including 57 selected stars most commonly used for navigation). It would clearly be impractical to list the GHA of each star for each hour of the year. Instead, the almanac makes use of the fact that stars are virtually fixed in their places. The almanac lists the GHA of a fixed point in the night sky, known as the first point of Aries (or just Aries); to this must be added a quantity called the *sidereal hour angle*, which gives the angles between the star itself and Aries (Fig. 1). The GHA of a star is therefore obtained by combining:

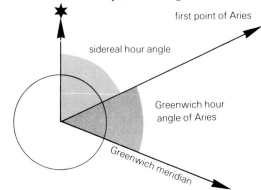

44.1 *GHA Aries and sidereal hour angle.*

1) The GHA of Aries for the hour (daily page)
2) The increment for minutes and seconds, using the Aries column of the table of increments and corrections.
3) The sidereal hour angle (SHA) of the star, from the star column of the daily page.

For example: To illustrate the use of the *Nautical Almanac*, the GHA and declination of the sun, moon, Venus and Aldebaran are given for 3 May 1980, 05 h 42 m 27 s.

	Sun	Moon	Venus	Aldebaran	
GHA 05 h	255°47′.4	40°54′.2 v = 10′.5	212°00′.8 v = 0.7	296°15′.1	(Aries)
Incr. 42 m 27 s	10°36′.8	10°07′.7	10°36′.8	10°38′.5	
v correction	–	7′.4	0′.5	–	
SHA	–	–	–	291°18′.6	
GHA	266°24′.2	51°09′.3	222°38′.1	598°12′.2	
				−360°	
				238°12′.2	
Dec 05 h	N15°42′.9 d = +0.7	S18°01′.3 d = +4.1	N27°38′.6 d = 0	N16°28′.0	
d correction	+0′.5	+2′.9	0.0	–	
Dec	N15°43′.4	S18°04′.2	N27°38′.6	N16°28′.0	

Table 2 *Increments and corrections*

42ᵐ   INCREMENTS AND CORRECTIONS   43ᵐ

42ᵐ	SUN PLANETS	ARIES	MOON	v or Corrⁿ d	v or Corrⁿ d	v or Corrⁿ d
s	° ′	° ′	° ′	′ ′	′ ′	′ ′
00	10 30·0	10 31·7	10 01·3	0·0 0·0	6·0 4·3	12·0 8·5
01	10 30·3	10 32·0	10 01·5	0·1 0·1	6·1 4·3	12·1 8·6
02	10 30·5	10 32·2	10 01·8	0·2 0·1	6·2 4·4	12·2 8·6
03	10 30·8	10 32·5	10 02·0	0·3 0·2	6·3 4·5	12·3 8·7
04	10 31·0	10 32·7	10 02·3	0·4 0·3	6·4 4·5	12·4 8·8
05	10 31·3	10 33·0	10 02·5	0·5 0·4	6·5 4·6	12·5 8·9
06	10 31·5	10 33·2	10 02·7	0·6 0·4	6·6 4·7	12·6 8·9
07	10 31·8	10 33·5	10 03·0	0·7 0·5	6·7 4·7	12·7 9·0
08	10 32·0	10 33·7	10 03·2	0·8 0·6	6·8 4·8	12·8 9·1
09	10 32·3	10 34·0	10 03·4	0·9 0·6	6·9 4·9	12·9 9·1
10	10 32·5	10 34·2	10 03·7	1·0 0·7	7·0 5·0	13·0 9·2
11	10 32·8	10 34·5	10 03·9	1·1 0·8	7·1 5·0	13·1 9·3
12	10 33·0	10 34·7	10 04·2	1·2 0·9	7·2 5·1	13·2 9·4
13	10 33·3	10 35·0	10 04·4	1·3 0·9	7·3 5·2	13·3 9·4
14	10 33·5	10 35·2	10 04·6	1·4 1·0	7·4 5·2	13·4 9·5
15	10 33·8	10 35·5	10 04·9	1·5 1·1	7·5 5·3	13·5 9·6
16	10 34·0	10 35·7	10 05·1	1·6 1·1	7·6 5·4	13·6 9·6
17	10 34·3	10 36·0	10 05·4	1·7 1·2	7·7 5·5	13·7 9·7
18	10 34·5	10 36·2	10 05·6	1·8 1·3	7·8 5·5	13·8 9·8
19	10 34·8	10 36·5	10 05·8	1·9 1·3	7·9 5·6	13·9 9·8
20	10 35·0	10 36·7	10 06·1	2·0 1·4	8·0 5·7	14·0 9·9
21	10 35·3	10 37·0	10 06·3	2·1 1·5	8·1 5·7	14·1 10·0
22	10 35·5	10 37·2	10 06·5	2·2 1·6	8·2 5·8	14·2 10·1
23	10 35·8	10 37·5	10 06·8	2·3 1·6	8·3 5·9	14·3 10·1
24	10 36·0	10 37·7	10 07·0	2·4 1·7	8·4 6·0	14·4 10·2
25	10 36·3	10 38·0	10 07·3	2·5 1·8	8·5 6·0	14·5 10·3
26	10 36·5	10 38·2	10 07·5	2·6 1·8	8·6 6·1	14·6 10·3
27	10 36·8	10 38·5	10 07·7	2·7 1·9	8·7 6·2	14·7 10·4
28	10 37·0	10 38·7	10 08·0	2·8 2·0	8·8 6·2	14·8 10·5
29	10 37·3	10 39·0	10 08·2	2·9 2·1	8·9 6·3	14·9 10·6
30	10 37·5	10 39·2	10 08·5	3·0 2·1	9·0 6·4	15·0 10·6
31	10 37·8	10 39·5	10 08·7	3·1 2·2	9·1 6·4	15·1 10·7
32	10 38·0	10 39·7	10 08·9	3·2 2·3	9·2 6·5	15·2 10·8
33	10 38·3	10 40·0	10 09·2	3·3 2·3	9·3 6·6	15·3 10·8
34	10 38·5	10 40·2	10 09·4	3·4 2·4	9·4 6·7	15·4 10·9
35	10 38·8	10 40·5	10 09·7	3·5 2·5	9·5 6·7	15·5 11·0
36	10 39·0	10 40·7	10 09·9	3·6 2·6	9·6 6·8	15·6 11·1
37	10 39·3	10 41·0	10 10·1	3·7 2·6	9·7 6·9	15·7 11·1
38	10 39·5	10 41·3	10 10·4	3·8 2·7	9·8 6·9	15·8 11·2
39	10 39·8	10 41·5	10 10·6	3·9 2·8	9·9 7·0	15·9 11·3
40	10 40·0	10 41·8	10 10·8	4·0 2·8	10·0 7·1	16·0 11·3
41	10 40·3	10 42·0	10 11·1	4·1 2·9	10·1 7·2	16·1 11·4
42	10 40·5	10 42·3	10 11·3	4·2 3·0	10·2 7·2	16·2 11·5
43	10 40·8	10 42·5	10 11·6	4·3 3·0	10·3 7·3	16·3 11·5
44	10 41·0	10 42·8	10 11·8	4·4 3·1	10·4 7·4	16·4 11·6
45	10 41·3	10 43·0	10 12·0	4·5 3·2	10·5 7·4	16·5 11·7
46	10 41·5	10 43·3	10 12·3	4·6 3·3	10·6 7·5	16·6 11·8
47	10 41·8	10 43·5	10 12·5	4·7 3·3	10·7 7·6	16·7 11·8
48	10 42·0	10 43·8	10 12·8	4·8 3·4	10·8 7·7	16·8 11·9
49	10 42·3	10 44·0	10 13·0	4·9 3·5	10·9 7·7	16·9 12·0
50	10 42·5	10 44·3	10 13·2	5·0 3·5	11·0 7·8	17·0 12·0
51	10 42·8	10 44·5	10 13·5	5·1 3·6	11·1 7·9	17·1 12·1
52	10 43·0	10 44·8	10 13·7	5·2 3·7	11·2 7·9	17·2 12·2
53	10 43·3	10 45·0	10 13·9	5·3 3·8	11·3 8·0	17·3 12·3
54	10 43·5	10 45·3	10 14·2	5·4 3·8	11·4 8·1	17·4 12·3
55	10 43·8	10 45·5	10 14·4	5·5 3·9	11·5 8·1	17·5 12·4
56	10 44·0	10 45·8	10 14·7	5·6 4·0	11·6 8·2	17·6 12·5
57	10 44·3	10 46·0	10 14·9	5·7 4·0	11·7 8·3	17·7 12·5
58	10 44·5	10 46·3	10 15·1	5·8 4·1	11·8 8·4	17·8 12·6
59	10 44·8	10 46·5	10 15·4	5·9 4·2	11·9 8·4	17·9 12·7
60	10 45·0	10 46·8	10 15·6	6·0 4·3	12·0 8·5	18·0 12·8

43ᵐ	SUN PLANETS	ARIES	MOON	v or Corrⁿ d	v or Corrⁿ d	v or Corrⁿ d
s	° ′	° ′	° ′	′ ′	′ ′	′ ′
00	10 45·0	10 46·8	10 15·6	0·0 0·0	6·0 4·4	12·0 8·7
01	10 45·3	10 47·0	10 15·9	0·1 0·1	6·1 4·4	12·1 8·8
02	10 45·5	10 47·3	10 16·1	0·2 0·1	6·2 4·5	12·2 8·8
03	10 45·8	10 47·5	10 16·3	0·3 0·2	6·3 4·6	12·3 8·9
04	10 46·0	10 47·8	10 16·6	0·4 0·3	6·4 4·6	12·4 9·0
05	10 46·3	10 48·0	10 16·8	0·5 0·4	6·5 4·7	12·5 9·1
06	10 46·5	10 48·3	10 17·0	0·6 0·4	6·6 4·8	12·6 9·1
07	10 46·8	10 48·5	10 17·3	0·7 0·5	6·7 4·9	12·7 9·2
08	10 47·0	10 48·8	10 17·5	0·8 0·6	6·8 4·9	12·8 9·3
09	10 47·3	10 49·0	10 17·8	0·9 0·7	6·9 5·0	12·9 9·4
10	10 47·5	10 49·3	10 18·0	1·0 0·7	7·0 5·1	13·0 9·4
11	10 47·8	10 49·5	10 18·2	1·1 0·8	7·1 5·1	13·1 9·5
12	10 48·0	10 49·8	10 18·5	1·2 0·9	7·2 5·2	13·2 9·6
13	10 48·3	10 50·0	10 18·7	1·3 0·9	7·3 5·3	13·3 9·6
14	10 48·5	10 50·3	10 19·0	1·4 1·0	7·4 5·4	13·4 9·7
15	10 48·8	10 50·5	10 19·2	1·5 1·1	7·5 5·4	13·5 9·8
16	10 49·0	10 50·8	10 19·4	1·6 1·2	7·6 5·5	13·6 9·9
17	10 49·3	10 51·0	10 19·7	1·7 1·2	7·7 5·6	13·7 9·9
18	10 49·5	10 51·3	10 19·9	1·8 1·3	7·8 5·7	13·8 10·0
19	10 49·8	10 51·5	10 20·2	1·9 1·4	7·9 5·7	13·9 10·1
20	10 50·0	10 51·8	10 20·4	2·0 1·5	8·0 5·8	14·0 10·2
21	10 50·3	10 52·0	10 20·6	2·1 1·5	8·1 5·9	14·1 10·2
22	10 50·5	10 52·3	10 20·9	2·2 1·6	8·2 5·9	14·2 10·3
23	10 50·8	10 52·5	10 21·1	2·3 1·7	8·3 6·0	14·3 10·4
24	10 51·0	10 52·8	10 21·3	2·4 1·7	8·4 6·1	14·4 10·4
25	10 51·3	10 53·0	10 21·6	2·5 1·8	8·5 6·2	14·5 10·5
26	10 51·5	10 53·3	10 21·8	2·6 1·9	8·6 6·2	14·6 10·6
27	10 51·8	10 53·5	10 22·1	2·7 2·0	8·7 6·3	14·7 10·7
28	10 52·0	10 53·8	10 22·3	2·8 2·0	8·8 6·4	14·8 10·7
29	10 52·3	10 54·0	10 22·5	2·9 2·1	8·9 6·4	14·9 10·8
30	10 52·5	10 54·3	10 22·8	3·0 2·2	9·0 6·5	15·0 10·9
31	10 52·8	10 54·5	10 23·0	3·1 2·2	9·1 6·6	15·1 10·9
32	10 53·0	10 54·8	10 23·3	3·2 2·3	9·2 6·7	15·2 11·0
33	10 53·3	10 55·0	10 23·5	3·3 2·4	9·3 6·7	15·3 11·1
34	10 53·5	10 55·3	10 23·7	3·4 2·5	9·4 6·8	15·4 11·2
35	10 53·8	10 55·5	10 24·0	3·5 2·5	9·5 6·9	15·5 11·2
36	10 54·0	10 55·8	10 24·2	3·6 2·6	9·6 7·0	15·6 11·3
37	10 54·3	10 56·0	10 24·4	3·7 2·7	9·7 7·0	15·7 11·4
38	10 54·5	10 56·3	10 24·7	3·8 2·8	9·8 7·1	15·8 11·5
39	10 54·8	10 56·5	10 24·9	3·9 2·8	9·9 7·2	15·9 11·5
40	10 55·0	10 56·8	10 25·2	4·0 2·9	10·0 7·3	16·0 11·6
41	10 55·3	10 57·0	10 25·4	4·1 3·0	10·1 7·3	16·1 11·7
42	10 55·5	10 57·3	10 25·6	4·2 3·0	10·2 7·4	16·2 11·7
43	10 55·8	10 57·5	10 25·9	4·3 3·1	10·3 7·5	16·3 11·8
44	10 56·0	10 57·8	10 26·1	4·4 3·2	10·4 7·5	16·4 11·9
45	10 56·3	10 58·0	10 26·4	4·5 3·3	10·5 7·6	16·5 12·0
46	10 56·5	10 58·3	10 26·6	4·6 3·3	10·6 7·7	16·6 12·0
47	10 56·8	10 58·5	10 26·8	4·7 3·4	10·7 7·8	16·7 12·1
48	10 57·0	10 58·8	10 27·1	4·8 3·5	10·8 7·8	16·8 12·2
49	10 57·3	10 59·0	10 27·3	4·9 3·6	10·9 7·9	16·9 12·3
50	10 57·5	10 59·3	10 27·5	5·0 3·6	11·0 8·0	17·0 12·3
51	10 57·8	10 59·6	10 27·8	5·1 3·7	11·1 8·0	17·1 12·4
52	10 58·0	10 59·8	10 28·0	5·2 3·8	11·2 8·1	17·2 12·5
53	10 58·3	11 00·1	10 28·3	5·3 3·8	11·3 8·2	17·3 12·5
54	10 58·5	11 00·3	10 28·5	5·4 3·9	11·4 8·3	17·4 12·6
55	10 58·8	11 00·6	10 28·7	5·5 4·0	11·5 8·3	17·5 12·7
56	10 59·0	11 00·8	10 29·0	5·6 4·1	11·6 8·4	17·6 12·8
57	10 59·3	11 01·1	10 29·2	5·7 4·1	11·7 8·5	17·7 12·8
58	10 59·5	11 01·3	10 29·5	5·8 4·2	11·8 8·6	17·8 12·9
59	10 59·8	11 01·6	10 29·7	5·9 4·3	11·9 8·6	17·9 13·0
60	11 00·0	11 01·8	10 29·9	6·0 4·4	12·0 8·7	18·0 13·1

45   Latitude by meridian altitude

There are some circumstances when it is particularly easy to obtain a position line from the observation of a body. The most generally useful of these 'short cut' observations is that for obtaining latitude by *meridian altitude*; this observation is made at local noon, when the sun is either due north or due south of the observer, depending on his latitude. This sight has a long and distinguished history; it was first used by the Portuguese navigators in the late 15th century, and has been in daily use by mariners all over the world to this day. It has the great virtues of providing a latitude without the need for special tables (except the *Nautical Almanac*), and without the need for precise GMT. This section only discusses meridian altitude of the sun; other bodies are not often used.

Principle The sun rises every day in the eastern sky and crosses the heavens to set in the western sky. At noon, local time, the sun is either due north or due south of the observer (i.e. it has the same longitude). The altitude of the sun at this moment can be simply processed to give a latitude, as shown in Figure 1. This is a cross-section of the earth through the meridian of longitude on which both the sun and the observer stand. The altitude of the sun can be converted to the zenith distance (= 90° − Alt.); the zenith distance is the distance from the observer to the geographical position or, in this special case, the difference in latitude between the observer and the GP. However, the latitude of the GP is known – it is equal to the declination of the sun at that moment. Thus, by combining zenith distance with declination, it is possible to derive latitude. The sun's declination changes slowly, so it does not matter if the precise GMT of the observation is not known.

45.1 *Noon altitude and latitude.*

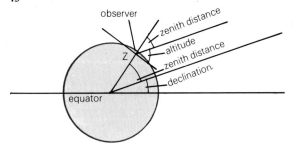

The actual crossing of the meridian is known as *meridian passage*, and the time at which this will happen is given in the *Nautical Almanac*. Meridian passage can happen in a number of different ways, as shown in Figure 2, depending on whether the sun is on the same side of the equator as the observer or not, and on whether the sun is closer to the equator than the observer, or further away. The rules for combining zenith distance and declination vary according to the circumstances; these rules become obvious if a diagram like one of those in Figure 2 is drawn for each case. Otherwise, the precepts given in the description of the method given below will always give the correct answer.

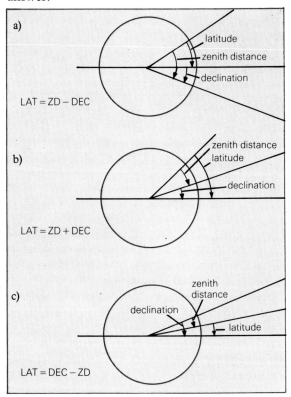

45.2 *Latitude and declination: (a) contrary name;*
(b) same name, declination less than latitude;
(c) same name, declination greater than latitude.

Preparation Meridian passage can be observed merely by watching the sun as it rises until it gets to its highest point in the sky, which is the moment of meridian passage. However, it is much more convenient to be able to predict the time of meridian passage to within a few minutes, to avoid wasting time and running the risk of missing the moment.

On the daily page of the nautical almanac, a figure is given for the meridian passage of the sun for each day (p. 139). This can be taken as the local mean time of meridian passage. The GMT of meridian passage can be obtained from this figure by applying a correction for the DR longitude, converted to time; easterly longitude is subtracted, westerly longitude added.

For example:
3 May 1980, a ship in DR longitude 12°15′W wishes to find the approximate time of meridian passage:

LMT mer pass	11 h 57 m	daily page
Long W in time		
(15° = 1 hr)	00 h 45 m	add W long
GMT	12 h 42 m	

Notes 1) It may be convenient to convert the GMT thus found to zone time, i.e., ship's clock time. In the above example, the ship would probably be keeping zone +1, so ship's time of meridian passage would be 11 h 42 m (+1).

2) It is quite easy to convert longitude to time by mental arithmetic, because

15° = 1 hour
1° = 4 minutes
15′ = 1 minute

A table for converting arc (angles) to time is given just before the table of increments and corrections in the *Nautical Almanac*.

Observing meridian altitude Come on deck about a quarter of an hour before the predicted time of meridian passage, and find the sun, putting it exactly on the horizon. Thereafter, observe the sun again at intervals of about a minute; if a gap has appeared between the lower limb of the sun and the horizon, increase the sextant altitude with the micrometer. The micrometer should *only* be adjusted in one direction – to increase the measured altitude. At noon, the sun will appear to 'hang' in the sky for several minutes, and then begin to fall. Do not adjust the sextant to follow the fall – it is the highest altitude reached that is required. Note the GMT of meridian passage (to the nearest minute or so), for later use in obtaining declination.

Calculating latitude The sextant altitude of meridian passage is converted to latitude by following these steps:

1) Convert sextant altitude to true altitude, as described on pages 130–3. Name the true altitude north or south to agree with its bearing at noon.

2) Obtain the True Zenith Distance (TZD) (= 90° – true altitude), and name it *opposite* to true altitude.

3) Find the declination of the sun for the GMT of the observation (see page 137); be sure to note the name (N or S) of the declination.

4) Combine the TZD and the declination:
same names – Add TZD and declination to give latitude of *same* name.
contrary names – Subtract smaller quantity from the greater to obtain latitude; name the latitude as the greater of TZD or declination.

Normally there is no difficulty in naming the latitude, as the DR position makes it obvious; however it may be possible for confusion to arise near to the equator. Following the rules given above will always cope with the situation, as the following examples show:

True altitude	80°N	80°N
TZD	10°S	10°S
Declination	9°N	11°N
Latitude (name as greater)	1°S	1°N

The following example shows the complete working of a sight for noon latitude by meridian altitude.

3 May 1980 12 h 45 m GMT: a ship in DR position 41°30′N, 12°15′W observes meridian altitude. Sextant altitude 64°22′.5 bearing south, index error +1′.5, height of eye 3 metres.

Sextant altitude	64°22′.5	
Index error	+ 1′.5	
	64°24′.0	
Dip	− 3′.0	
Apparent altitude	64°21′.0	
Correction	+ 15′.5	
True altitude	64°36′.5 S	(rule 1)
True zenith distance (90° − TA)	25°23′.5 N	(rule 2)
Declination (12 h) N15°48′.0 + (d)0′.5	15°48′.5 N	(see page 137)
Latitude at 1245 GMT	41°12′.0 N	(rule 4)

46 Noon longitude by equal altitudes

Noon longitude by equal altitudes is a particularly simple way of establishing longitude once a day (at local noon), which requires only a sextant, the *Nautical Almanac* and an accurate source of GMT. In conjunction with an observation of meridian passage for latitude, it offers the ocean navigator a daily position with very little effort; for much of any ocean passage, a daily position will be quite sufficient.

The principle of this type of sight is very simple. At meridian passage, the observer and the sun's geographical position have the same longitude. If the exact GMT of meridian passage can be established, then the observer's longitude is equal to the GHA of the sun (which is another way of expressing the longitude of the GP). It is not possible to obtain the GMT of meridian passage by direct observation, as the sun's altitude is changing very slowly at meridian passage and it appears to 'hang' in the sky for several minutes. The procedure adopted is to observe the altitude of the sun while it is still changing quite rapidly, at some suitable time before noon, and note the GMT. The sun will then rise to meridian passage (when a latitude would normally be obtained), and then sinks; the navigator notes the exact GMT at which the sun reaches the same altitude as the observation before noon. The GMT of meridian passage is half way between the two GMTs observed (Fig. 1).

The observations

The first step in observing the longitude by this method is to work out the predicted time of meridian passage (pages 142–3); this time will also be needed for the latitude sight at noon. Then work out the best time for the forenoon altitude by the following rule of thumb:

Combine the DR latitude and the declination (degrees only), by adding if contrary name and subtracting the smaller from the larger if names are the same. Make the first observation the same number of minutes before predicted meridian passage.

For example:

Latitude   45°N
Dec   15°N
Combined 30°N

Therefore make the first observation 30 minutes before meridian passage.

Latitude   30°S
Dec   10°N
Combined 40°

First observation made 40 minutes before meridian passage.

Note: If by following this rule, the result comes to more than an hour (60 minutes) before noon, avoid using this method if possible; the simplifying assumptions that it makes start to break down, and longitudes may be significantly in error.

When the predicted time arrives, take a sextant altitude of the sun and record this with the precise

46.1 *Principle of noon longitude by equal altitudes.*

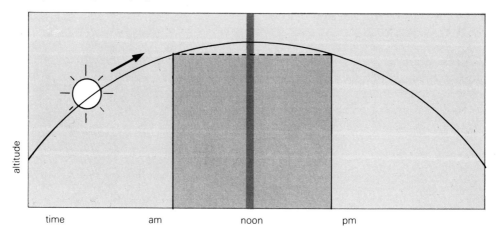

GMT of the observation; there is no need to apply any correction to the sextant altitude thus obtained. If there is cloud in the sky, it would be a prudent precaution to make several observations at intervals, in case the sun is intermittently obscured in the afternoon. With several sights to play with, you would be unlucky not to match up at least one of the forenoon sights.

Afternoon observation If the ship has not changed latitude since the first observation, nor the sun changed declination, it is merely necessary to set the same altitude on the sextant as was observed in the forenoon, observe the sun as it sinks and then note the exact GMT at which it touches the horizon; as with the forenoon observation, there is no need to apply any correction for index error, dip, refraction or semidiameter, provided the height of eye is the same for both observations.

If, as is more generally the case, the ship has changed her latitude in the interval between the sights and/or the sun has changed its declination, then a correction must be applied to the sextant altitude for the second observation.

Ship movement The difference in latitude between the DR of the forenoon sight and the (predicted) DR of the afternoon sight must be worked out. This difference in latitude (in minutes of arc) must be *added* to the first sextant altitude if the ship is moving *towards* the sun, and subtracted if the ship is moving away.

Change in declination The rate of change of declination, in minutes of arc per hour, is given in the *Nautical Almanac*; it is the quantity d at the foot of the sun column. Given this value and the total time between the two observations, it is possible to work out a correction to be applied to the sextant, to be *added* if the sun is moving *towards* the ship, and subtracted if it is moving away.

For example:

On 3 May 1980, a ship in DR latitude 52°N wishes to observe noon longitude by equal altitudes. Declination is 16°N, so the chosen time to observe is (52 − 16 =) 36 minutes before meridian passage. Ship's course 180 (true), speed 6 knots. From the *Nautical Almanac*, d for 3 May is 0.7 and the sun is moving north (the northerly declination is increasing). Total time between observations 2 × 36 m = 1 hr 12 m or 1.2 hours.

The ship movement correction in this case is 7′.2 (1.2 hours on course 180 at 6 knots); the ship is north of the sun and moving south, so this correction must be added to the sextant altitude.

The declination correction is 0′.8 (d of 0′.7 for 1.2 hours); the sun is south of the ship and moving north, so this correction too must be added.

The total correction is therefore 8′.0, to be added to the sextant altitude of the forenoon observation.

Having made the observations before and after noon, the two times recorded are used to work out the GMT of meridian passage by simple averaging, thus:

GMT of first sight	10 h 59 m 49 s
GMT of second sight	12 h 11 m 59 s
Added together	23 h 11 m 48 s
Divide by 2 = GMT mer pass	11 h 35 m 54 s

The actual longitude is found by looking out the sun's GHA for the GMT thus found:

GHA 11 h	345°47′.8
Increment 35 m 54 s	8°58′.5
GHA (= longitude west)	354°46′.3

Or, subtracting from 360°, long = 5°13′.7 East

Note: Unlike longitude, GHA is always measured west of the Greenwich meridian. To convert GHA to longitude, the rule is:

If GHA is less than 180°, longitude west = GHA

If GHA is more than 180°, longitude east = 360° − GHA

A complete example is given on the following page.

Complete example: The example below completes that on page 143, which showed how the latitude was worked out from meridian passage. The additional information needed for longitude by equal altitude is that the ship is in DR position 41°30′N, 12°15′W, steering north at 7 knots. The predicted time of meridian passage is 3 May 1980 12 h 45 m GMT. Latitude − declination = 41° − 16° = 25°.

First observation 58°17′.1 at   12 h 17 m 47 s GMT

This observation was taken about 25 minutes before meridian passage, so the second will be approximately 25 minutes after, a total interval of 50 minutes.

Ship movement correction
(50 m at 7 knots)   −6′.0
(−ve as ship is moving due north away from the sun)
Declination correction
(50 m at d = 0′.7)   +0′.6
(+ve as sun is moving north towards the ship)
Total correction   −5′.4
So sextant altitude for pm
sight   58°17′.1 − 5′.4
                                  = 58°11′.7

The second observation with this sextant altitude was made at:

	13 h 07 m 27 s GMT
First observation	12 h 17 m 47 s GMT
(add)	25 h 25 m 14 s
meridian passage (divide by two)	12 h 42 m 37 s GMT
GHA for 12 h on 3 May	0°47′.8
Increment 42 m 37 s	10°39′.3
Therefore longitude = (add)	11°27′.1 W

Notes:

1) This method is not suitable for use when the sun is low in the sky at noon, i.e. in winter, especially in higher latitudes.

2) It is also unsuitable for high-speed craft, where latitude corrections may become large. Its use should be confined to vessels travelling at ten knots or less.

3) If the sky clouds over in the afternoon, it may not be possible to complete the observation; in this case, the forenoon observation can be worked out as a general position line (see pages 156–7) and thus not wasted, though the angle of cut with the noon latitude may be rather acute.

4) In an emergency it is possible to get some idea of longitude even without a sextant. In a slow-moving craft (such as a liferaft), it may be possible to record the GMT at which the sun clears the eastern horizon in the morning, and touches the western horizon in the evening; the mean of these two times is (rather approximately) the longitude.

47 The general position line; intercepts

The astronomical position lines so far described rely on the special circumstance that the body is on the same meridian as the observer, that is, the LHA of the body is 0°. For the sun, this happens at local noon, and offers two simple and excellent solutions to the position line problem – for latitude and for longitude. However it is not generally so simple to convert a sextant altitude and time into a position line; the process is still not difficult, but requires some new ideas, new techniques and new tables. For the general solution of astronomical position lines, this book uses the *Sight Reduction Tables for Air Navigation* (in Britain, AP 3270; in the US, Pub. 249). This publication is in three volumes; volumes 2 and 3 are used for general solutions and volume 1 deals with star sights (see pages 158–60).

At first glance, the general astronomical position line is easy enough to work out; the GHA and declination of the body at the moment of observation define the geographical position (see pages 137–41), whilst the true sextant altitude (converted to true zenith distance) (see page 124) gives the distance of the ship from the GP. The position line is therefore a circle with radius equal to the true zenith distance, centred on the GP. The difficulty that arises is purely one of scale; the zenith distance may be several thousand miles, and it is quite impossible to plot a position line as described with any pretence at accuracy; on a chart or globe of suitable scale to take to sea, even the thickness of a pencil line may represent tens of miles on the surface.

Except in very rare circumstances (see page 126), the direct plotting of GP and zenith distance is quite impracticable. Instead, a mathematical trick known as an *intercept* is brought into play, to allow the position line to be plotted directly on the chart in use, at a practical scale. The intercept is derived by following this argument (and see Fig. 1):

1) Choose a convenient position close to the ship's actual (but unknown) position.
2) Calculate the distance between this chosen position and the GP of the body.
3) Compare this distance with the true distance measured on the sextant. The difference in the distances is known as the *intercept*, and it shows by how much the true distance from the GP is more or less than the calculated value from the chosen position.
4) Another quantity, the bearing of the GP (known as the *azimuth* of the body), must also be obtained, either by taking a compass bearing of the body observed, or from the tables.
5) Given the intercept and the azimuth, the position line can be plotted, as shown in Figure 2. The position line is technically part of a circle, but because the GP is so far away, the line can be assumed to be straight, running in a direction at right angles to the azimuth.

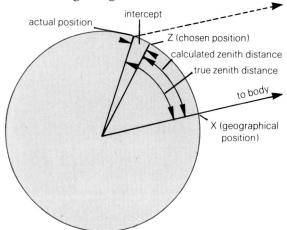

47.1 *Principle of the intercept method.*

47.2 *Plotting a position line using the intercept.*

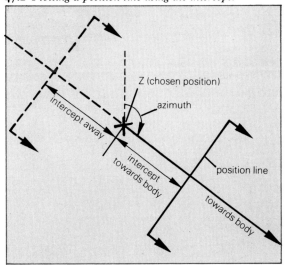

The function of all the various methods of *sight reduction* is to provide the answers for step 2 (distance to the GP from the chosen position) and step 4 (the azimuth of the body). These are both problems in spherical trigonometry, though the navigator need not let this fact dismay him. In these modern days of microelectronics, the problems are easily solved by calculator or computer (see page 165); otherwise, various methods have been developed over the years to give the practical seaman an easy route to the answers he needs. The primary method chosen for this book is the use of the *Sight Reduction Tables for Air Navigation* (AP 3270, Pub. 249). Other methods are described on pages 164–5.

Sight Reduction Tables for Air Navigation (AP 3270, Pub. 249) As the name implies, these tables were devised for use by aviators. They are also very suitable for use in yachts, because, at the price of an unimportant loss of precision, they are quick and easy to use. Volume 1 deals only with certain stars, and is used on pages 158–60. Volumes 2 and 3 provide general solutions to the two problems for all bodies with a declination of less than 30° north or south; this includes the sun, moon and planets, and 27 of the most important navigational stars. For normal use, this is quite sufficient. Specimen pages from Volume 3 are shown on pages 149 and 151.

The tables must be entered with three quantities:

1) Latitude of the chosen position; this must be a whole number of degrees. It selects the page at which the tables are opened.
2) Declination of the body – the degrees part only; this selects the column within the page. Detailed selection of the page and column also depends on the actual value of the declination (0–14° or 15°–29°), and on whether the declination has the same or contrary name to the latitude; page and column headings make this clear.
3) The local hour angle, which is a combination of the Greenwich hour angle from the *Nautical Almanac* and the chosen longitude. This quantity must be a whole number of degrees. It selects the line on the page where the solutions lie.

There are two outputs from the tables:

1) The calculated altitude (Hc). This is the altitude that would be observed if the ship were exactly at the chosen position; it can be compared directly with the observed altitude (Ho) to obtain the intercept. The tables give altitude rather than zenith distance to avoid an additional calculation without affecting the answer. The calculated altitude is given to the nearest minute of arc.
2) The azimuth angle (Z); this can be converted to azimuth (the true bearing of the GP) by following the precepts given at the top and foot of the page, depending on LHA and latitude.

The use of the tables is very slightly complicated by the need for interpolation, as described below.

The chosen position Having made an observation and extracted the body's GHA and declination from the *Nautical Almanac*, the next step is to choose the position for entry to the *Sight Reduction Tables*. The choice of position is somewhat confined, unlike some other methods, by the special requirements of the tables.

Latitude: The chosen latitude should be the whole number of degrees closest to the DR latitude. Thus if the DR latitude is 50°17'N, choose 50°N; if the DR latitude is 34°46'S, choose 35°S.

Longitude: The longitude must be chosen so that it is close to the DR longitude; also it must have a value which, when combined with the GHA of the body, yields an LHA which is a whole number of degrees. Easterly longitude is added, westerly longitude is subtracted from GHA to give LHA. Thus, if the DR longitude is 17°30'W and the GHA is 332°17'.2:

GHA	332°17'.2
Long W (chosen)	17°17'.2
LHA	315°

or, for DR longitude 112°30'E, GHA 17°22'.3:

GHA	17°22'.3
Long E (chosen)	112°37'.7
LHA	130°

Entering the tables

1) Choose the page according to chosen latitude, same or contrary name and declination range (0°–14° or 15°–29°).
2) Find the line appropriate to the LHA, either on the extreme left or extreme right of the page; it may be necessary to turn over the page to find the LHA required.
3) Find the intersection of the line of LHA and

LAT 50°

LAT 50°

DECLINATION (15°–29°) SAME NAME AS LATITUDE

DECLINATION (15°–29°) SAME NAME AS LATITUDE

N. Lat. {LHA greater than 180°...... Zn=Z / LHA less than 180°...... Zn=360−Z}

S. Lat. {LHA greater than 180°...... Zn=180−Z / LHA less than 180°...... Zn=180+Z}

Table I *Extract from AP3270 (USA, Pub. 249).*

the column corresponding to the number of degrees in the declination. Write down the three quantities, Hc, *d*, and Z.

4) Enter the correction table (Table 5, also supplied on a loose card), to correct the calculated altitude for the minutes of declination. *d* across the top of the table finds the correct column; run down the column to the line appropriate to the number of minutes in the declination.

5) Apply the correction just obtained to the calcu-lated altitude, with the same sign as *d*.

This results in the calculated altitude which is compared with the true altitude to give the intercept.

6) Take the value of Z given in the table, and process it as directed by the instructions at top and bottom of the page; this give the azimuth of the body.

All that remains is the plotting of the position line, which is described on page 152.

TABLE 5.—Correction to Tabulated Altitude for Minutes of Declination

d /	1	2	3	4	5	6	7	8	9	10	11	12	13	14	15	16	17	18	19	20	21	22	23	24	25	26	27	28	29	30	31	32	33	34	35	36	37	38	39	40	41	42	43	44	45	46	47	48	49	50	51	52	53	54	55	56	57	58	59	60

Table 2 *Extract from AP3270 (USA, Pub. 249).*

48   Plotting the position line

The whole purpose of the sight reduction process is to produce three pieces of information which allow the position line to be plotted; they are:

The chosen position

The intercept, towards or away from the body

The azimuth

The basic method of plotting the position line is shown in Figure 1. First, the chosen position is marked, with the name of the body observed; if several bodies are observed at the same time (as for example in a set of star sights), then *each sight will have its own chosen position.*

The next step is to lay off the azimuth -either towards the body or away from it (the reciprocal of the azimuth), according to the way the intercept was named. If the true altitude was greater than the calculated altitude, then the ship was actually closer to the GP than the chosen position, and the

intercept is *towards*; a smaller true altitude than calculated altitude means that the ship was further from the GP than the chosen position, and the intercept is marked *away*.

The intercept is now marked along the azimuth line, to give a point (A) which is at the correct true distance from the geographical position – it is a point on the position line.

The final step is to draw the position line itself. To be exact, the position line is a circle with its centre at the GP, but because this circle has, in general, a very large radius, the position line can be regarded as being a straight line in the area immediately surrounding the ship. The position line can be drawn through point A, at right angles to the azimuth. The line can be made as long or as short as desired, and it is conventional to mark it at each end with an arrow-head pointing towards the GP, as shown; the reason for this is explained below.

48.1 *Plotting the position line.*

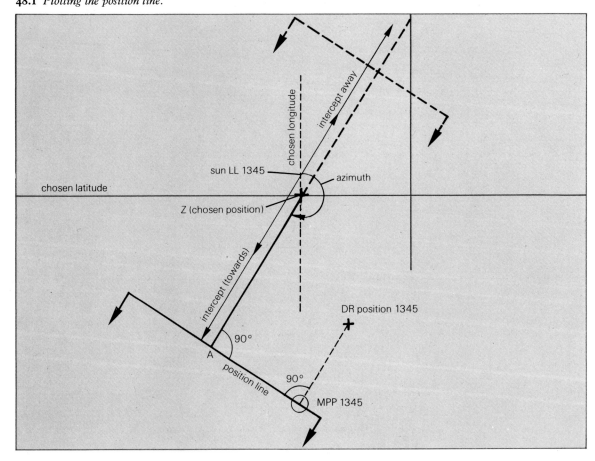

Most probable position When a single position line only is available, the navigator will wish to revise his DR to take into account the new information given by the position line. Provided that the position line is considered reliable, the MPP is usually selected at the point on the position line closest to the DR, as shown in Figure 2.

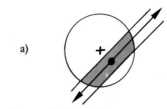

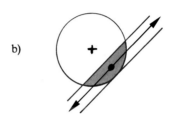

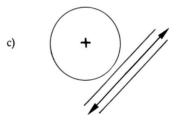

48.2 *Most probable position.*

Fixes An astronomical position line is exactly the same, from a position finding point of view, as any other position line; it can be used for fixing in just the same way. A fix requires the intersection of two (or more) position lines related to the same time. Position lines from the simultaneous observation of two bodies suitably placed in azimuth can yield a fix, or one of the position lines could be derived from a sounding or a radio bearing or any other source. Figure 3 illustrates the plotting of a fix from simultaneous observations of the sun and moon; note that each body has its own chosen position. Using AP 3270 (Pub. 249), the chosen latitudes will be the same, but the longitudes differ. It very often happens that only one position line can be obtained at a particular time, and another becomes available later. The most common example is the use of the sun; one observation

48.3 *Astronomical fix from simultaneous observations of sun and moon.*

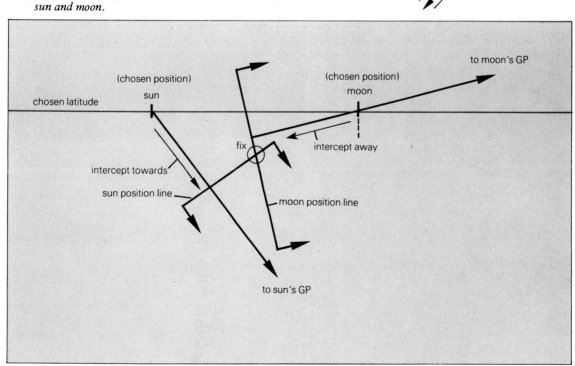

yields a position line, but it is not possible to get another position line from the sun which will intersect the first until sufficient time has passed for the sun's azimuth to change. This time interval is likely to be several hours, by which time the ship will have moved from the first position line. This problem is solved by use of the transferred position line idea (see pages 77–79). Figure 4 illustrates one of the classic fixes using the sun – a morning observation when the sun was still rising in the east, followed by a meridian altitude at local noon; the first position line is transferred to the same time as the second, the so-called *sun-run-mer alt* fix. If the noon latitude sight cannot be taken for any reason, the same procedure can be followed using a second sun observation at a convenient time, the *sun-run-sun* fix.

Plotting without a chart It may well happen that no chart of a suitable scale for plotting sights is available; ocean charts, for example, are generally on such a small scale that it is impossible to plot positions and intercepts accurately. The three most practical ways of making up a suitable chart of the locality in which the vessel lies are:

1) Use a plotting sheet; these are blank 'charts' specially printed for this very purpose, covering various bands of latitude. These sheets carry a fixed longitude scale and various scales of latitude, and are used like an ordinary chart.
2) Latitude and longitude graduations can be taken from any chart of a suitable scale that covers the same latitude as the DR, and transferred to a sheet of paper.
3) Latitude and longitude scales can be manufactured on a sheet of paper; first choose an appropriate scale for latitude (for example one centimetre to one minute of latitude), and then make the longitude scale by using the equation:

Minutes of longitude = minutes of latitude × cos (lat). Table 1 gives the cosines of angles between 0° and 75°, for use if a calculator is not available.

Reducing errors with multiple position lines
When three or more position lines are drawn, they will very rarely meet in a point, giving rise to a 'cocked hat' (Fig. 5). In establishing the most probable position, it is possible to reduce certain errors in the position lines by *bisecting the external*

48.4 *Sun-run-mer alt fix.*

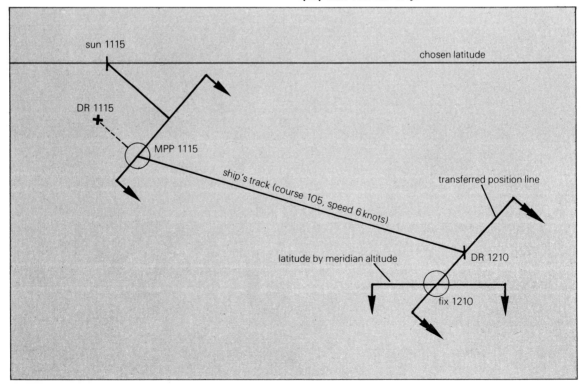

angles, as shown. Note that under certain circumstances, the MPP can lie *outside* the cocked hat (Fig. 5b). This process reduces any systematic errors in the observations considerably, and also helps to reduce the random errors to some extent.

48.5 *Reducing errors with a 'cocked hat'.*

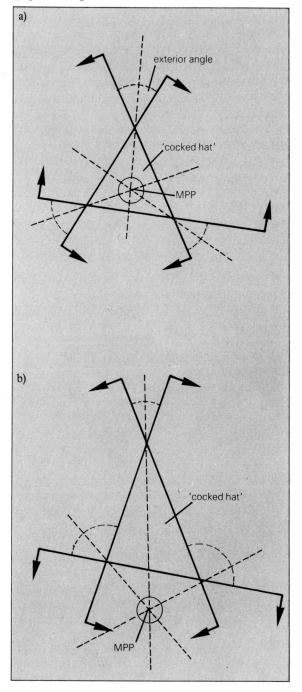

Table 1 Scale conversion table for longitude

Lat°		Lat°		Lat°		Lat°		Lat°	
0	1.000	1	1.000	2	0.999	3	0.999	4	0.998
5	0.996	6	0.995	7	0.993	8	0.990	9	0.988
10	0.985	11	0.982	12	0.978	13	0.974	14	0.970
15	0.966	16	0.961	17	0.956	18	0.951	19	0.946
20	0.940	21	0.934	22	0.927	23	0.921	24	0.914
25	0.906	26	0.899	27	0.891	28	0.883	29	0.875
30	0.866	31	0.857	32	0.848	33	0.839	34	0.829
35	0.819	36	0.809	37	0.799	38	0.788	39	0.777
40	0.766	41	0.755	42	0.743	43	0.731	44	0.719
45	0.707	46	0.695	47	0.682	48	0.669	49	0.656
50	0.643	51	0.629	52	0.616	53	0.602	54	0.588
55	0.574	56	0.559	57	0.545	58	0.530	59	0.515
60	0.500	61	0.485	62	0.469	63	0.454	64	0.438
65	0.423	66	0.407	67	0.391	68	0.375	69	0.358

49 General position line – summary and proforma

This section summarizes the steps that must be followed to obtain a general astronomical position line. Reference is made to the pages where the detailed procedures for each step are described. Also given is a proforma which can be used as a model for the navigator's own observations, with a worked example.

The basic procedure can be summarized as follows:

1) Select the body to be observed and the approximate time. Check the sextant and measure its index error (see page 127). Make sure that the watch to be used for recording time has recently been compared with GMT.

2) Make the observation(s) and record the time and sextant altitude for each. Time is required to the nearest second, altitude to the nearest 0.2 minutes of arc. If making a series of observations of the same body, average the results (see page 129).

3) On the sight form, record:
   a) The DR position   1
   b) The body (and limb) observed   2
   c) The height of eye   3
   d) The index error   4
   e) The date and approximate zone time   5
   f) The watch error on GMT   6
   g) The (averaged) watch time   7
   h) The (averaged) sextant altitude   8

4) Work out the Greenwich date and time, by applying the zone number to the zone time. 9
   Find the GMT of the observation by applying the watch error to the watch time.   10

5) Open the *Nautical Almanac* to the daily page appropriate to the *Greenwich date*; for the hour of GMT, record:
   a) The GHA of the body (GHA Aries for a star)   11
   b) v (moon, planets) or SHA (star)   12
   c) Declination (and name)   13
   d) d (not for star) and sign by inspection   14
   e) Horizontal parallax (HP) for the moon   15

6) Open the *Nautical Almanac* to the section of the increments and corrections table for the minutes of GMT. Record:

a) The increment to GHA for the minutes and seconds of GMT. Use the correct column   16
b) The v correction, if appropriate   17
c) The d correction (or estimate mentally) 18
   This has the same sign as given to d.

7) Combine the above figures to obtain the exact GHA and declination for the instant of observation:
   a) Add together GHA, the increment and the v correction or SHA to obtain GHA   19
   b) Add or subtract the d correction according to its sign to obtain declination.   20

8) Choose a position for entry to the tables:
   a) Latitude – the nearest whole number of degrees to the DR.   21
   b) Longitude – the nearest longitude to the DR that will make the LHA a whole number of degrees (see page 148).   22
   Then apply the chosen longitude to the GHA to obtain LHA (add E long, subtract W long). 23

9) Choose volume 2 or volume 3 of the *Sight Reduction Tables* (AP 3270, Pub. 249) according to the chosen latitude; find the page in the correct volume according to:
   The chosen latitude.
   Whether latitude and declination have the same or contrary names.
   The range of declination (0–14° or 15°–29°). This will narrow the choice of pages to two, one of which will have the LHA in either the extreme left or extreme right hand column.
   From the selected page, in the column with the degrees of declination and the line with LHA, record:
   a) The quantity labelled Hc   24
   b) The quantity d (not the same as d in the *Nautical Almanac*)   25
   c) The azimuth angle, Z

10) Work out the azimuth of the body by following the precepts given at the top or bottom of the page.   26

11) Enter the Interpolation table (Table 5, also supplied on a loose card), with d across the top and the nearest minute of declination down the side. Record the altitude correction, with the same sign as d, and apply it to Hc, to give the calculated altitude.   27

12) Now find the observed altitude (Ho) as follows:
   a) Apply index error to the sextant altitude.
   b) From the altitude correction tables (at the front of the *Nautical Almanac*, also on a loose card), find the dip appropriate to the height of eye; apply this to obtain apparent altitude   **28**
   c) Enter the correction table appropriate to the body with apparent altitude to get the altitude correction for refraction, semi-diameter etc. (The moon has its own tables). Apply the correction to apparent altitude to get observed altitude.   **29**

13 Subtract the lesser of true and calculated altitude from the other to obtain the intercept. Name this 'towards' if the true altitude is greater, otherwise name it 'away'.   **30**

14) The position line may now be plotted on the chart, laying off the intercept towards or away from the azimuth, from the chosen position (see page 147) (Fig. 1).

49.1 *Astronomical position line plotted.*

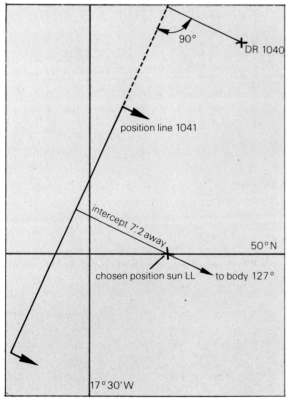

Pro forma and example

DR 50°15′N, 17°10′W **1**	Chosen lat 50°N **21** HE 3 m **3**
Body **2**	Sun LL
Zone date/time **5**	3 May 1980 09 h 40 m
Zone	+1 h
Greenwich date **9**	3 May 1980 10 h 40 m
Watch time **7**	10 h 41 m 17 s
Watch error **6**	01 m 02 s slow (+)
GMT **10**	10 h 42 m 19 s
GHA hrs **11** *v* **12**	330°47′.7 *v* −
Incr m,s **16**	10°34′.8
v Cor or SHA **17**	−
GHA **19**	341°22′.5
Chos long **22**	17°22′.5 W
LHA **23**	324°
Dec **13** *d* **14**	N15°46′.5 *d* + 0′.7
d Cor **18**	+0′.5
Dec **20**	N15°47′.0 SAME as lat
Hc **24** *d* **25**	44°28′ *d* + 51′
Cor	+40′
Calc alt **27**	45°08′
Z	127°
Azimuth (Zn) **26**	127°
Sext alt **8**	44°47′.2
Index error **4**	+1′.2
	44°48′.4
Dip **28**	−3′.0
App alt	44°45′.4
Cor **29**	+15′.0
Moon cor (HP =) **15**	
Moon cor **2**	
True alt	45°00′.8
Calc alt	45°08′
Intercept **30**	7′.2 AWAY from 127°
Chos pos	50°N, 17°22′.5 W
	(see Fig. 1 for the plotted position line)

50 Star sight using seven selected stars (AP 3270 Vol 1 [US Pub. 229])

The *Sight Reduction Tables for Air Navigation* (AP 3270, Pub. 249), in the interests of saving space and weight, are confined to declinations between 0° and 30°N or S. Whilst this allows reduction of sun, moon and planet sights, there are only 27 of the main navigational stars with declinations in this range. To make better use of the navigational stars, volume 1 of the sight reduction tables provides solutions for seven selected stars for all combinations of latitude and LHA Aries. The stars selected are chosen on the basis of the most favourable distribution in altitude and azimuth.

The great advantage of a fix derived from star sights is that several can be observed at (more or less) the same time to provide a number of position lines; not only does this give an immediate fix without the need to transfer a position line, but it also gives confidence in the fix if three or more position lines intersect closely. However, it is not easy to take star sights from the deck of a yacht unless conditions are very good. Even so, considerable practice is needed to get good results.

To observe the altitude of a star, you must be able to see both the star and the horizon. In practical terms, this confines the time at which such sights can be taken to a few minutes after sunset and a few minutes before sunrise. Exactly how long is available to make the observations depends on the latitude; in the tropics, it can be very short.

Predicting twilight The first step in observing stars is to predict the time at which they will be visible. This is generally accepted as being when the sun is 6° below the horizon, a time known as civil twilight. This is given on the daily pages of the *Nautical Almanac* (Table 1). The procedure is as follows:

1) In the civil twilight column appropriate to either dawn or dusk, select the local mean time of civil twilight for the DR latitude; interpolate by eye if necessary.

2) To the LMT thus obtained, apply the DR longitude (add W long, subtract E long) to obtain the GMT of civil twilight.

3) Correct the GMT according to the zone being kept on board, to obtain the time of civil twilight by the ship's clock. This is the

Lat.	Twilight Naut.	Civil	Sunrise	Moonrise 3	4	5	6
°	h m	h m	h m	h m	h m	h m	h m
N 72	////	////	01 23	01 45	■	■	■
N 70	////	////	02 12	00 14	01 53	03 05	03 24
68	////	00 13	02 43	24 56	00 56	01 58	02 35
66	////	01 35	03 05	24 22	00 22	01 22	02 04
64	////	02 10	03 23	23 57	24 56	00 56	01 40
62	00 11	02 35	03 37	23 38	24 36	00 36	01 22
60	01 24	02 55	03 50	23 22	24 19	00 19	01 07
N 58	01 57	03 10	04 00	23 09	24 06	00 06	00 53
56	02 20	03 24	04 09	22 57	23 54	24 42	00 42
54	02 38	03 35	04 17	22 47	23 43	24 32	00 32
52	02 53	03 45	04 25	22 38	23 34	24 24	00 24
50	03 06	03 54	04 31	22 30	23 26	24 16	00 16
45	03 31	04 12	04 45	22 13	23 08	23 59	24 44
N 40	03 51	04 27	04 56	21 59	22 54	23 45	24 32
35	04 06	04 39	05 06	21 47	22 42	23 33	24 22
30	04 19	04 49	05 15	21 37	22 31	23 23	24 12
20	04 39	05 06	05 29	21 19	22 13	23 05	23 56
N 10	04 54	05 20	05 42	21 04	21 57	22 50	23 43
0	05 07	05 32	05 53	20 49	21 42	22 35	23 30
S 10	05 18	05 43	06 05	20 35	21 27	22 21	23 16
20	05 28	05 54	06 17	20 20	21 11	22 06	23 03
30	05 37	06 06	06 31	20 02	20 53	21 48	22 47
35	05 42	06 12	06 39	19 52	20 42	21 38	22 37
40	05 47	06 19	06 48	19 41	20 30	21 26	22 27
45	05 52	06 27	06 58	19 27	20 16	21 12	22 14
S 50	05 58	06 37	07 11	19 10	19 59	20 55	21 59
52	06 00	06 41	07 17	19 03	19 51	20 47	21 52
54	06 03	06 45	07 24	18 54	19 41	20 38	21 44
56	06 06	06 50	07 31	18 44	19 31	20 28	21 35
58	06 08	06 56	07 39	18 33	19 20	20 17	21 25
S 60	06 12	07 02	07 48	18 20	19 06	20 04	21 13

Lat.	Sunset	Twilight Civil	Naut.	Moonset 3	4	5	6
°	h m	h m	h m	h m	h m	h m	h m
N 72	22 40	////	////	02 28	■	■	■
N 70	21 46	////	////	04 00	04 07	04 46	06 19
68	21 14	////	////	04 40	05 05	05 53	07 07
66	20 51	22 25	////	05 07	05 39	06 28	07 38
64	20 33	21 47	////	05 28	06 04	06 54	08 01
62	20 18	21 21	////	05 45	06 23	07 14	08 19
60	20 06	21 01	22 35	05 59	06 39	07 31	08 34
N 58	19 55	20 45	22 00	06 12	06 53	07 44	08 47
56	19 46	20 31	21 36	06 22	07 04	07 56	08 58
54	19 37	20 20	21 17	06 31	07 15	08 07	09 08
52	19 30	20 10	21 02	06 40	07 24	08 16	09 17
50	19 23	20 01	20 49	06 47	07 32	08 24	09 24
45	19 09	19 42	20 23	07 03	07 49	08 42	09 41
N 40	18 58	19 27	20 04	07 16	08 03	08 56	09 54
35	18 48	19 15	19 48	07 28	08 15	09 08	10 06
30	18 39	19 05	19 35	07 37	08 26	09 19	10 16
20	18 25	18 48	19 15	07 54	08 44	09 37	10 33
N 10	18 12	18 34	19 00	08 09	09 00	09 53	10 47
0	18 00	18 22	18 47	08 23	09 14	10 07	11 01
S 10	17 49	18 10	18 36	08 37	09 29	10 22	11 15
20	17 36	17 59	18 25	08 51	09 45	10 38	11 30
30	17 22	17 47	18 16	09 08	10 03	10 56	11 47
35	17 14	17 41	18 11	09 18	10 13	11 06	11 56
40	17 05	17 34	18 06	09 29	10 25	11 18	12 07
45	16 54	17 25	18 00	09 43	10 39	11 32	12 20
S 50	16 42	17 16	17 55	09 59	10 57	11 50	12 36
52	16 36	17 12	17 52	10 06	11 05	11 58	12 44
54	16 29	17 07	17 50	10 15	11 14	12 07	12 52
56	16 22	17 02	17 47	10 24	11 24	12 17	13 01
58	16 14	16 57	17 44	10 35	11 36	12 28	13 11
S 60	16 04	16 51	17 41	10 48	11 49	12 42	13 23

Day	SUN Eqn. of Time 00h	12h	Mer. Pass.	MOON Mer. Pass. Upper	Lower	Age	Phase
	m s	m s	h m	h m	h m	d	
3	03 08	03 11	11 57	02 11	14 36	18	◐
4	03 14	03 17	11 57	03 02	15 28	19	
5	03 20	03 22	11 57	03 55	16 21	20	

Table 1 *Extract from sunrise, sunset and twilight table.*

approximate time at which observations will be possible.

For example: DR position 50°N, 17°30'W on 4 May 1980
Required, the time of dawn civil twilight

LMT	03 h 54 m
Long W 17°30′ (in time)	01 h 10 m (see page 143)
GMT	05 h 04 m
Zone in force	+1
Zone time of civil twilight	04 h 04 m (+1)

Predicting the star position The next step is to predict the approximate altitudes and azimuths of the selected stars. This is necessary because the sky at civil twilight is still very light and the stars are barely visible (or not visible at all) to the naked eye. The only reliable way of finding the stars you are looking for is to search the correct part of the sky with the sextant telescope. If the sky is dark enough for the stars to be plainly visible to the naked eye, then it is almost certain that the horizon is too dark for accurate observation.

1) Using the LMT of civil twilight (step 1 of the previous example), enter the Aries column on the opposite page to obtain the LHA of Aries at civil twilight; add the increment for the minutes of LMT (see page 140) and round off the result to the nearest whole degree of LHA Aries.

2) Enter AP 3270 volume 1 with arguments latitude (nearest whole degree to the DR lat) and LHA.

3) Extract the names, altitudes and azimuths of the seven selected stars. Note which stars are printed in capital letters (bright stars) and which three are marked with asterisks (the best three of the seven selected).

For example: Following on from the previous example, we have LMT of civil twilight at 03 h 54 m

LHA Aries 03 h	267°09′.3
Incr 54 m	13°32′.2
LHA Aries (to nearest degree)	281°
Latitude	50°N

	Alt (Hc)	Az (Zn)
*Mirfak	18°39′	032
Alpheratz	27°26′	077
*ALTAIR	46°36′	156
Rasalhague	49°55′	207
*ARCTURUS	29°09′	266
Alkaid	44°01′	299
Kochab	56°00′	336

Note It will be helpful when searching for the stars

to convert the azimuths to magnetic bearings by applying variation, so that the compass can be used to help find them.

Making the observations Come on deck with the sextant and watch about a quarter of an hour before the predicted time of civil twilight, and begin searching for the first star to be observed; at dawn, avoid the temptation to start too early, before the horizon has become firm.

Select the order in which you will look for the stars on the following basis:

At dawn, look in the lighter (eastern) part of the sky before the western sky; look for faint stars before bright ones.

At dusk, look in the darker (eastern) sky before the western sky; look for bright stars before faint ones.

Having decided which star to look for, set its predicted altitude on the sextant and sweep the sky on the compass bearing established from the predicted azimuth. By searching slowly and carefully from side to side and up and down, the star should appear within the field of the sextant telescope. Provided the bearing and altitude are approximately as predicted, the chances of observing the wrong star are small. Bring the star to the horizon in the usual way, and record the time. If the duration of twilight is short, as it is in the tropics, it may only be possible to take one sight of each star. Star sights should not be hurried, but it is important not to waste time.

Sights during the night If the horizon is bright, it is sometimes possible to take star sights throughout the night; this generally is possible when the moon is near full. Use the sextant without the telescope fitted, and avoid using the moon itself or any star close to it. The position line resulting from such an observation is likely to have a 95 per cent error of five miles or more, so it should be used with caution.

Reduction and plotting Reduction of the sights follow a similar, but rather simpler course as the general position line described on page 152. The following summary and Figure 1 should make the process plain.

1) The following steps must be applied to each star individually, so that each has its own chosen position, LHA Aries and calculated altitude.

2) For the GMT of the observation, find the GHA Aries. **I**

3) Choose a longitude close to the DR to make the LHA Aries a whole number, and choose the latitude as a whole number of degrees nearest the DR. **2**

4) Enter volume I of the tables with lat and LHA Aries for each star, and extract the calculated altitude (Hc) and azimuth (Zn). **3**

5) Correct the sextant altitude and compare the true altitude with the calculated altitude to obtain the intercept. **4**

6) Plot the position lines in the normal way. See page 154 for advice on reducing errors in a 'cocked hat'.

The fix is plotted in Figure 1; the final position, after bisecting the exterior angles (see page 155) is 50°07′.2N, 17°27′.5W.

Precession and nutation AP 3270 Volume I is published for a particular year; in other years, variations in the orbit of the earth, known as precession and nutation, introduce errors into the final fix. A table is supplied with the volume to correct this if desired; except at the end of the life of the tables, this correction does not matter very much. Full instructions are given with the correction table.

50.1 *Plotting the fix*

DR 50°10′N, 17°30′W Chosen lat 50°N HE 2 m

Body:	Mirfak	Altair	Arcturus	
ZD/Time	4 May 1980	0410 (+1)		
Zone		+1		
Greenwich date	4 May 1980	0510		
Watch time	05 h 07 m 22 s	05 h 08 m 31 s	05 h 09 m 54 s	
Watch error	12 s	12 s	12 s fast	
GMT	05 h 07 m 10 s	05 h 08 m 19 s	05 h 09 m 42 s	
GHA Aries	297°14′.2	297°14′.2	297°14′.2	
Incr	1°47′.8	2°05′.1	2°25′.9	
GHA	299°02′.0	299°19′.3	299°40′.1	**I**
Chos long	17°02′.0W	17°19′.3W	17°40′.1W	**2**
LHA Aries	282°	282°	282°	
Hc	19°00′	46°51′	28°30′	**3**
Zn	032	157	266	
Sext alt	19°02′.3	46°45′.1	28°25′.6	
Index error	+1′.1	+1′.1	+1′.1	
	19°03′.4	46°46′.2	28°26′.7	
Dip	−2′.5	−2′.5	−2′.5	
App alt	19°00′.9	46°43′.7	28°24′.2	
Correction	−2′.8	−0′.9	−1′.8	
Obs alt	18°58′.1	46°42′.8	28°22′.4	
Intercept	1′.9 from	8′.2 from	7′.6 from	**4**
Azimuth	032	157	266	
Chos pos	50°N	50°N	50°N	
	17°02′.0W	17°19′.3W	17°40′.1W	

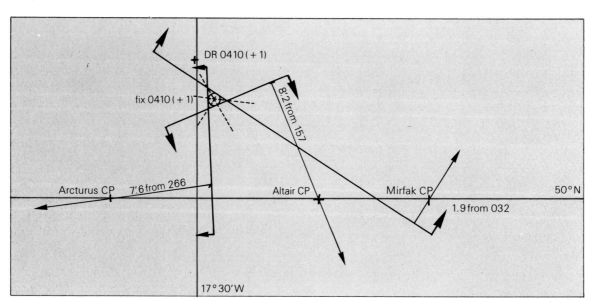

51 Latitude by polaris. Compass checking

Latitude by Polaris

Scientific astronomical navigation began when Arab travellers first used their astrolabes to find their latitude by observing the Pole Star (Polaris). This historical and very easy observation for latitude can still be very useful in the northern hemisphere, although Polaris is not a very bright star and is therefore quite hard to observe.

The value of Polaris is that it lies very close to the axis of the earth, and it is permanently (almost) over the north pole; in other words, it has a declination of (about) 90°N (Fig. 1). The important consequence is that the altitude of Polaris is 90° at the north pole, 0° from the equator, and in between the altitude is equal to the latitude of the observer. In actual fact, the declination of Polaris is about 89°10'N, so the GP of the star moves around the pole in a circle of about 50 miles radius. Various small corrections must therefore be applied to the altitude to obtain latitude; these are given in the Pole Star tables at the end of the *Nautical Almanac*.

Observing Polaris Polaris is not a very bright star, so it can sometimes be difficult to find before the horizon has gone. Set the sextant to the DR latitude and search in the north, and Polaris should appear within the telescope field. Take the altitude, and note GMT to the nearest minute. If Polaris cannot be found at twilight, it is a good subject for night-time observation, because the altitude changes very slowly, and hence the navigator can take his time over the sight; a bright, clear night with a moon is best, and the sextant telescope should be removed. The 95 per cent error of such a sight will be greater than at twilight, probably five miles or more.

Calculating the latitude The latitude is obtained by following these steps:

1) Using the GMT of the observation and the DR longitude, work out the LHA Aries.
2) Correct the sextant altitude for index error, dip and refraction to obtain observed altitude.
3) Enter the Pole Star tables in the *Nautical Almanac* to find the three corrections to be applied. The table is divided into columns, each covering a band of 10° of LHA Aries.
   a) Find the appropriate column according to LHA Aries.
   b) Within the column, find the first correction for LHA Aries, interpolating by eye.
   c) In the same column, find the second correction for the DR latitude in the second table.
   d) Still in the same column, find the correction for the month in the third table.
   e) Add all three corrections to the observed altitude and subtract 1° from the answer, to obtain latitude.

For example: In DR position 51°30'N, 3°45'E at 20 h 42 m GMT, 5 May 1980, the sextant altitude of Polaris is 50°58'.2. I.E. +2'.2, H.E. 3 m

Aries GHA 20 h	163°50'.3
Incr 42 m	10°31'.7
GHA Aries	174°22'.0
Long E	3°45'
LHA Aries	178°07'
Sext alt	50°58'.2
Index error	+2'.2
	51°00'.4
Dip	−3'.0
App alt	50°57.4
Cor	−0'.8
Observed alt	50°56'.6
a_0	1°39'.5
a_1	0'.6
a_2	1'.0
Subtract 1° from sum to give latitude	51°37'.7N

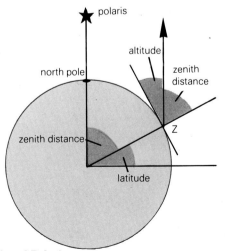

51.1 *Position of Polaris.*

POLARIS (POLE STAR) TABLES, 1980
FOR DETERMINING LATITUDE FROM SEXTANT ALTITUDE AND FOR AZIMUTH

L.H.A. ARIES	0°– 9°	10°– 19°	20°– 29°	30°– 39°	40°– 49°	50°– 59°	60°– 69°	70°– 79°	80°– 89°	90°– 99°	100°– 109°	110°– 119°
	a_0	a_0	a_0	a_0	a_0	a_0	a_0	a_0	a_0	a_0	a_0	a_0
0	0 17·5	0 13·3	0 10·6	0 09·4	0 09·7	0 11·5	0 14·7	0 19·4	0 25·2	0 32·0	0 39·7	0 48·0
1	17·0	13·0	10·4	09·3	09·8	11·7	15·1	19·9	25·8	32·8	40·5	48·8
2	16·5	12·7	10·2	09·3	09·9	12·0	15·5	20·4	26·5	33·5	41·3	49·7
3	16·1	12·4	10·1	09·3	10·0	12·3	16·0	21·0	27·1	34·3	42·1	50·5
4	15·7	12·1	09·9	09·3	10·2	12·6	16·4	21·5	27·8	35·0	43·0	51·4
5	0 15·2	0 11·8	0 09·8	0 09·3	0 10·4	0 12·9	0 16·9	0 22·1	0 28·5	0 35·8	0 43·8	0 52·2
6	14·8	11·5	09·7	09·4	10·6	13·3	17·3	22·7	29·2	36·6	44·6	53·1
7	14·4	11·3	09·6	09·4	10·8	13·6	17·8	23·3	29·9	37·3	45·4	53·9
8	14·1	11·0	09·5	09·5	11·0	14·0	18·3	23·9	30·6	38·1	46·3	54·8
9	13·7	10·8	09·4	09·6	11·2	14·3	18·8	24·6	31·3	38·9	47·1	55·7
10	0 13·3	0 10·6	0 09·4	0 09·7	0 11·5	0 14·7	0 19·4	0 25·2	0 32·0	0 39·7	0 48·0	0 56·5
Lat.	a_1	a_1	a_1	a_1	a_1	a_1	a_1	a_1	a_1	a_1	a_1	a_1
0	0·5	0·6	0·6	0·6	0·6	0·5	0·5	0·4	0·3	0·3	0·2	0·2
10	·5	·6	·6	·6	·6	·5	·5	·4	·4	·3	·3	·2
20	·5	·6	·6	·6	·6	·6	·5	·5	·4	·4	·3	·3
30	·6	·6	·6	·6	·6	·6	·6	·5	·5	·4	·4	·4
40	0·6	0·6	0·6	0·6	0·6	0·6	0·6	0·5	0·5	0·5	0·5	0·5
45	·6	·6	·6	·6	·6	·6	·6	·6	·6	·5	·5	·5
50	·6	·6	·6	·6	·6	·6	·6	·6	·6	·6	·6	·6
55	·6	·6	·6	·6	·6	·6	·6	·6	·7	·7	·7	·7
60	·6	·6	·6	·6	·6	·6	·7	·7	·7	·7	·8	·8
62	0·7	0·6	0·6	0·6	0·6	0·6	0·7	0·7	0·8	0·8	0·8	0·8
64	·7	·6	·6	·6	·6	·6	·7	·7	·8	·8	·9	0·9
66	·7	·6	·6	·6	·6	·7	·7	·8	·8	0·9	0·9	1·0
68	0·7	0·6	0·6	0·6	0·6	0·7	0·7	0·8	0·9	1·0	1·0	1·0
Month	a_2	a_2	a_2	a_2	a_2	a_2	a_2	a_2	a_2	a_2	a_2	a_2
Jan.	0·7	0·7	0·7	0·7	0·7	0·7	0·7	0·7	0·7	0·7	0·6	0·6
Feb.	·6	·7	·7	·7	·7	·8	·8	·8	·8	·8	·8	·8
Mar.	·5	·5	·6	·6	·7	·7	·8	·8	·8	·9	·9	·9
Apr.	0·3	0·4	0·4	0·5	0·6	0·6	0·7	0·7	0·8	0·9	0·9	0·9
May	·2	·3	·3	·4	·4	·5	·5	·6	·7	·8	·8	·9
June	·2	·2	·2	·2	·3	·3	·4	·5	·5	·6	·7	·7
July	0·2	0·2	0·2	0·2	0·2	0·3	0·3	0·3	0·4	0·5	0·5	0·6
Aug.	·4	·3	·3	·3	·2	·2	·3	·3	·3	·3	·4	·4
Sept.	·5	·5	·4	·4	·3	·3	·3	·3	·3	·3	·3	·3
Oct.	0·7	0·7	0·6	0·5	0·5	0·4	0·4	0·3	0·3	0·3	0·3	0·3
Nov.	0·9	0·8	·8	·7	·7	·6	·5	·5	·4	·4	·3	·3
Dec.	1·0	1·0	0·9	0·9	0·8	0·8	0·7	0·6	0·6	0·5	0·4	0·4
Lat.	AZIMUTH											
0	0·4	0·3	0·1	0·0	359·8	359·7	359·6	359·4	359·4	359·3	359·2	359·2
20	0·4	0·3	0·1	0·0	359·8	359·7	359·5	359·4	359·3	359·2	359·2	359·1
40	0·5	0·3	0·2	0·0	359·8	359·6	359·4	359·3	359·1	359·1	359·0	358·9
50	0·6	0·4	0·2	0·0	359·7	359·5	359·3	359·1	359·0	358·9	358·8	358·7
55	0·7	0·5	0·2	0·0	359·7	359·5	359·2	359·0	358·9	358·7	358·6	358·6
60	0·8	0·5	0·2	359·9	359·7	359·4	359·1	358·9	358·7	358·5	358·4	358·4
65	0·9	0·6	0·3	359·9	359·6	359·3	358·9	358·7	358·4	358·3	358·1	358·1

Latitude = Apparent altitude (corrected for refraction) − 1° + a_0 + a_1 + a_2

The table is entered with L.H.A. Aries to determine the column to be used; each column refers to a range of 10°. a_0 is taken, with mental interpolation, from the upper table with the units of L.H.A. Aries in degrees as argument; a_1, a_2 are taken, without interpolation, from the second and third tables with arguments latitude and month respectively. a_0, a_1, a_2 are always positive. The final table gives the azimuth of *Polaris*.

Table 1 *Extract from Pole Star tables.*

Compass checking

The prudent navigator will wish to check his compass at regular intervals, to make sure that no unexpected error has crept in. When coasting, it is generally easy enough to find transits of shore objects for this purpose (see page 34), but away from land, this is not possible. However, it is possible to find the true bearing of any heavenly body (i.e. its azimuth) at any time, and this can be compared with its compass bearing to find the compass error (allowing for variation).

The body most commonly observed for compass checking is the sun. The easiest way of finding its bearing is to use a shadow pin (Fig. 2); some compasses are fitted with one, or it may be possible to improvise a short, vertical pin over the pivot of

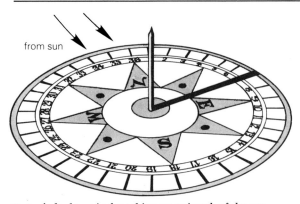

51.2 *A shadow pin for taking an azimuth of the sun.*

the compass card. The shadow of the pin reaches across the card to indicate the *reciprocal* of the sun's bearing; subtract 180° to get the bearing. In the absence of a shadow pin, the bearing of the sun when it is high in the sky demands some form of azimuth ring on the compass, fitted with a mirror (Fig. 3). This is rarely available in a yacht, so the most common time for checking a compass is near rising and setting, when the sun is low in the sky. Even so, some form of pelorus (see page 32) may be needed if the compass is unfavourably sited.

Having measured the sun's bearing (or that of any other identified body, for that matter), it is necessary to establish its azimuth. Over the years, a large number of different ways of doing this have been devised, such as special tables and diagrams; however, the yacht navigator need only bother with the two or three that are most convenient:

51.3 *Azimuth ring.*

1) *Sight Reduction Tables for Air Navigation* One of the two quantities required for the general astronomical position line is the azimuth. The GMT at which the bearing was taken is converted to LHA and declination. Entering these quantities, together with latitude, into the tables will give the azimuth. GMT is only needed to the nearest minute.
2) An alternative, though slightly more involved process is to use the azimuth or ABC tables published in most yacht almanacs and nautical tables. Layouts vary for these tables, and the instructions given in each volume should be followed. This method also requires LHA, declination and latitude.
3) The simplest method, and the most generally useful, is to take the bearing of the sun at sunrise or sunset, when its altitude is 0°. *Note:* Due to refraction, the true altitude of the sun is 0° when the lower limb is approximately half the sun's diameter above the horizon. The sun's azimuth can then be determined by the method of *amplitudes*. A table of amplitudes (one is given on page 193) is entered with latitude and declination; the result given is the bearing of the sun, either east (on rising) or west (on setting) from true north (declination N) or true south (declination S).

For example: 5 May 1980, in DR position 27°S, 122°W, the sun at sunset bore 280° by steering compass. Variation 6°E. Required, the compass error:

Lat	27°S
Dec (from *Nautical Almanac*)	16°N
Amplitude (from table on page 193)	N72°W
True bearing	360° − 72° = 288
Magnetic bearing	288° − 6°E = 282M
Compass bearing	280C
So compass error	2°E

Identifying planets

When observing planets, which are normally very bright and distinctive when compared with stars, the *Nautical Almanac* gives advice on identification. Normally no confusion is likely.

52 Sight reduction – alternative methods

Over the years, many different ways of calculating the zenith distance (or the calculated altitude) and azimuth have been published, all designed in one way or another to simplify the navigator's task. Most of these have been superseded by the tables for rapid sight reduction which are now published; however, it is as well for the navigator to have at least a glancing knowledge of other methods, in case he finds himself on a vessel which does not carry the tables he is used to using.

Alternative Nautical Almanacs

Various yachting and small ship almanacs are published, containing (amongst many other things) the ephemeral data for astronomical bodies. These generally follow a different layout from the *Nautical Almanac* used in this book; the purpose of this is to save space in the volume, by providing discrete values of GHA and declination at wider intervals and relying more on interpolation tables. As a result, such almanacs are slightly more difficult to use, and the values obtained can be somewhat less accurate, though entirely sufficient for yacht navigation. Anyone who has mastered the methods described in this book should have no difficulty in using such tables by following the instructions given with them. The advantage, of course, is that it is possible to carry most of the information that the yachtsman needs on all aspects of navigation within the covers of one volume.

Certain pre-programmed navigational calculators are able to provide ephemeral data on the sun for a number of years at the touch of a button.

Alternative methods of sight reduction
Sight reduction tables for marine navigation
These tables are published in six volumes, by the British Admiralty as NP 401 and by the US Defense Mapping Agency Hydrographic/Topographic Center as Pub. No. 229. Each volume covers a 16° band of latitude for all possible combinations of local hour angle and declinations to 90° (same or contrary name). Calculated altitudes (Hc) are given to the nearest 0.1 minute of arc, and azimuth angles (Z) to the nearest 0.1 degree.

The tables are identical in principle to the *Sight Reduction Tables for Air Navigation* (AP 3270 Pub. 249) used in this book, although the layout is different. The only difference in use is a slightly more involved table for interpolating for the minutes and decimals of declination, required to maintain the extra precision offered by the main tables. Once this interpolation table has been mastered, the method is just as quick and easy as the air tables.

The advantages of this method over the air tables are:
1) Calculated altitudes are given to 0.1 minutes of arc, rather than to one minute (though this improved precision will rarely benefit the yacht navigator in normal conditions).
2) Solutions can be found for all bodies, rather than just those with declinations less than 30°.

The disadvantages are:
1) For world-wide coverage, six volumes are required, rather than the three volumes of AP 3270 (Pub. 249). This will increase cost and stowage requirements, but may be of little significance for a yacht which only sails in a limited area.
2) There is no equivalent to AP 3270 (Pub. 249) Volume 1 (seven selected stars), so choosing suitable stars and reducing their observations is more difficult.

The haversine method This was the most widely used method of sight reduction used at sea before the widespread introduction of rapid sight reduction tables; it requires tables of natural and log haversines and log cosines (haversine (A) = $\frac{1}{2}(1 - \text{cosine A})$), which are often to be found in small craft almanacs and always in books of nautical tables; some tables contain natural and log versines rather than haversines, but the method is the same.

The 'raw ingredients' for the haversine method are the same as for any other – latitude, declination and local hour angle, but there is no need to choose a position; the DR position can be used directly. The procedure is then as follows:
1) From the tables, extract:
   a) The log haversine of the LHA
   b) The log cosine of the DR latitude
   c) The log cosine of the declination
   Add them together; discard the tens figure in the sum (the second figure to the left of the decimal point).

2) Find the sum thus obtained in the log haversine table, and extract the natural haversine that corresponds with it.
3) Combine the DR latitude and the declination (same names, subtract smaller from greater, contrary names add). Look up the natural haversine of this angle.
4) Add this natural haversine to the natural haversine found in step 2.
5) Look up the result of this addition in the natural haversine table. The angle to which it corresponds is the calculated zenith distance of the body.
6) Subtract the CZD from 90° to get the calculated altitude.
7) Use the ABC tables to find the azimuth.
8) Compare the calculated altitude with the true altitude to obtain the intercept, and plot the position line *from the DR position.*

Other short methods There is a host of other short methods for reducing a sight – Ageton, Driesenstock, Sadler and many more, each with their own adherents. If you find one you like, stick with it, but you should always be aware that some have limitations.

Computers and calculators Sight reduction is a problem admirably suited to computers or calculators. Various specialized calculators are available specifically for this problem; some of them also contain the data needed to work out the GHA and declination of the sun. An ordinary calculator needs to be of the scientific type (i.e. with trigonometric functions), and should also be programmable; a simple calculator can be used, but so many key-strokes are needed that a blunder is very likely. The equations for calculated altitude and azimuth, given DR latitude, declination and LHA, are on page 185.

PASSAGE MAKING

53 Passage planning

The amount of planning and preparation that a navigator makes before undertaking a passage will depend very much on his temperament. Some will make very detailed preparations indeed, on the basis that plans and calculations made in peace and comfort ashore will be much more useful and easy that similar work at sea, where he may have to cope with the motion of the boat, tiredness, possibly seasickness, and all of the host of factors which make navigation at sea difficult and liable to blunders. Another navigator may take the attitude that, whilst some preparation is obviously essential, detailed plans are bound to be changed by circumstances and are therefore a waste of time. The balance probably lies somewhere between these two extremes.

The following check-list is divided into essential items and useful ones; it does not include items which are the province of the skipper, rather than the navigator – crew considerations, provisions and fuel, customs clearances and the like. There is one factor amongst these that can have particular importance for the navigator. When going foreign, many countries require a yacht to enter at a particular port or ports for customs and immigration formalities; this obviously affects the route chosen.

Essential

1) *Books and charts* Make sure that you have all the books and charts that you are going to need, and that they are up to date. Small scale charts are needed for planning, medium scale for the actual conduct of the passage and large-scale harbour plans for the arrival. You should carry charts to cover *anywhere* you might conceivably find yourself, even if diverted by heavy weather; there is nothing more unnerving than being blown off the chart into the unknown. Harbour plans of any possible port of refuge are also needed, though in an emergency it is possible to make up a sketch plan of a port from information in the *Pilot* and the *Light List*, which will be sufficiently accurate for a cautious approach.

2) *The route* Using the *Pilot* and the charts, choose the route to be followed. For ocean passages, this will rarely be direct (see page 182), but for shorter passages, the most direct route is generally best. However, diversions should be made to give a good offing to dangerous or uncomfortable areas, or to approach some prominent navigational mark that can give a position check. Traffic separation schemes must either be followed correctly, crossed at right angles or avoided entirely. One can also plan to take advantage of a fair tide or avoid a foul one, at least in the early stages of a passage. After twelve hours or so, such planning is less valuable, as circumstances will almost certainly have changed.

Having chosen the route, plot it carefully on the passage charts and note the course and distance for each leg. Examine the tracks drawn on the chart minutely to make absolutely sure that they do not take the ship into some hitherto unnoticed danger. Plot and record any clearing lines that may be needed to keep the ship clear of dangers.

3) *Navigational aids* Make a note of the lights, radio beacons and other navigational aids which may be used during the passage, and consider the route afresh to make sure that you will make the best use of them.

4) *Tides* Work out from the tide tables the times of high and low water for the departure port around the proposed time of departure, the times of high water for the standard port to which tidal stream predictions are referred, and the times and heights of high and low water for the destination for a suitable period either side of the anticipated time of arrival. Consider that there may be times when the depth of water may make it impossible or unsafe to enter the destination port – a factor all too easily overlooked at the end of an exhausting and difficult passage.

If using a tidal stream atlas, it is helpful to write the actual times beside each chartlet, so that the appropriate one can be found at a glance.

5) *Refuges* Imagine all the difficult circumstances that may arise on passage, and consider a suitable course of action for each – whether to run for shelter, stand off until conditions improve or make for some harbour of refuge.

The actual decision will have to be made at the time, but thought in advance makes the decision much easier.

6) *Tools* Check the tools of your trade – pencils, erasers, dividers, parallel rulers and protractors – make sure they are present and in good order. Also check the compasses (is the steering compass corrected?), log, MFDF equipment and sextant (if carried). Make sure they are in working order and that spare, fresh batteries are carried. A torch (flashlight) with spare batteries is invaluable in case of electrical trouble.

These points must be checked particularly carefully when sailing in someone else's boat. Many navigators carry their own tools around with them from boat to boat.

7) *Weather forecast* Immediately before sailing, a detailed weather forecast, including a synoptic chart, should be obtained. This will form the basis upon which subsequent broadcast forecasts can be interpreted

Useful
8) *Lists* Lists of courses and distances, lights and other objects of navigational interest can be prepared and pinned up over the chart table, for use both by the navigator and the rest of the crew. A particularly useful list is one of frequencies, callsigns and sequence numbers of all radio beacons in the vicinity (this can also be written on the chart by the position of each beacon).

9) *Tidal streams* Details of tidal streams at key points in the passage (e.g. turning marks) can be noted on the chart – especially the times at which the tidal stream starts to run fair or foul.

10) *Dipping ranges* The range at which lights on the route will be raised or dipped can be worked out (page 192), and drawn as a circle on the chart; it is then only necessary to take a bearing of the light as it dips to obtain an instant fix (see pages 71–72).

54 On passage

Departure

On clearing the harbour, the first step is to take a *departure fix*, as a starting point for the dead reckoning, which begins at once. This fix is often a pinpoint (see page 82) on the outer buoy of the harbour approach channel. The fix should be marked on the chart and in the log, with the time and log reading. From this time on, the navigator must insist that the watch on deck keep a careful record of courses sailed and distances run in the log book, so that the dead reckoning can be maintained.

Coasting

Whilst coasting, or travelling parallel to a coast which is in sight, the DR should be plotted at regular intervals – at least once an hour. At the same time, fixes by observations of shore objects should be taken whenever the opportunity offers – again, once an hour is a good target to aim for. On each occasion, the DR and the fix should be compared, to detect any gross errors which may have occurred in either.

Whilst coasting, it can be difficult to identify shore marks positively as they come into view. As new objects appear, they can be *shot up*, by fixing the ship with position lines from objects already identified, and at the same time taking a compass bearing of the unidentified object. This bearing can then be plotted in reverse from the fix obtained; the resulting line will pass through (or close to) the unidentified object.

Keep an eye open for any transits (ranges) that may come into view (see page 68). Not only is a transit an easy and accurate position line; it also offers an opportunity to check the steering compass, which should be done as often as possible.

Monitoring

One of the navigator's basic functions is to monitor what is happening to the boat. Not only does this mean being aware of planned or spontaneous changes of course or speed; it also means watching the crew (especially the helmsman), to make sure that what the watch on deck write in the log is correct. Like any other equipment, helmsmen need to be calibrated (see pages 52–3), and the

accuracy of log entries must also be assessed. Checking should be done unobtrusively, to avoid offence.

There are very many occasions, especially when racing, when the dominant requirement is boat speed, rather than the slavish holding of a particular course. These are circumstances that the navigator must accept, merely insisting that the small but frequent course changes are properly entered in the log book. In racing yachts, it is not uncommon for log entries to be required every fifteen minutes, as well as on all course changes. Cruising yachts need not be quite so meticulous, but hourly log readings should be entered even in mid-Atlantic. The deck watch will not mind – it breaks the monotony of a long watch, and gives someone a chance to warm up and put the kettle on.

Because of the relatively detached position the navigator often enjoys, he may be best placed to keep an eye on changes outside the boat itself. The watch on deck, preoccupied by sailing the boat, keeping a lookout and adjusting the sails, may be slow to appreciate the significance of a gradual wind shift or a changing sky; and a watch fresh on deck after leaving their bunks have nothing to compare what they see now with what has happened in the past few hours. A navigator outside the watch system provides a valuable continuity that is hard to manage in any other way.

Tactics (sailing vessels)

Beating When beating to windward, the cardinal principle is to keep the destination in the wind's eye (Fig. 1). First take the making tack, the tack which points up best towards the mark; when the mark is upwind, work up towards it with a series of relatively short tacks; in this way, you will always be well placed to take any advantage of wind shifts as they occur. Do not tack too often, especially when the mark is some distance away, but make the tacks shorter as you get closer.

If you have reason to believe that a wind shift is coming, then keep over towards the direction from where the new wind will come (Fig. 2). When the shift comes, you will be in a good position to make use of it; however, do not gamble too heavily, in case the shift never comes.

When beating, an old adage which rarely lets

54.1 *Tactics when beating.*

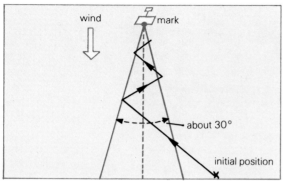

54.2 *Making the best of an anticipated wind-shift.*

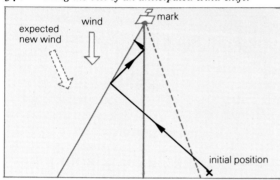

54.3 *Tacking downwind.*

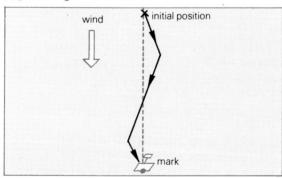

54.4 *Lee-bowing the tide.*

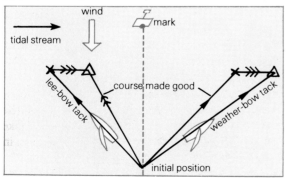

you down says 'always tack when headed off'. If the header heralds a permanent wind-shift, then you are using it straight away; if the header is only temporary, it is simple enough to tack back if desired.

Off the wind It is almost always wise to work a little way to windward as the opportunity offers, to protect yourself against a last-minute header.

Running A dead run is a slow and uncomfortable point of sailing, and one which causes the helmsman a lot of worry. It will almost always pay to luff up a little, put the wind on the quarter and go onto a broad reach. It means that you have further to travel, as you must *tack downwind* to reach your objective (Fig. 3), but the increase in speed and comfort makes it worth while. Exactly how far one should luff up depends on the boat, the wind strength and the sea, but 10° to 15° would probably be about right. As when beating, it is necessary to watch for wind shifts and gybe when needed.

Light airs The principle here is for the helmsman to keep the boat moving, in almost any direction. Some progress is better than no progress, and the small distances travelled mean that the navigator's life is not made too difficult by the variable courses steered.

If the speed of the boat through the water is not sufficient to stem the tide, then kedge immediately, and keep the kedge down until you are sure that you can do better without it. Many a race has been won with judicious use of the kedge anchor.

The foregoing remarks are, of course, addressed to the racing yachtsman; in light airs, the cruising man sensibly puts on the engine.

Beating across the tide On a beat where the tide is running at right angles (or nearly so) to the track, then the tack which puts the tide on the lee bow gets you towards the destination more quickly than the other (Fig. 4). If the tidal stream is constant, the lee-bow tack offers no advantage as one has to go on the other tack sometime or other and lose what you have gained. If, however, the tidal stream is going to slacken or even reverse its direction, then the lee-bow tack does indeed pay. Ideally, you would tack at the turn of the tide, to lee-bow the new tidal stream, or perhaps when you reach a position where the tidal stream has weakened.

55 Navigating at night, in fog and in heavy weather

Navigating at night

Navigation during the hours of darkness is often thought to be difficult but, if anything, the reverse is true. The process of keeping the dead reckoning is unchanged, and many types of position line can be obtained in exactly the same way as during the day – soundings, radio bearings, radar, and advanced electronic aids all work equally well in darkness or in daylight, though in one or two cases with reduced accuracy due to changes in the ionosphere. It is only visual observations that change; as twilight falls, visible objects gradually slide into the gloom, to be replaced by a pattern of twinkling, blinking lights – a pattern which may be easier to understand than the often meagre view of a distant coastline by day.

Whilst night navigation is not difficult, it does require a little preparation. The chart table must be fitted with a suitable light – not so bright as to dazzle the navigator and disturb the watch below, but bright enough to read the chart easily; a map light on a flexible stalk is almost ideal, though the addition of a dimmer improves it. A torch (flashlight) and batteries are needed in case the main lights fail. An illuminated magnifying glass is a valuable aid for anyone whose reading vision is not what it was.

The hand bearing compass must also be illuminated; most are fitted either with a luminous capsule or a built-in bulb and battery. If neither is fitted, or if the lamp fails, a pocket torch will be needed to light up the compass card to read off the bearing of a light.

Night vision In the dark, the human eye makes certain physiological adjustments to improve its performance in low light conditions. These adjustments take time – at least twenty minutes – so the navigator should avoid destroying his own or anyone else's night vision by flashing bright lights around. It is thought that red light damages night adaption relatively little, so some people prefer to use red lights at the chart table or wear red goggles.

In low light, the most sensitive part of the eye is not at the centre of the field of view, but at the edge (*peripheral vision*). If you are looking for an object in the dark, it is a mistake to stare; rather, keep the eyes moving all around and keep alert for the object in the corner of your eye.

Binoculars Suitable binoculars can make it easier to see things at night. The prime quality needed is light-gathering power, which is found in binoculars with large diameter lenses at the far end (the objective lens). 50 mm diameter is about the largest diameter that is readily available. The second factor is magnification and the allied question of field of view. On the unsteady platform of a yacht, too much magnification makes the binocular impossible to hold sufficiently still to be useful. The best compromise is a magnification of seven times; therefore the most suitable specification for marine binoculars is 7×50 mm.

Identifying lights The first step that must be taken on seeing a light is to identify it beyond question. This means watching for the character and colour of the light, and timing it *with a stop watch*. Timing the period of a light by counting or guessing is potentially dangerous, as the light may thereby be wrongly identified. Match the character, colour and period with those of lights printed on the chart to make the identification; be on your guard for lights with identical characters and periods, although these are usually a long way apart.

Looms A bright light beyond the horizon can be seen as a faint patch of light scattered in the air, known as the *loom* of the light. Large towns, factories and harbour installations can often be detected at some distance by their looms. The most valuable application of the loom is with navigational lights whose beams are formed by rotating lenses. The loom of such a light can be identified and a bearing taken when it is still well below the horizon.

Navigating in fog

Navigating in fog stretches the nerves and requires as much accuracy as can possibly be found, but it is not of itself hard to do.

Dead reckoning In fog, the DR becomes of paramount importance and must be kept up faithfully. If opportunity offers before the fog comes down, a good fix should be taken for a departure, and the DR plotted and assessed thereafter. This may be hard during a race, if the wind is also very light; the yacht will be going in all directions to try and make progress, leading to a plot which resembles the rambles of a drunken spider. The 95 per cent error of the DR will still be growing, and must be considered when deciding on the safety of a particular course of action.

Fixing aids All available fixing aids must be used to help reduce uncertainties in the DR. The echo sounder (if fitted) should be left on as much as possible, for insurance against running aground as much as for position lines. Electronic aids should be used to the full, especially radar which helps with collision avoidance as well as navigation. Some information can be gleaned from fog signals; too much reliance should not be placed on bearings of fog signals taken by ear, as the fog may distort the transmission of sound. On the other hand, hearing a faint fog signal (such as a bell on a buoy) is good evidence that the buoy is quite close; provided the buoy can be identified beyond doubt, this can be very helpful. If it is safe to do so, there is much to be said for homing on to such a fog signal to find and identify the buoy positively (by reading the name painted on it if necessary), to obtain a pinpoint and re-start the DR.

Navigating in heavy weather

In heavy weather everything, including navigation, is more difficult. The motion of the boat, tiredness, fright, seasickness, wet and cold are among the many handicaps the navigator has to fight.

Chart and log book Guard these carefully, as you may need them very badly later on for a second attempt at the DR when conditions improve. Keep both as dry as possible; consider whether it is essential for the chart to be kept on the chart table all the time. Wet hats should be taken off before working on the chart, and the near edge of the chart protected – wet oilskins rubbing against a wet chart will destroy it, and possibly some priceless information, in seconds.

Dead reckoning Keep this as carefully as possible in the conditions, bearing in mind that both course and speed are liable to very large errors. If lying ahull, hove to or running before under bare poles, course and distance can only

be guessed at from watching the yacht as she moves in the water.

Fixing Fixing aids can be few, especially if the heavy winds bring poor visibility with them. Visual bearings can be taken with difficulty and considerable error, as can MFDF radio bearings. Radio bearings should be repeated over and over again until some sort of consistency emerges. Radar and advanced electronic aids keep working, though radar needs proper adjustment of the clutter controls. You should not be surprised if the violent conditions cause such equipment to break down. Astronomical position lines are almost impossible to take because the horizon is obscured by huge waves nearby, but patience and practice may give you something to work on. Watch your own safety while using the sextant, and try to prevent it getting soaked.

Leeway Leeway is by far the most important and difficult factor to estimate in heavy weather. In general it is safe to say that there will be much more leeway than you expect; this arises in three ways:

1) Normal leeway caused by the pressure of the wind on the topsides and rig of the boat.
2) 'Dumping' by breaking waves. Every time the boat is picked up by a wave which breaks under her, she will be put down some distance to leeward. Each 'dump' may not move the boat very far, but over a period of time they add up.
3) Surface water movement, a sort of short-term current caused by friction between the wind and the surface of the sea. This obviously depends upon the strength of the wind and the length of time it has been blowing. It will persist for some hours after the wind that caused it moderates.

Overall, the effect of leeway is such that it no longer is sensible to treat it as a change in the course, as is done for most DR work (see page 60). Instead, the leeway can be treated as a current, the direction being downwind, and the speed at the guess of the navigator. In extreme conditions, this 'leeway current' can easily reach three knots, but will depend upon the boat and the conditions of the moment. The leeway current is naturally quite independent of any progress the boat might be making on her own account; the current must be added to the boat's course and speed.

56 Landfall

The most critical and exciting moment of any passage other than one that involves only coasting, is the landfall. However long or short a time the ship has been out of sight of land, there is a period of anxiety whilst waiting for the landfall to appear, and a great feeling of pleasure and relief when it finally shows up.

There is no other time in a passage when the principles of random error described in this book assume greater importance. A landfall can be considered as the whittling down of uncertainty. Beforehand, the 95 per cent error circle is large (sometimes very large); as land is approached and position lines based on the shore become available, the error circle is reduced until eventually it can be made so small as to be relatively unimportant and the navigator can set off on the final stages of the passage in safety and confidence.

The actual ways in which the error circle can be progressively reduced vary so much with individual circumstances that it is difficult to give specific advice. The example which follows is fairly typical of the situation which may occur at the end of a longish passage out of sight of land; it is imaginary, and designed mainly to illustrate the principles upon which the navigator should base his thinking.

The example supposes that a yacht is approaching the coast after an ocean passage. The weather has been overcast, and the last astronomical fix is now some five hundred miles behind. The navigator has been running his DR, and reckons that his 95 per cent error circle has a radius of 50 miles. By the time he gets within about 150 miles of the coast (three times his error circle radius), he begins to feel the need for better information (Fig. 1).

He first tries to take bearings of MF radio beacons on the coast; he manages to pick up two, but they are both near the limit of their range, and are situated quite close together. After correcting the bearings for half convergency (see page 114), he plots them, and decides to allow a 95 per cent error of 10° (Fig. 2). The resulting fix is poor, but better than the DR in that the error zone is much smaller. The fix is not too far from the DR, well inside the DR's error circle, so he considers the fix (as far as it goes) as being trustworthy. As the error zone is

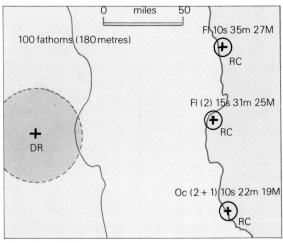

56.1 *Landfall – phase 1.*

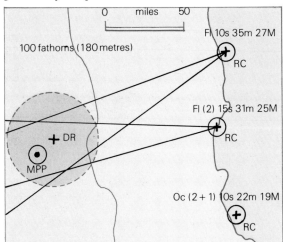

56.2 *Landfall – phase 2.*

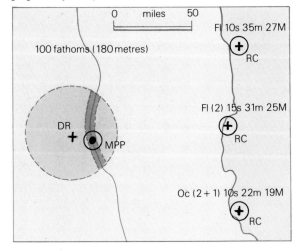

56.3 *Landfall – phase 3.*

56.4 *Landfall – phase 4.*

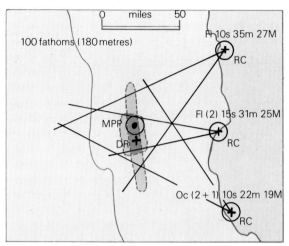

56.5 *Landfall – phase 5.*

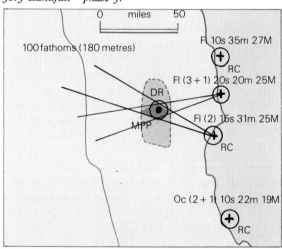

56.6 *The landfall complete.*

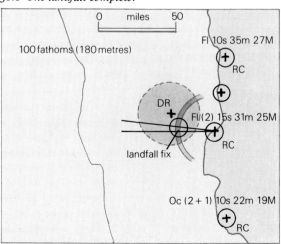

long and thin, it tells him more about his line of approach than his distance offshore.

Meanwhile, the navigator has been running his echo sounder from time to time, and some time after the radio fix he picks up the 100 fathom (180 m) line, traditionally regarded as the edge of the continental shelf. By now it is dusk, so radio bearings are for the moment unreliable, but the sounding can be used to reduce the error zone of the previous fix, which has by now grown a little through errors in the DR since the fix was taken (Fig. 3). The 100 fathom line runs more or less parallel with the coast, so he now has a much better idea how far off he is.

Later on, when the ionosphere has settled down, he tries another radio fix, and this time manages to get bearings on three beacons (Fig. 4). He notices that all three signals show signs of fading and that the nulls are not very sharp; he concludes that night effect is present, and decides to use the same 95 per cent error as before, 10°. However, the beacons are now closer and the angle of cut is better, so the fix has a smaller error circle than the one he has been using up to that time, and therefore he has improved his situation.

Some time after midnight, he sees the faint loom of two powerful landfall lights ahead. At first they are so faint and intermittent they do nothing but reassure him that land does actually exist, but as time goes by he is first able to make a positive identification, and then take useful bearings (Fig. 5). The angle of cut is not too good, but the bearings themselves are quite accurate, and the navigator uses a 95 per cent error of 4°. His error circle has now been reduced to something less than four miles across the track, and perhaps six or seven along it.

Finally, just before dawn, the landfall light for which he has been aiming is raised above the horizon. He takes a long, careful bearing (95 per cent error of 2°), and looks up the range in the table (see page 192), which has a 95 per cent error of about half a mile (Fig. 6). The landfall is complete, and the navigator can thankfully give new instructions to the watch on deck and go and get some well-earned sleep.

The problems of making a landfall are by no means confined to ocean sailing. Skipping across a wide bay, or crossing a narrow sea produce exactly the same situation, though the magnitudes of the errors may be smaller; on the other hand, in such circumstances there may be more off-lying dangers to worry about, so the situation is no easier. In poor visibility, a landfall after three miles can be more difficult than one made after 3,000 miles.

Planning the landfall

Making a landfall can be simplified to some extent by a little pre-planning. First, the actual point for the landfall should be selected with some care. It should be prominent, well marked and (if possible) free from off-lying dangers. Many of the great capes of the world have been used as landfall points.

Secondly, it should be possible to choose the time at which landfall is expected. The best time is to raise the shore lights just before dawn, as in the example above. This means that, provided visibility is all right, the light can be identified from its loom at some distance, and the process of raising it gives a valuable position line. If the destination port lies close to the landfall, it can then be entered in daylight. Unless the coast is very distinctive, it is hard to identify features at a distance in daylight, and the navigator can remain in doubt for some time after sighting land. Self-deception is very easy under these circumstances, and the navigator may persuade himself he is in a quite different position from his real one. If circumstances allow, a position line from the sun can help sort out such problems; navigators often forget about their sextants when land is in sight.

For a short passage, the time of landfall can be decided (more or less) by choosing the time of departure. On a long passage, where time is probably of less importance anyway, there is much to be gained by standing off for a while, so as to make the final approach to the coast at night.

57 Pilotage

Pilotage is the term used to describe navigation in harbours and narrow channels, where big ships would carry a pilot. Most of the normal tools of navigation are of little use, but it is during this phase of the passage that the yacht comes closest to danger. It would be a great pity to ruin an otherwise immaculate passage by putting the ship aground in the last half-mile, so pilotage deserves just as much attention as any other aspect of navigation.

The major contribution towards successful pilotage is preparation; study the chart carefully, read the *Pilot Book* and any other information, and try to form some sort of image in your mind as to what you should look for. Whilst your impression of the general scenery will almost certainly be wrong, such prominent objects as churches, beacons and breakwaters should show up as expected. Blind pilotage using radar requires very careful preparation indeed, as it can be difficult to distinguish between buoys and nearby small craft. The course and distance between each mark should be written down in advance.

The time of day can make a considerable difference to the ease of pilotage. It is much easier to feel your way up a long, winding buoyed channel at night (provided the buoys are lit) as each buoy can be identified positively by its light. During the day in a big river, this is not so easy; if in doubt, go right up to the buoy and read the name painted on it. It is not a bad idea to tick off each buoy on the chart as it is passed, as it is surprisingly easy to lose track of where you have got to.

On the other hand, it is best to enter a harbour, especially a busy one, during the day. At night it is very much harder to judge distance, and navigational marks can easily get lost in street lighting, flashing advertisement signs and traffic lights. Harbours are constantly being altered or improved, so there may well be obstructions or other changes which do not appear on your chart; it is much easier to avoid such hazards in daylight.

When entering pilotage waters, make ready by putting the *Pilot* (weighted open at the right page) and the chart (in a plastic cover if it is raining) by the helm. A hand bearing compass and binoculars will also be needed. The echo sounder will

naturally be running, and you will have worked out the state of the tide in advance, so you will be able to reduce the soundings in your head; you will also know what tidal streams to expect in different parts of the approach. A decision to be taken at this stage is whether you should take on a pilot or whether you can manage on your own. There is no disgrace involved in taking on a pilot, and it may well be the sensible and seamanlike thing to do.

The first essential on entering pilotage waters is to make sure you know exactly where you are to begin with; some form of pinpoint is best, such as passing close by the outer buoy of the approach channel. Thereafter you should keep track of the buoys as they pass on the chart, the compass course between them, the depth of water and the tidal stream. Conning by eye needs practice, as the view from sea level is at first confusing and hard to relate to the plan view given by the chart. It is necessary to watch the compass, as tidal streams or currents may otherwise lead you into trouble. In Figure 1, a yacht is steering for a buoy, but a cross-tide is running. If the navigator paid no attention to the compass, he would approach the buoy along a curve which might well set him into danger.

In all pilotage, you should take your time, and not go thrusting forward into the unknown. Keep an anchor ready for letting go, so that if necessary you can stop for a good long think.

57.1 *Steering for a buoy without allowing for tide or watching the compass.*

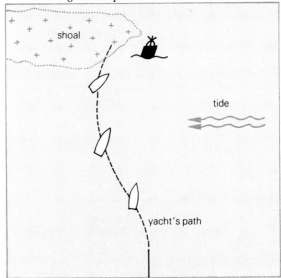

57.2 *Use transits where available.*

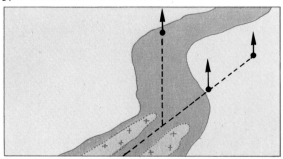

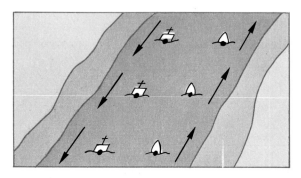

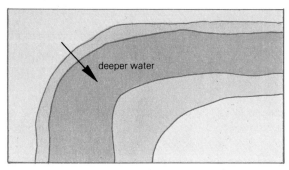

deeper water

57.3 (Centre) *Keeping clear of the main channel if depth of water permits.*

57.4 (Above) *Deeper water is generally on the outside of river bends.*

When following a long, winding channel, make use of any transits or leading lines that may be available (Fig. 2). The rule of the road at sea requires you to keep to the starboard hand of the channel, but if possible you should keep out of the deep water channel intended for big ships altogether (Fig. 3). Very often, there is plenty of water for a yacht on the 'wrong' side of the channel buoys; the correct place for a yacht in such circumstances, from everyone's point of view, is outside the channel. When following a river, the temptation to cut corners should be resisted; deeper water is normally to be found at the outside of a bend (Fig. 4).

In the final stages of the approach, you come into contact once again with the rest of the human race, in the form of harbour officials and the like who may or may not be pleased to see you. It is important to keep your temper and to listen to any instructions you may be given very carefully. Occasionally, it may be neither safe nor sensible to do what officials say, and polite obstinacy usually wins the day.

Make sure that your berth is as satisfactory as possible – that you will not dry out, perhaps, or if drying out is inevitable there are suitable conditions for this to be done safely – a firm bottom, a stout wall to lean against, ample fendering and suitable bollards. The berth should be as far protected from prevailing weather as possible and clear of passing traffic. Decisions or arguments at this stage can make you visit much more agreeable.

58 Plane sailing

Plane sailing (sometimes written: plain sailing) is a way of keeping up a dead reckoning position without actually plotting it on a chart, or of calculating the direction and distance of one point on the surface of the earth from another. Plane sailing can only be used over relatively short distances, because it assumes that the earth is flat (a plane) over the region of interest; the practical limit beyond which this assumption starts to introduce noticeable errors is about 600 miles.

What is required for plane sailing is a way of converting a particular direction and distance into a change of latitude and longitude, or conversely a way of converting changes in latitude and longitude into a direction and a distance. This problem is divided into two parts:

1) Solving the right-angled triangle on the surface of the earth, to give north-south distance in miles and east-west distance in miles from a known direction and distance, or *vice versa* (Fig. 1).

2) Because the nautical mile and the minute of latitude are equivalent, the north-south distance in miles is the same as the change in latitude and is known as the difference in latitude (D lat). However, the minute of longitude is only equivalent to the nautical mile at the equator, so in general the east-west distance in miles (known as the departure) must be converted to minutes of longitude (difference in longitude, D long), depending upon the latitude; the higher the latitude, the closer the meridians come and the shorter the minute of longitude becomes.

Plane sailing makes use of four equations, which can either be worked out on a pocket calculator (see page 185) or by means of a traverse table (see below). The equations are:

Departure = D long cos (mid latitude) (1)
Departure = distance sin (direction) (2)
D lat   = distances cos (direction) (3)

and, dividing (2) by (3):

$$\tan (\text{direction}) = \frac{\text{departure}}{\text{D lat}} \quad (4)$$

In the equations, mid-latitude is the latitude mid-way between the starting latitude and the finishing latitude.

58.1 *The plane triangle.*

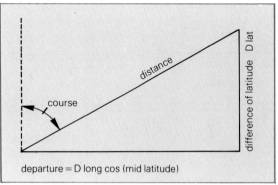

departure = D long cos (mid latitude)

The plane sailing problems that a navigator may wish to solve generally take one of two forms:

1) *To find the direction and distance between two known points*: The mid latitude, D lat and D long can be worked out, and departure obtained from equation (1). Either (2) or (3) can be used to find the distance, and (4) gives the direction.

2) *To find the position after following a given direction for a given distance*: D lat and departure can be found from equations (2) and (3). From the D lat, the finishing latitude can be found, and hence the mid latitude. Equation (1) then gives the D long.

The traverse table

To help the navigator solve these equations (especially in the days before pocket calculators were invented), the traverse table was devised. A part of one page of a traverse table is shown in Table 1. A double page is provided for each degree of direction, and the various columns provide distance, D lat, departure, and D long. The traverse table only covers 45° of direction, as the values then start to repeat themselves. For the sample page shown, the four directions shown at the top of the page (025°, 155°, 205° and 335°) require that the column headings at the top of the page be used; for the directions at the bottom of the page (065°, 115°, 245° and 295°), the column headings at the bottom of the page should be used.

Thus, to find the D lat and departure for a direction of 025° and a distance of 170 miles, it is only necessary to consult the table on the page with 025° at distance 170 miles to find D lat 154.1

Table 1 *Extract from traverse tables.*

E60

TRAVERSE TABLE

25°

335°   025°

205°   155°

DIST	D.LAT	DEP	DIST	D.LAT	DEP	DIST	D.LAT	DEP	DIST	D.LAT	DEP	DIST	D.LAT	DEP
D.long	*Dep*		*D.long*	*Dep*		*D.long*	*Dep*		*D.long*	*Dep*		*D.long*	*Dep*	
1	00·9	00·4	61	55·3	25·8	121	109·7	51·1	181	164·0	76·5	241	218·4	101·9
2	01·8	00·8	62	56·2	26·2	122	110·6	51·6	182	164·9	76·9	242	219·3	102·3
3	02·7	01·3	63	57·1	26·6	123	111·5	52·0	183	165·9	77·3	243	220·2	102·7
4	03·6	01·7	64	58·0	27·0	124	112·4	52·4	184	166·8	77·8	244	221·1	103·1
5	04·5	02·1	65	58·9	27·5	125	113·3	52·8	185	167·7	78·2	245	222·0	103·5
6	05·4	02·5	66	59·8	27·9	126	114·2	53·2	186	168·6	78·6	246	223·0	104·0
7	06·3	03·0	67	60·7	28·3	127	115·1	53·7	187	169·5	79·0	247	223·9	104·4
8	07·3	03·4	68	61·6	28·7	128	116·0	54·1	188	170·4	79·5	248	224·8	104·8
9	08·2	03·8	69	62·5	29·2	129	116·9	54·5	189	171·3	79·9	249	225·7	105·2
10	09·1	04·2	70	63·4	29·6	130	117·8	54·9	190	172·2	80·3	250	226·6	105·7
11	10·0	04·6	71	64·3	30·0	131	118·7	55·4	191	173·1	80·7	251	227·5	106·1
12	10·9	05·1	72	65·3	30·4	132	119·6	55·8	192	174·0	81·1	252	228·4	106·5
13	11·8	05·5	73	66·2	30·9	133	120·5	56·2	193	174·9	81·6	253	229·3	106·9
14	12·7	05·9	74	67·1	31·3	134	121·4	56·6	194	175·8	82·0	254	230·2	107·3
15	13·6	06·3	75	68·0	31·7	135	122·4	57·1	195	176·7	82·4	255	231·1	107·8
16	14·5	06·8	76	68·9	32·1	136	123·3	57·5	196	177·6	82·8	256	232·0	108·2
17	15·4	07·2	77	69·8	32·5	137	124·2	57·9	197	178·5	83·3	257	232·9	108·6
18	16·3	07·6	78	70·7	33·0	138	125·1	58·3	198	179·4	83·7	258	233·8	109·0
19	17·2	08·0	79	71·6	33·4	139	126·0	58·7	199	180·4	84·1	259	234·7	109·5
20	18·1	08·5	80	72·5	33·8	140	126·9	59·2	200	181·3	84·5	260	235·6	109·9
21	19·0	08·9	81	73·4	34·2	141	127·8	59·6	201	182·2	84·9	261	236·5	110·3
22	19·9	09·3	82	74·3	34·7	142	128·7	60·0	202	183·1	85·4	262	237·5	110·7
23	20·8	09·7	83	75·2	35·1	143	129·6	60·4	203	184·0	85·8	263	238·4	111·1
24	21·8	10·1	84	76·1	35·5	144	130·5	60·9	204	184·9	86·2	264	239·3	111·6
25	22·7	10·6	85	77·0	35·9	145	131·4	61·3	205	185·8	86·6	265	240·2	112·0
26	23·6	11·0	86	77·9	36·3	146	132·3	61·7	206	186·7	87·1	266	241·1	112·4
27	24·5	11·4	87	78·8	36·8	147	133·2	62·1	207	187·6	87·5	267	242·0	112·8
28	25·4	11·8	88	79·8	37·2	148	134·1	62·5	208	188·5	87·9	268	242·9	113·3
29	26·3	12·3	89	80·7	37·6	149	135·0	63·0	209	189·4	88·3	269	243·8	113·7
30	27·2	12·7	90	81·6	38·0	150	135·9	63·4	210	190·3	88·7	270	244·7	114·1
31	28·1	13·1	91	82·5	38·5	151	136·9	63·8	211	191·2	89·2	271	245·6	114·5
32	29·0	13·5	92	83·4	38·9	152	137·8	64·2	212	192·1	89·6	272	246·5	115·0
33	29·9	13·9	93	84·3	39·3	153	138·7	64·7	213	193·0	90·0	273	247·4	115·4
34	30·8	14·4	94	85·2	39·7	154	139·6	65·1	214	193·9	90·4	274	248·3	115·8
35	31·7	14·8	95	86·1	40·1	155	140·5	65·5	215	194·9	90·9	275	249·2	116·2
36	32·6	15·2	96	87·0	40·6	156	141·4	65·9	216	195·8	91·3	276	250·1	116·6
37	33·5	15·6	97	87·9	41·0	157	142·3	66·4	217	196·7	91·7	277	251·0	117·1
38	34·4	16·1	98	88·8	41·4	158	143·2	66·8	218	197·6	92·1	278	252·0	117·5
39	35·3	16·5	99	89·7	41·8	159	144·1	67·2	219	198·5	92·6	279	252·9	117·9
40	36·3	16·9	100	90·6	42·3	160	145·0	67·6	220	199·4	93·0	280	253·8	118·3
41	37·2	17·3	101	91·5	42·7	161	145·9	68·0	221	200·3	93·4	281	254·7	118·8
42	38·1	17·7	102	92·4	43·1	162	146·8	68·5	222	201·2	93·8	282	255·6	119·2
43	39·0	18·2	103	93·3	43·5	163	147·7	68·9	223	202·1	94·2	283	256·5	119·6
44	39·9	18·6	104	94·3	44·0	164	148·6	69·3	224	203·0	94·7	284	257·4	120·0
45	40·8	19·0	105	95·2	44·4	165	149·5	69·7	225	203·9	95·1	285	258·3	120·4
46	41·7	19·4	106	96·1	44·8	166	150·4	70·2	226	204·8	95·5	286	259·2	120·9
47	42·6	19·9	107	97·0	45·2	167	151·4	70·6	227	205·7	95·9	287	260·1	121·3
48	43·5	20·3	108	97·9	45·6	168	152·3	71·0	228	206·6	96·4	288	261·0	121·7
49	44·4	20·7	109	98·8	46·1	169	153·2	71·4	229	207·5	96·8	289	261·9	122·1
50	45·3	21·1	110	99·7	46·5	170	154·1	71·8	230	208·5	97·2	290	262·8	122·6
51	46·2	21·6	111	100·6	46·9	171	155·0	72·3	231	209·4	97·6	291	263·7	123·0
52	47·1	22·0	112	101·5	47·3	172	155·9	72·7	232	210·3	98·0	292	264·6	123·4
53	48·0	22·4	113	102·4	47·8	173	156·8	73·1	233	211·2	98·5	293	265·5	123·8
54	48·9	22·8	114	103·3	48·2	174	157·7	73·5	234	212·1	98·9	294	266·5	124·2
55	49·8	23·2	115	104·2	48·6	175	158·6	74·0	235	213·0	99·3	295	267·4	124·7
56	50·8	23·7	116	105·1	49·0	176	159·5	74·4	236	213·9	99·7	296	268·3	125·1
57	51·7	24·1	117	106·0	49·4	177	160·4	74·8	237	214·8	100·2	297	269·2	125·5
58	52·6	24·5	118	106·9	49·9	178	161·3	75·2	238	215·7	100·6	298	270·1	125·9
59	53·5	24·9	119	107·9	50·3	179	162·2	75·6	239	216·6	101·0	299	271·0	126·4
60	54·4	25·4	120	108·8	50·7	180	163·1	76·1	240	217·5	101·4	300	271·9	126·8
D.long		*Dep*	*D.long*		*Dep*	*D.long*		*Dep*	*D.long*		*Dep*	*D.long*		*Dep*
DIST	DEP	D.LAT	DIST	DEP	D.LAT	DIST	DEP	D.LAT	DIST	DEP	D.LAT	DIST	DEP	D.LAT

N

295°   065°

245°   115°

65°

miles, departure 71.8 miles. This departure can be converted to D long by opening the traverse table at the page appropriate to the mid latitude and entering the columns headed *D long* and *dep*. Assume in the previous example that the mid latitude was 65° (use the bottom column headings). A departure of 71.8 miles gives a D long of 170 minutes of longitude, or 2°50′. From the D lat and the D long thus obtained, the finishing position can be established from the starting position; D lat is either north or south depending on the direction (north in this example), and similarly D long is east or west (east in the example).

The converse process of finding a direction and distance between two positions is a little more involved. First establish the mid latitude and convert D long to departure. Then scan through the tables until the values of D lat and departure are found matching each other. The distance column then shows the distance, and the page shows the direction (to be interpreted according to whether D lat is north or south, and dep is east or west).

DR by traverse table

It can sometimes be convenient to keep up the dead reckoning by traverse table rather than plot-ting on a chart; the most likely occasion for this is when working on a small-scale ocean chart, when accurate plotting becomes almost impossible. The following example shows the method:

Time	Course	Distance	D lat N	D lat S	Dep E	Dep W
1200–1800	240	41	–	35.5	–	20.5
1800–0100	275	50	4.4	–	–	49.8
0100–1130	220	69	–	52.9	–	44.4
Current	060	18	9.0	–	15.6	–
			13.4	88.4	15.6	114.7
				–13.4		–15.6
Total D lat and departure				75.0S		99.1W

Start lat	29°40′N		Start long	44°20′W
D lat	1°15′S		D long	1°53′.3W
End lat	28°25′N		End long	46°13′.3W
Mid lat	29°N	, so D long = 113′.3 = 1°53′.3W		

For interest, the traverse table also shows that the course and distance made good over the period was:

233° — 125 n miles.

59 Mercator and great circle sailings

Mercator sailing

The ocean navigator may sometimes want to calculate the course to steer and the distance to run between two positions which are a long way apart – too far for the basic assumption that the earth is flat used in plane sailing to be valid. For distances greater than about 600 miles, mercator sailing should be used instead, which requires a special table to be found in books of nautical tables, called 'meridional parts for the terrestial spheroid'.

Without going too deeply into theory, mercator sailing is to some extent the converse of plane sailing. In plane sailing, D lat is held constant and D long is changed into departure; in mercator sailing, the D long is held constant and the D lat is changed into a quantity called DMP (difference of meridional parts) by using the table. The DMP is formed by taking out the meridional parts of the starting and the finishing latitudes and subtracting (adding if the track crosses the equator).

The two basic formulae for mercator sailing are:

$$\tan (\text{course}) = \frac{\text{D long}}{\text{DMP}} \qquad (1)$$

$$\text{distance} = \frac{\text{D lat}}{\cos (\text{course})} \text{ or D lat sec (course)} \quad (2)$$

(The first form is easier to use with a pocket calculator)

The results given by these formulae are exact for any distance travelled. They give the course to steer (rhumb line) and distance between the points, though it must be remembered that the resulting distance will not be the shortest possible distance between the points; this is found by great circle sailing (see below), if required.

For example: What is the rhumb line course and distance from New York (40°45′N, 74°00′W) to Bermuda (32°45′N, 65°00′W)?

New York lat 40°45′N	mer part 2666.48	long 74°00′W
Bermuda lat 32°45′N	mer part 2069.01	long 65°00′W
D lat 8°S	DMP 597.47	D long 9°E
= 480′S		= 540′E

$$\tan (\text{course}) = \frac{\text{D long}}{\text{DMP}} = \frac{540}{597.47} = 0.90381$$

$$\text{Course} = S42°E = 138$$

$$\text{distance} = \text{D lat sec (course)} = 480 \sec (42°) = 645.9 \text{ miles}$$

It is, of course, possible to invert the formulae if desired to solve the converse problem of finding the finishing position given the starting position and the course and distance sailed.

Great circle sailing

As has been pointed out, the shortest distance between two points on the earth's surface is on the great circle that joins them. The difference in distance between the great circle track and the rhumb line can be considerable in longer passages. For example, the great circle distance between San Francisco and Yokohama is 4517 miles, while the rhumb line distance is 4723 miles – a difference of 206 miles or the best part of two days sailing in a small craft. Of course, distance is not everything, and a sailing craft in particular will plan a route with many other factors in mind (see page 182); however, there is no point in sailing unnecessary miles if they can be avoided, so a consideration of the great circle track should be an important part of the planning.

There are two ways of determining the great circle track between two points; the graphical method described first is the more satisfactory, as it allows for the plotting of intermediate positions on a mercator chart for detailed planning. The tabular method can be used if no gnomonic chart is available, or as a quick check on the distance involved.

Graphical method The graphical method of determining a great circle track requires a gnomonic passage planning chart (see pages 16–7). On this chart, great circles are represented by straight lines. Therefore, the great circle track between two points can be found by drawing a straight line between them (Fig. 1a). The track should then be divided into convenient lengths (say every 10° of longitude), and the intermediate positions on the track recorded; these positions can then be transferred to a mercator chart, and the courses and distances of the various legs worked out, either by drawing or (preferably) by mercator sailings (Fig. 1b).

By comparing Figures 1a and 1b, it is clear that the great circle track always takes the ship closer to the pole than the rhumb line. This can take the ship into undesirably high latitudes on occasion. Thus, the great circle from the Lizard to New York

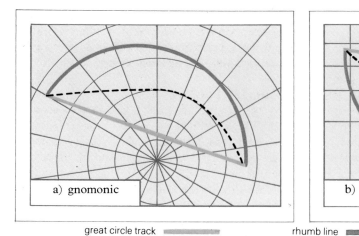 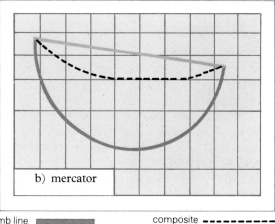

great circle track ▪▪▪▪▪▪▪ rhumb line ▪▪▪▪▪ composite ----------

59.1 *Rhumb line, great circle and composite tracks on (a) gnomonic (b) mercator projections.*

comes within the iceberg region in winter, and a great circle from Tasmania to Cape Horn takes one within 1000 miles of the south pole! To avoid such hazards whilst still keeping the distance as short as possible, a *composite track* is used. In this case, a limiting latitude is chosen, beyond which the ship will not go. A great circle track to this latitude is followed, and the ship then sails due east or west along the limiting parallel until it is in a position to start following another great circle track to the destination.

Tabular method The problem of finding the great circle distance between two points is exactly the same as finding the calculated zenith distance between a chosen position and the geographical position of a heavenly body; therefore, the various methods of sight reduction can be applied to this problem. *The Sight Reduction Tables for Marine Navigation* (NP 401) and the haversine method can be used in all cases; the *Sight Reduction Tables for Air Navigation* (AP 3270 Vols 2 and 3) can only be used if the latitude of the destination is less than 30°N or S.

The method consists of entering the tables with the following quantities:

1) Starting latitude as latitude
2) Finishing latitude as declination (same or contrary name as appropriate)
3) Difference in longitude as LHA

With the haversine method, the answer comes out directly as zenith distance, which can be converted to distance in miles by multiplying the degrees by 60. The *Sight Reduction Tables* give the calculated altitude; this must be subtracted from 90° to give zenith distance before being converted to miles. The azimuth of the body corresponds with the initial heading for the great circle track.

A complication with this method is that it is not so easy to obtain intermediate points on the track for course changes. This can be done by plotting a suitable distance (of a day or two's sail) along the initial heading and finding the position reached, then re-computing the next great circle heading using the position reached as the starting position. Plotting a composite track by this method is very involved and best avoided if possible.

Note: The great circle track only offers significant benefits in higher latitudes and if the desired course is mainly east or west. In other circumstances, great circle sailings can be ignored.

60 Ocean passage planning

When considering an ocean passage, careful planning is an important and enjoyable aspect of the whole enterprise. A small craft is very much at the mercy of the elements, so the shortest route may not necessarily be the quickest. A sailing craft, in particular, will be able to 'afford' a substantial detour if the result is constant, moderate and favourable winds; to fall into an area of light, contrary or gale force winds can set a passage back by days or weeks.

Planning needs to begin with a study of the *Pilot Charts* (or routing charts) of the area; these give a wealth of information about the conditions that may be met, generally organized on a monthly basis throughout the year. A very large number of considerations need to be taken into account when planning an ocean passage, and the following list contains merely those most commonly regarded as important; it is for the individual to decide what is important from his own point of view.

1) *The plan* The owner or skipper (who may also be the navigator) will have a certain plan in mind – places to be visited or avoided, time available and so on. The owner's wife may offer frequent modifications.

2) *The vessel* The actual course of action decided upon may be influenced by the size and stowage capacity of the craft. Extra ports of call may be needed to replenish fuel, water or provisions.

3) *The crew* Crew considerations may also modify the plan, requiring extra ports of call for crew changes. Perhaps such ports must be chosen for the air links available for crew travel.

4) *Prevailing winds* For a sailing yacht, the route must be chosen to give the maximum chance of fair winds, preferably moderate in strength. Pages 88–9 give a general impression of global winds in the (northern) summer and (northern) winter, but much more detailed information is given on the pilot charts. Note in particular how the area of trade winds and the doldrums between moves north or south according to the season. In the Indian Ocean, monsoons are of major importance.

5) *Currents* A contrary current can have a very bad effect on passage times, and should be avoided if possible. A general view of global currents is shown on page 89, but (again) more detailed information should be gleaned from the pilot chart.

6) *Tropical revolving storms* Variously known as hurricanes, typhoons or cyclones, these intense storms should be avoided; many yachts have survived these dangerous storms, but many others have not. Tropical storms are notoriously unpredictable, and may be encountered outside their 'proper' season (see pages 92–3).

7) *Fog, ice, etc* The pilot chart also gives details of regions liable to fog, icebergs or pack ice; clearly, such areas should be avoided if possible.

8) *Gales and calms* Gales, even if favourable in direction, are far from comfortable; calms are time-consuming and frustrating, and perhaps the most likely condition to spoil the enjoyment of the whole crew. A week spent slatting in the same spot will drive the most placid soul into fits of gibbering rage. Keep away (if you can!).

Isochrones In the early part of this century, the German Hydrographic Office published some fascinating charts, which show the average duration (in days) of sailing ship journeys; the source of the data was an analysis of many hundreds of sailing ship logs. Specimens are given in Figure 1. Whilst the numbers attached to each contour represent days for large sailing ships, and hence are unlikely to relate to smaller sailing yachts, the general impression the charts give is likely to remain valid. An idea of the most favourable route can be gained by seeing where the contours 'bulge' in the general direction in which you wish to go. Thus Figure 1a, outward bound from the Lizard, suggests a course for the Cape of Good Hope, which leads close to the Portuguese coast and the Cape Verde Islands, thence across to within a few hundred miles of the South American coast, and generally south or south-west until about latitude 25° south, when course can be shaped ESE for Cape Town. Figure 1d shows that, because of the prevailing westerlies, it is always quicker to round Cape Horn rather than the Cape of Good Hope when bound from the Pacific into the Atlantic.

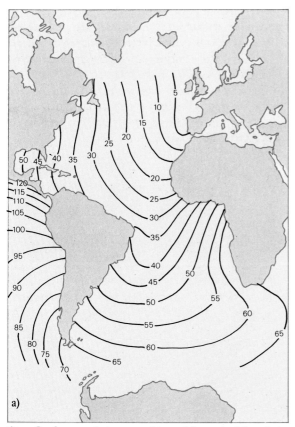

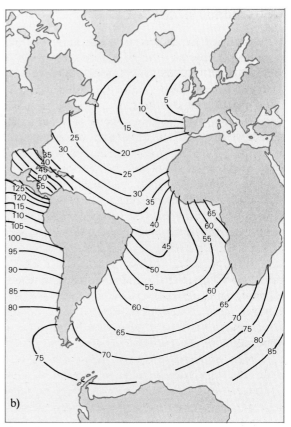

60.1 *Isochrones: (a) outward bound from the Lizard; (b) homeward bound for the Lizard; (c) from* *Cape Horn and Cape of Good Hope; (d) to Cape Horn and Cape of good Hope.*

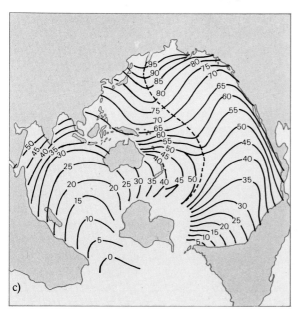

61 Pocket calculators

A pocket calculator can be a powerful aid for someone who is used to using one, provided he bears in mind that it is a vulnerable piece of equipment which is liable to fail in the adverse conditions found at sea. There must always be some form of back-up available (generally books of tables) which does not suffer from this drawback.

Calculator types

Calculators are available in a bewildering profusion, to suit all pockets and all levels of expertise. They range from specialized pre-programmed devices made specifically for use in navigation, to others which can be programmed either by inserting chips or cards, or by hand. Non-programmable calculators may be *scientific*, i.e. with trigonometrical and other functions, or purely arithmetical ($+$, $-$, $\times$, $\div$).

A simple arithmetical calculator is not a great deal of use to a navigator, as most of the useful formulae require trig. or square root functions which means a scientific calculator. The most common source of error with a calculator is pressing the wrong button by mistake; therefore, the fewer key-strokes that need to be made, the better. This points towards a programmable calculator if possible. One drawback with calculators programmed by hand (rather than by inserting cards or memory modules) is that the programme is lost when the calculator is switched off, which can be inconvenient. Some calculators are fitted with a special type of memory which is maintained by the battery when the calculator is switched off, and so programmes and data are not lost. As with all types of equipment, the buyer must balance the needs of the job against the depth of his pocket.

Care of the calculator

The calculator faces two big risks – of being dropped or thrown about, and of getting wet. The utmost care must be taken to guard against both of these. The calculator must be held firmly when in use and immediately put away afterwards in a safe, dry place. A good way of protecting it from water is to seal it inside a transparent plastic bag; the keys can be operated and the display read through the plastic.

Many calculators, especially those with a light-emitting diode display (bright, red numbers), have a limited battery life. Spare batteries must be carried; if it is possible either to run the calculator or to recharge its battery from the ship's supply, this is an advantage.

Equations

The following useful formulae can generally be adapted to the calculator in use; the more elaborate ones become time-consuming and liable to button-pressing errors if attempted on any other than programmable machines.

Speed, time and distance

$$\text{Speed (knots)} = \frac{\text{distance (n miles)}}{\text{time (hours)}}$$

Converting metres to fathoms and feet

$$\text{Metres} = \text{feet} \times 0.305$$
$$= \text{fathoms} \times 1.83$$

Range by narrow horizontal angle (see page 70)

$$\text{Range of midpoint} = \frac{\text{distance between objects}}{2 \times \tan \text{(measured angle)}}$$

Range by sound echo

$$\text{Range (n miles)} = \text{time (seconds)} \times 0.0904$$

Half convergency (see page 114)

$$\text{Half convergency (degrees)} = \tfrac{1}{2} \text{D long (degrees)} \times \sin \text{(mean lat)} \tfrac{1}{2}$$

Range by vertical sextant angle (see page 71)

For short ranges (foot of the object visible)

$$\text{Distance (n miles)} = \frac{\text{height (metres)}}{1852 \times \tan \text{(angle)}}$$

For all circumstances

$$R = \cos(H_s - D)\left\{ -\frac{\sin(H_s - D)}{0.0002493} + \left[\left(\frac{\sin(H_s - D)}{0.0002439} \right)^2 + \frac{h_s - h_o}{0.2258} \right]^{\frac{1}{2}} \right\}$$

Where:

R = range to base of object (n miles)
H_s = sextant altitude corrected for index error (deg, min)
D = Dip of observer's horizon (min)
h_s = height of object above sea level (metres)
h_o = height of observer above sea level (metres)

The tables on pages 187–191 are based on this formula, which is after Guier W.H., *Navigation* (USA) Vol 15 No. 4 (1968) p. 368

Dipping distance of lights (see page 71)

Use the formula above with a sextant altitude of 0 — i.e., enter the value of the dip as a negative quantity.

Dip of a short sea horizon

When practising astronomical sights, it may happen that the sea horizon is obscured by intervening land. This formula gives a figure for dip which should be used instead of the normal dip found in the *Nautical Almanac*

$$\text{Dip (minutes)} = \frac{1.85 \times H}{D} + 0.423 \times D$$

Where:

H = height of eye (metres)
D = Distance to short horizon (n miles)

Plane sailing (see page 177)

Departure = D long cos (mid latitude)
Departure = distance sin (direction)
D lat = distance cos (direction)

$$\text{Direction} = \tan^{-1}\left(\frac{\text{departure}}{\text{D lat}}\right)$$

Note: If using a calculator with polar to rectangular co-ordinate conversion keys, note that the x direction in mathematics is conventionally east; D lat must go in the y register and departure in the x register.

Mercator sailing (see page 180)

Course

$$= \tan^{+1}\frac{\pi\,(\text{Lon}_1 - \text{Lon}_2)}{180\{\text{in}\tan[45 + \frac{1}{2}\text{Lat}_2] - \text{in}\tan[45 + \frac{1}{2}\text{Lat}_1]\}}$$

Distance = $60(\text{Lon}_2 - \text{Lon}_1)\cos(\text{Lat})$
if cos C = 0

$$= \frac{60(\text{lat}_2 - \text{Lat}_1)}{\cos(C)}\ \text{otherwise}$$

Great circle sailing (see page 181)

Distance = $60 \times \cos^{-1}[\sin(\text{Lat}_1)\sin(\text{Lat}_2)$
$+ \cos(\text{Lat}_1)\cos(\text{Lat}_2)\cos(\text{D Long})]$

Course angle

$$= \cos^{-1}\left[\frac{\sin(\text{Lat}_2) - \sin(\text{Lat}_1)\cos\left(\dfrac{D}{60}\right)}{\sin\left(\dfrac{D}{60}\right)\cos\text{Lat}_1}\right]$$

Course = course angle
if $\sin(\text{Lon}_2 - \text{Lon}_1) < 0$
= 360° − course angle
if $\sin(\text{Lon}_2 - \text{Lon}_1) \geq 0$

Note: S latitudes and E longitudes are entered as negative
Avoid passing through the poles
Do not compute a course of north or south

Interpolating Greenwich hour angle (see page 140)

First express the minutes and seconds of GMT as decimals of an hour:
Decimal = mins/60 + secs/3600.
Increment
= Decimal of hour × 15° (sun, planets)
× 15°02′.5 (Aries)
× 14°19′.0 (moon)

v corrections (if appropriate) are needed additionally.

Sight reduction (see page 165)

$H_c = \sin^{-1}[\sin(D)\sin(L)$
$+ \cos(D)\cos(L)\cos(\text{LHA})]$

$$Z = \cos^{-1}\left[\frac{\sin(D) - \sin(L)\sin(H_c)}{\cos(L)\cos(H_c)}\right]$$

$Z_n = Z$ where sin LHA < 0
= 360° − Z where sin LHA ≥ 0

Note: S latitudes and declinations are entered as negative

Where H_c = calculated altitude
D = declination
L = latitude
LHA = local hour angle
Z = azimuth angle
Z_n = azimuth

Amplitude (see page 163)

$$\text{Amplitude} = \cos^{-1}\left[\frac{\sin(D)}{\cos(L)}\right]$$

Feet and metres conversion table

Feet		Metres	Feet		Metres
3.3	1	.3	167.2	51	15.6
6.6	2	.6	170.5	52	15.9
9.8	3	.9	173.8	53	16.2
13.1	4	1.2	177.0	54	16.5
16.4	5	1.5	180.3	55	16.8
19.7	6	1.8	183.6	56	17.1
23.0	7	2.1	186.9	57	17.4
26.2	8	2.4	190.2	58	17.7
29.5	9	2.7	193.4	59	18.0
32.8	10	3.1	196.7	60	18.3
36.1	11	3.4	200.0	61	18.6
39.3	12	3.7	203.3	62	18.9
42.6	13	4.0	206.6	63	19.2
45.9	14	4.3	209.8	64	19.5
49.2	15	4.6	213.1	65	19.8
52.5	16	4.9	216.4	66	20.1
55.7	17	5.2	219.7	67	20.4
59.0	18	5.5	223.0	68	20.7
62.3	19	5.8	226.2	69	21.0
65.6	20	6.1	229.5	70	21.4
68.9	21	6.4	232.8	71	21.7
72.1	22	6.7	236.1	72	22.0
75.4	23	7.0	239.3	73	22.3
78.7	24	7.3	242.6	74	22.6
82.0	25	7.6	245.9	75	22.9
85.2	26	7.9	249.2	76	23.2
88.5	27	8.2	252.5	77	23.5
91.8	28	8.5	255.7	78	23.8
95.1	29	8.8	259.0	79	24.1
98.4	30	9.2	262.3	80	24.4
101.6	31	9.5	265.6	81	24.7
104.9	32	9.8	268.9	82	25.0
108.2	33	10.1	272.1	83	25.3
111.5	34	10.4	275.4	84	25.6
114.8	35	10.7	278.7	85	25.9
118.0	36	11.0	282.0	86	26.2
121.3	37	11.3	285.2	87	26.5
124.6	38	11.6	288.5	88	26.8
127.9	39	11.9	291.8	89	27.1
131.1	40	12.2	295.1	90	27.5
134.4	41	12.5	298.4	91	27.8
137.7	42	12.8	301.6	92	28.1
141.0	43	13.1	304.9	93	28.4
144.3	44	13.4	308.2	94	28.7
147.5	45	13.7	311.5	95	29.0
150.8	46	14.0	314.8	96	29.3
154.1	47	14.3	318.0	97	29.6
157.4	48	14.6	321.3	98	29.9
160.7	49	14.9	324.6	99	30.2
163.9	50	15.3	327.9	100	30.5

Metre and fathom conversion table

Fath		Metres	Fath		Metres
.5	1	1.8	27.9	51	93.3
1.1	2	3.7	28.4	52	95.2
1.6	3	5.5	29.0	53	97.0
2.2	4	7.3	29.5	54	98.8
2.7	5	9.2	30.1	55	100.7
3.3	6	11.0	30.6	56	102.5
3.8	7	12.8	31.1	57	104.3
4.4	8	14.6	31.7	58	106.1
4.9	9	16.5	32.2	59	108.0
5.5	10	18.3	32.8	60	109.8
6.0	11	20.1	33.3	61	111.6
6.6	12	22.0	33.9	62	113.5
7.1	13	23.8	34.4	63	115.3
7.7	14	25.6	35.0	64	117.1
8.2	15	27.5	35.5	65	119.0
8.7	16	29.3	36.1	66	120.8
9.3	17	31.1	36.6	67	122.6
9.8	18	32.9	37.2	68	124.4
10.4	19	34.8	37.7	69	126.3
10.9	20	36.6	38.3	70	128.1
11.5	21	38.4	38.8	71	129.9
12.0	22	40.3	39.3	72	131.8
12.6	23	42.1	39.9	73	133.6
13.1	24	43.9	40.4	74	135.4
13.7	25	45.8	41.0	75	137.3
14.2	26	47.6	41.5	76	139.1
14.8	27	49.4	42.1	77	140.9
15.3	28	51.2	42.6	78	142.7
15.8	29	53.1	43.2	79	144.6
16.4	30	54.9	43.7	80	146.4
16.9	31	56.7	44.3	81	148.2
17.5	32	58.6	44.8	82	150.1
18.0	33	60.4	45.4	83	151.9
18.6	34	62.2	45.9	84	153.7
19.1	35	64.1	46.4	85	155.6
19.7	36	65.9	47.0	86	157.4
20.2	37	67.7	47.5	87	159.2
20.8	38	69.5	48.1	88	161.0
21.3	39	71.4	48.6	89	162.9
21.9	40	73.2	49.2	90	164.7
22.4	41	75.0	49.7	91	166.5
23.0	42	76.9	50.3	92	168.4
23.5	43	78.7	50.8	93	170.2
24.0	44	80.5	51.4	94	172.0
24.6	45	82.4	51.9	95	173.9
25.1	46	84.2	52.5	96	175.7
25.7	47	86.0	53.0	97	177.5
26.2	48	87.8	53.6	98	179.3
26.8	49	89.7	54.1	99	181.2
27.3	50	91.5	54.6	100	183.0

Range by vertical sextant angle – 5 to 15 metres

Arguments are: sextant altitude in minutes (corrected for index error and dip) and height of object minus height of eye (metres). Range is given in nautical miles.

Angle (mins)	Height in metres										
	5	6	7	8	9	10	11	12	13	14	15
−5	13.6	13.8	14.1	14.4	14.6	14.9	15.1	15.4	15.6	15.8	16.1
−4	11.5	11.8	12.1	12.4	12.7	13.0	13.2	13.5	13.7	14.0	14.2
−3	9.5	9.9	10.2	10.5	10.8	11.1	11.4	11.7	12.0	12.2	12.5
−2	7.7	8.1	8.4	8.8	9.1	9.5	9.8	10.1	10.3	10.6	10.9
−1	6.0	6.5	6.9	7.3	7.6	8.0	8.3	8.6	8.9	9.2	9.4
0	4.7	5.2	5.6	6.0	6.3	6.7	7.0	7.3	7.6	7.9	8.2
1	3.7	4.1	4.5	4.9	5.2	5.6	5.9	6.2	6.5	6.8	7.0
2	2.9	3.3	3.7	4.0	4.4	4.7	5.0	5.3	5.6	5.8	6.1
3	2.3	2.7	3.0	3.4	3.7	4.0	4.3	4.5	4.8	5.1	5.3
4	1.9	2.3	2.6	2.9	3.1	3.4	3.7	3.9	4.2	4.4	4.7
5	1.6	1.9	2.2	2.5	2.7	3.0	3.2	3.5	3.7	3.9	4.1
6	1.4	1.7	1.9	2.2	2.4	2.6	2.8	3.1	3.3	3.5	3.7
7	1.2	1.5	1.7	1.9	2.1	2.3	2.5	2.7	2.9	3.1	3.3
8	1.1	1.3	1.5	1.7	1.9	2.1	2.3	2.5	2.6	2.8	3.0
9	1.0	1.2	1.4	1.5	1.7	1.9	2.1	2.2	2.4	2.6	2.7
10	.9	1.1	1.2	1.4	1.6	1.7	1.9	2.1	2.2	2.4	2.5
12	.8	.9	1.0	1.2	1.3	1.5	1.6	1.7	1.9	2.0	2.2
14	.7	.8	.9	1.0	1.2	1.3	1.4	1.5	1.6	1.8	1.9
16	.6	.7	.8	.9	1.0	1.1	1.2	1.3	1.5	1.6	1.7
18	.5	.6	.7	.8	.9	1.0	1.1	1.2	1.3	1.4	1.5
20	.5	.6	.6	.7	.8	.9	1.0	1.1	1.2	1.3	1.4
22	.4	.5	.6	.7	.7	.8	.9	1.0	1.1	1.2	1.2
24	.4	.5	.5	.6	.7	.8	.8	.9	1.0	1.1	1.1
26	.4	.4	.5	.6	.6	.7	.8	.8	.9	1.0	1.1
28	.3	.4	.5	.5	.6	.7	.7	.8	.9	.9	1.0
30	.3	.4	.4	.5	.6	.6	.7	.7	.8	.9	.9
32	.3	.3	.4	.5	.5	.6	.6	.7	.7	.8	.9
34	.3	.3	.4	.4	.5	.5	.6	.7	.7	.8	.8
36	.3	.3	.4	.4	.5	.5	.6	.6	.7	.7	.8
38	.2	.3	.3	.4	.4	.5	.5	.6	.6	.7	.7
40	.2	.3	.3	.4	.4	.5	.5	.6	.6	.6	.7
42	.2	.3	.3	.4	.4	.4	.5	.5	.6	.6	.7
44	.2	.3	.3	.3	.4	.4	.5	.5	.5	.6	.6
46	.2	.2	.3	.3	.4	.4	.4	.5	.5	.6	.6
48	.2	.2	.3	.3	.3	.4	.4	.5	.5	.5	.6
50	.2	.2	.3	.3	.3	.4	.4	.4	.5	.5	.6
52	.2	.2	.2	.3	.3	.4	.4	.4	.5	.5	.5
54	.2	.2	.2	.3	.3	.3	.4	.4	.4	.5	.5
56	.2	.2	.2	.3	.3	.3	.4	.4	.4	.5	.5
58	.2	.2	.2	.3	.3	.3	.4	.4	.4	.4	.5
60	.2	.2	.2	.2	.3	.3	.3	.4	.4	.4	.5

Range by vertical sextant angle – 18 to 48 metres

Arguments are: sextant altitude in minutes (corrected for index error and dip) and height of object minus height of eye (metres). Range is given in nautical miles.

Angle (mins)	Height in metres										
	18	21	24	27	30	33	36	39	42	45	48
0	8.9	9.6	10.3	10.9	11.5	12.1	12.6	13.1	13.6	14.1	14.6
1	7.8	8.5	9.2	9.8	10.4	11.0	11.5	12.0	12.5	13.0	13.4
2	6.9	7.5	8.2	8.8	9.4	9.9	10.5	11.0	11.5	11.9	12.4
3	6.0	6.7	7.3	7.9	8.5	9.0	9.5	10.0	10.5	11.0	11.4
4	5.4	6.0	6.6	7.2	7.7	8.2	8.7	9.2	9.7	10.1	10.6
5	4.8	5.4	5.9	6.5	7.0	7.5	8.0	8.5	8.9	9.4	9.8
6	4.3	4.9	5.4	5.9	6.4	6.9	7.4	7.8	8.2	8.7	9.1
7	3.9	4.4	4.9	5.4	5.9	6.3	6.8	7.2	7.6	8.1	8.5
8	3.5	4.0	4.5	5.0	5.4	5.9	6.3	6.7	7.1	7.5	7.9
9	3.2	3.7	4.1	4.6	5.0	5.4	5.8	6.2	6.6	7.0	7.4
10	3.0	3.4	3.8	4.3	4.7	5.1	5.4	5.8	6.2	6.6	6.9
11	2.7	3.2	3.6	4.0	4.3	4.7	5.1	5.5	5.8	6.2	6.5
12	2.6	2.9	3.3	3.7	4.1	4.4	4.8	5.1	5.5	5.8	6.1
13	2.4	2.8	3.1	3.5	3.8	4.2	4.5	4.8	5.1	5.5	5.8
14	2.2	2.6	2.9	3.3	3.6	3.9	4.2	4.6	4.9	5.2	5.5
15	2.1	2.4	2.8	3.1	3.4	3.7	4.0	4.3	4.6	4.9	5.2
20	1.6	1.9	2.1	2.4	2.6	2.9	3.1	3.4	3.6	3.9	4.1
25	1.3	1.5	1.7	1.9	2.2	2.4	2.6	2.8	3.0	3.2	3.4
30	1.1	1.3	1.5	1.6	1.8	2.0	2.2	2.3	2.5	2.7	2.9
35	.9	1.1	1.3	1.4	1.6	1.7	1.9	2.0	2.2	2.3	2.5
40	.8	1.0	1.1	1.2	1.4	1.5	1.6	1.8	1.9	2.0	2.2
45	.7	.9	1.0	1.1	1.2	1.3	1.5	1.6	1.7	1.8	1.9
50	.7	.8	.9	1.0	1.1	1.2	1.3	1.4	1.5	1.6	1.8
55	.6	.7	.8	.9	1.0	1.1	1.2	1.3	1.4	1.5	1.6
60	.6	.6	.7	.8	.9	1.0	1.1	1.2	1.3	1.4	1.5
65	.5	.6	.7	.8	.9	.9	1.0	1.1	1.2	1.3	1.4
70	.5	.6	.6	.7	.8	.9	.9	1.0	1.1	1.2	1.3
75	.4	.5	.6	.7	.7	.8	.9	1.0	1.0	1.1	1.2
80	.4	.5	.6	.6	.7	.8	.8	.9	1.0	1.0	1.1
85	.4	.5	.5	.6	.7	.7	.8	.8	.9	1.0	1.0
90	.4	.4	.5	.6	.6	.7	.7	.8	.9	.9	1.0
95	.4	.4	.5	.5	.6	.6	.7	.8	.8	.9	.9
100	.3	.4	.4	.5	.6	.6	.7	.7	.8	.8	.9
105	.3	.4	.4	.5	.5	.6	.6	.7	.7	.8	.8
110	.3	.4	.4	.5	.5	.6	.6	.7	.7	.8	.8
115	.3	.3	.4	.4	.5	.5	.6	.6	.7	.7	.8
120	.3	.3	.4	.4	.5	.5	.6	.6	.6	.7	.7

Range by vertical sextant angle – 50 to 100 metres

Arguments are: sextant altitude in minutes (corrected for index error and dip) and height of object minus height of eye (metres). Range is given in nautical miles.

Angle (mins)	50	55	60	65	70	75	80	85	90	95	100
					Height in metres						
0	14.9	15.6	16.3	17.0	17.6	18.2	18.8	19.4	20.0	20.5	21.0
1	13.7	14.5	15.2	15.8	16.5	17.1	17.7	18.2	18.8	19.4	19.9
2	12.7	13.4	14.1	14.7	15.4	16.0	16.6	17.2	17.7	18.3	18.8
3	11.7	12.4	13.1	13.8	14.4	15.0	15.6	16.2	16.7	17.2	17.8
4	10.9	11.5	12.2	12.9	13.5	14.1	14.6	15.2	15.8	16.3	16.8
5	10.1	10.7	11.4	12.0	12.6	13.2	13.8	14.3	14.9	15.4	15.9
6	9.4	10.0	10.6	11.3	11.8	12.4	13.0	13.5	14.1	14.6	15.1
7	8.7	9.4	10.0	10.6	11.1	11.7	12.2	12.8	13.3	13.8	14.3
8	8.1	8.8	9.3	9.9	10.5	11.0	11.6	12.1	12.6	13.1	13.6
9	7.6	8.2	8.8	9.3	9.9	10.4	10.9	11.4	11.9	12.4	12.9
10	7.1	7.7	8.3	8.8	9.3	9.9	10.4	10.8	11.3	11.8	12.3
11	6.7	7.3	7.8	8.3	8.8	9.3	9.8	10.3	10.8	11.2	11.7
12	6.3	6.9	7.4	7.9	8.4	8.9	9.3	9.8	10.3	10.7	11.1
13	6.0	6.5	7.0	7.5	8.0	8.4	8.9	9.3	9.8	10.2	10.6
14	5.7	6.2	6.6	7.1	7.6	8.0	8.5	8.9	9.3	9.8	10.2
15	5.4	5.9	6.3	6.8	7.2	7.6	8.1	8.5	8.9	9.3	9.7
20	4.3	4.7	5.0	5.4	5.8	6.2	6.5	6.9	7.3	7.6	8.0
25	3.5	3.8	4.2	4.5	4.8	5.1	5.4	5.8	6.1	6.4	6.7
30	3.0	3.3	3.5	3.8	4.1	4.4	4.6	4.9	5.2	5.5	5.7
35	2.6	2.8	3.1	3.3	3.6	3.8	4.0	4.3	4.5	4.8	5.0
40	2.3	2.5	2.7	2.9	3.1	3.4	3.6	3.8	4.0	4.2	4.4
45	2.0	2.2	2.4	2.6	2.8	3.0	3.2	3.4	3.6	3.8	4.0
50	1.8	2.0	2.2	2.4	2.5	2.7	2.9	3.1	3.3	3.4	3.6
55	1.7	1.8	2.0	2.2	2.3	2.5	2.6	2.8	3.0	3.1	3.3
60	1.5	1.7	1.8	2.0	2.1	2.3	2.4	2.6	2.7	2.9	3.0
65	1.4	1.6	1.7	1.8	2.0	2.1	2.3	2.4	2.5	2.7	2.8
70	1.3	1.4	1.6	1.7	1.8	2.0	2.1	2.2	2.4	2.5	2.6
75	1.2	1.4	1.5	1.6	1.7	1.8	2.0	2.1	2.2	2.3	2.4
80	1.2	1.3	1.4	1.5	1.6	1.7	1.8	2.0	2.1	2.2	2.3
85	1.1	1.2	1.3	1.4	1.5	1.6	1.7	1.8	1.9	2.1	2.2
90	1.0	1.1	1.2	1.3	1.4	1.5	1.6	1.7	1.8	1.9	2.0
95	1.0	1.1	1.2	1.3	1.4	1.5	1.6	1.6	1.7	1.8	1.9
100	.9	1.0	1.1	1.2	1.3	1.4	1.5	1.6	1.7	1.8	1.8
105	.9	1.0	1.1	1.1	1.2	1.3	1.4	1.5	1.6	1.7	1.8
110	.8	.9	1.0	1.1	1.2	1.3	1.3	1.4	1.5	1.6	1.7
115	.8	.9	1.0	1.0	1.1	1.2	1.3	1.4	1.4	1.5	1.6
120	.8	.8	.9	1.0	1.1	1.2	1.2	1.3	1.4	1.5	1.5
125	.7	.8	.9	1.0	1.0	1.1	1.2	1.3	1.3	1.4	1.5
130	.7	.8	.9	.9	1.0	1.1	1.1	1.2	1.3	1.4	1.4
135	.7	.8	.8	.9	1.0	1.0	1.1	1.2	1.2	1.3	1.4
140	.7	.7	.8	.9	.9	1.0	1.1	1.1	1.2	1.3	1.3
145	.6	.7	.8	.8	.9	1.0	1.0	1.1	1.1	1.2	1.3
150	.6	.7	.7	.8	.9	.9	1.0	1.0	1.1	1.2	1.2
155	.6	.7	.7	.8	.8	.9	1.0	1.0	1.1	1.1	1.2
160	.6	.6	.7	.8	.8	.9	.9	1.0	1.0	1.1	1.2

Range by vertical sextant angle – 150 to 650 metres

Arguments are: sextant altitude in minutes (corrected for index error and dip) and height of object minus height of eye (metres). Range is given in nautical miles.

					Height in metres						
Angle (mins)	150	200	250	300	350	400	450	500	550	600	650
0	25.8	29.8	33.3	36.5	39.4	42.1	44.6	47.1	49.4	51.5	53.7
1	24.6	28.6	32.1	35.3	38.2	40.9	43.5	45.9	48.2	50.4	52.5
2	23.5	27.5	31.0	34.1	37.1	39.8	42.3	44.7	47.0	49.2	51.3
3	22.4	26.4	29.9	33.0	36.0	38.7	41.2	43.6	45.9	48.1	50.2
4	21.4	25.4	28.8	32.0	34.9	37.6	40.1	42.5	44.8	47.0	49.1
5	20.5	24.4	27.8	31.0	33.9	36.5	39.1	41.5	43.7	45.9	48.0
6	19.6	23.5	26.9	30.0	32.9	35.5	38.1	40.4	42.7	44.9	47.0
7	18.7	22.6	26.0	29.0	31.9	34.6	37.1	39.4	41.7	43.9	46.0
8	17.9	21.7	25.1	28.1	31.0	33.6	36.1	38.5	40.7	42.9	45.0
9	17.2	20.9	24.2	27.3	30.1	32.7	35.2	37.5	39.8	41.9	44.0
10	16.5	20.1	23.4	26.4	29.2	31.8	34.3	36.6	38.8	41.0	43.0
11	15.8	19.4	22.6	25.6	28.4	31.0	33.4	35.7	37.9	40.1	42.1
12	15.2	18.7	21.9	24.8	27.6	30.1	32.6	34.9	37.1	39.2	41.2
13	14.6	18.1	21.2	24.1	26.8	29.3	31.8	34.0	36.2	38.3	40.3
14	14.0	17.4	20.5	23.4	26.1	28.6	31.0	33.2	35.4	37.5	39.5
15	13.5	16.8	19.9	22.7	25.4	27.8	30.2	32.5	34.6	36.7	38.7
20	11.3	14.3	17.1	19.7	22.2	24.5	26.8	28.9	31.0	32.9	34.9
25	9.6	12.3	14.9	17.3	19.6	21.8	23.9	25.9	27.8	29.7	31.6
30	8.3	10.8	13.1	15.3	17.4	19.5	21.4	23.3	25.2	27.0	28.7
35	7.3	9.5	11.6	13.7	15.6	17.5	19.4	21.2	22.9	24.6	26.2
40	6.5	8.5	10.5	12.3	14.1	15.9	17.6	19.3	20.9	22.5	24.1
45	5.9	7.7	9.5	11.2	12.9	14.5	16.1	17.7	19.2	20.7	22.2
50	5.3	7.0	8.7	10.3	11.8	13.4	14.9	16.3	17.8	19.2	20.6
55	4.9	6.4	8.0	9.4	10.9	12.3	13.7	15.1	16.5	17.8	19.1
60	4.5	5.9	7.4	8.7	10.1	11.5	12.8	14.1	15.4	16.6	17.9
65	4.2	5.5	6.8	8.1	9.4	10.7	11.9	13.2	14.4	15.6	16.8
70	3.9	5.1	6.4	7.6	8.8	10.0	11.2	12.3	13.5	14.6	15.8
75	3.6	4.8	6.0	7.1	8.3	9.4	10.5	11.6	12.7	13.8	14.9
80	3.4	4.5	5.6	6.7	7.8	8.9	9.9	11.0	12.0	13.0	14.0
85	3.2	4.3	5.3	6.4	7.4	8.4	9.4	10.4	11.4	12.4	13.3
90	3.1	4.0	5.0	6.0	7.0	8.0	8.9	9.9	10.8	11.7	12.7
95	2.9	3.8	4.8	5.7	6.6	7.6	8.5	9.4	10.3	11.2	12.1
100	2.8	3.7	4.6	5.4	6.3	7.2	8.1	8.9	9.8	10.7	11.5
105	2.6	3.5	4.3	5.2	6.0	6.9	7.7	8.5	9.4	10.2	11.0
110	2.5	3.3	4.2	5.0	5.8	6.6	7.4	8.2	9.0	9.8	10.5
115	2.4	3.2	4.0	4.8	5.5	6.3	7.1	7.8	8.6	9.4	10.1
120	2.3	3.1	3.8	4.6	5.3	6.1	6.8	7.5	8.3	9.0	9.7
125	2.2	2.9	3.7	4.4	5.1	5.8	6.5	7.2	8.0	8.7	9.4
130	2.1	2.8	3.5	4.2	4.9	5.6	6.3	7.0	7.7	8.3	9.0
135	2.0	2.7	3.4	4.1	4.7	5.4	6.1	6.7	7.4	8.0	8.7
140	2.0	2.6	3.3	3.9	4.6	5.2	5.9	6.5	7.1	7.8	8.4
145	1.9	2.5	3.2	3.8	4.4	5.0	5.7	6.3	6.9	7.5	8.1
150	1.8	2.5	3.1	3.7	4.3	4.9	5.5	6.1	6.7	7.3	7.9
155	1.8	2.4	3.0	3.6	4.1	4.7	5.3	5.9	6.5	7.0	7.6
160	1.7	2.3	2.9	3.4	4.0	4.6	5.1	5.7	6.3	6.8	7.4

Range by vertical sextant angle – 150 to 650 metres

Arguments are: sextant altitude in degrees (corrected for index error and dip) and height of object minus height of eye (metres). Range is given in nautical miles.

Height in metres

Angle (degrees)	150	200	250	300	350	400	450	500	550	600	650
0	25.8	29.8	33.3	36.5	39.4	42.1	44.6	47.1	49.4	51.5	53.7
1	4.5	5.9	7.4	8.7	10.1	11.5	12.8	14.1	15.4	16.6	17.9
2	2.3	3.1	3.8	4.6	5.3	6.1	6.8	7.5	8.3	9.0	9.7
3	1.5	2.1	2.6	3.1	3.6	4.1	4.6	5.1	5.6	6.1	6.6
4	1.2	1.5	1.9	2.3	2.7	3.1	3.5	3.8	4.2	4.6	5.0
5	.9	1.2	1.5	1.8	2.2	2.5	2.8	3.1	3.4	3.7	4.0
6	.8	1.0	1.3	1.5	1.8	2.1	2.3	2.6	2.8	3.1	3.3
7	.7	.9	1.1	1.3	1.5	1.8	2.0	2.2	2.4	2.6	2.9
8	.6	.8	1.0	1.2	1.3	1.5	1.7	1.9	2.1	2.3	2.5
9	.5	.7	.9	1.0	1.2	1.4	1.5	1.7	1.9	2.0	2.2
10	.5	.6	.8	.9	1.1	1.2	1.4	1.5	1.7	1.8	2.0
11	.4	.6	.7	.8	1.0	1.1	1.2	1.4	1.5	1.7	1.8
12	.4	.5	.6	.8	.9	1.0	1.1	1.3	1.4	1.5	1.6
13	.4	.5	.6	.7	.8	.9	1.1	1.2	1.3	1.4	1.5
14	.3	.4	.5	.6	.8	.9	1.0	1.1	1.2	1.3	1.4
15	.3	.4	.5	.6	.7	.8	.9	1.0	1.1	1.2	1.3

Table of half convergency

Arguments are difference in longitude and mean latitude. Half convergency (in degrees) is applied towards the equator.

D long (degrees)

Mid lat	1	2	3	4	5	6	7	8	9	10	11	12
10	.1	.2	.3	.3	.4	.5	.6	.7	.8	.9	1.0	1.0
15	.1	.3	.4	.5	.6	.8	.9	1.0	1.2	1.3	1.4	1.6
20	.2	.3	.5	.7	.9	1.0	1.2	1.4	1.5	1.7	1.9	2.1
25	.2	.4	.6	.8	1.1	1.3	1.5	1.7	1.9	2.1	2.3	2.5
30	.3	.5	.8	1.0	1.3	1.5	1.8	2.0	2.3	2.5	2.8	3.0
35	.3	.6	.9	1.1	1.4	1.7	2.0	2.3	2.6	2.9	3.2	3.4
40	.3	.6	1.0	1.3	1.6	1.9	2.2	2.6	2.9	3.2	3.5	3.9
45	.4	.7	1.1	1.4	1.8	2.1	2.5	2.8	3.2	3.5	3.9	4.2
50	.4	.8	1.1	1.5	1.9	2.3	2.7	3.1	3.4	3.8	4.2	4.6
55	.4	.8	1.2	1.6	2.0	2.5	2.9	3.3	3.7	4.1	4.5	4.9
60	.4	.9	1.3	1.7	2.2	2.6	3.0	3.5	3.9	4.3	4.8	5.2
65	.5	.9	1.4	1.8	2.3	2.7	3.2	3.6	4.1	4.5	5.0	5.4
70	.5	.9	1.4	1.9	2.3	2.8	3.3	3.8	4.2	4.7	5.2	5.6

Geographical range (dipping range) of lights

Arguments are: height of object and height of eye both in metres. Range is given in nautical miles

Ht. of object (m)	Height of eye (metres)								
	2	3	4	5	6	7	8	9	10
5	7.7	8.3	8.9	9.4	9.8	10.2	10.6	11.0	11.3
6	8.1	8.8	9.3	9.8	10.3	10.7	11.1	11.4	11.8
7	8.5	9.2	9.8	10.3	10.7	11.1	11.5	11.8	12.2
8	8.9	9.6	10.1	10.6	11.1	11.5	11.9	12.2	12.6
9	9.3	9.9	10.5	11.0	11.4	11.9	12.2	12.6	12.9
10	9.6	10.3	10.8	11.3	11.8	12.2	12.6	12.9	13.3
11	9.9	10.6	11.2	11.7	12.1	12.5	12.9	13.3	13.6
12	10.3	10.9	11.5	12.0	12.4	12.8	13.2	13.6	13.9
13	10.6	11.2	11.8	12.3	12.7	13.1	13.5	13.9	14.2
14	10.8	11.5	12.1	12.6	13.0	13.4	13.8	14.2	14.5
15	11.1	11.8	12.3	12.8	13.3	13.7	14.1	14.4	14.8
16	11.4	12.0	12.6	13.1	13.6	14.0	14.3	14.7	15.0
17	11.6	12.3	12.9	13.4	13.8	14.2	14.6	15.0	15.3
18	11.9	12.6	13.1	13.6	14.1	14.5	14.9	15.2	15.6
19	12.1	12.8	13.4	13.9	14.3	14.7	15.1	15.5	15.8
20	12.4	13.0	13.6	14.1	14.5	15.0	15.3	15.7	16.0
22	12.8	13.5	14.1	14.6	15.0	15.4	15.8	16.2	16.5
24	13.3	13.9	14.5	15.0	15.4	15.9	16.2	16.6	16.9
26	13.7	14.4	14.9	15.4	15.9	16.3	16.7	17.0	17.4
28	14.1	14.8	15.3	15.8	16.3	16.7	17.1	17.4	17.8
30	14.5	15.2	15.7	16.2	16.7	17.1	17.5	17.8	18.2
32	14.9	15.5	16.1	16.6	17.0	17.5	17.8	18.2	18.5
34	15.2	15.9	16.5	17.0	17.4	17.8	18.2	18.6	18.9
36	15.6	16.3	16.8	17.3	17.8	18.2	18.6	18.9	19.3
38	15.9	16.6	17.2	17.7	18.1	18.5	18.9	19.3	19.6
40	16.3	16.9	17.5	18.0	18.4	18.9	19.2	19.6	19.9
42	16.6	17.3	17.8	18.3	18.8	19.2	19.6	19.9	20.3
44	16.9	17.6	18.2	18.6	19.1	19.5	19.9	20.2	20.6
46	17.2	17.9	18.5	19.0	19.4	19.8	20.2	20.6	20.9
48	17.5	18.2	18.8	19.3	19.7	20.1	20.5	20.9	21.2
50	17.8	18.5	19.1	19.6	20.0	20.4	20.8	21.2	21.5
55	18.6	19.2	19.8	20.3	20.7	21.2	21.5	21.9	22.2
60	19.3	19.9	20.5	21.0	21.4	21.8	22.2	22.6	22.9
65	19.9	20.6	21.2	21.7	22.1	22.5	22.9	23.3	23.6
70	20.6	21.2	21.8	22.3	22.7	23.2	23.5	23.9	24.2
75	21.2	21.9	22.4	22.9	23.4	23.8	24.2	24.5	24.9
80	21.8	22.5	23.0	23.5	24.0	24.4	24.8	25.1	25.5
85	22.4	23.0	23.6	24.1	24.5	25.0	25.3	25.7	26.0
90	22.9	23.6	24.2	24.7	25.1	25.5	25.9	26.3	26.6
95	23.5	24.1	24.7	25.2	25.6	26.1	26.4	26.8	27.1
100	24.0	24.7	25.2	25.7	26.2	26.6	27.0	27.3	27.7
110	25.0	25.7	26.3	26.8	27.2	27.6	28.0	28.4	28.7
120	26.0	26.7	27.2	27.7	28.2	28.6	29.0	29.3	29.7
130	27.0	27.6	28.2	28.7	29.1	29.5	29.9	30.3	30.6
140	27.9	28.5	29.1	29.6	30.0	30.5	30.8	31.2	31.5
150	28.7	29.4	30.0	30.5	30.9	31.3	31.7	32.1	32.4
160	29.6	30.3	30.8	31.3	31.8	32.2	32.6	32.9	33.3

Table of amplitudes in degrees

Arguments are: declination (top) and latitude (side); apply eastward on rising and westward on setting, from north or south according to name of declination. Below latitude 10, use 90°-declination.

													Declination											
Latitude	0	1	2	3	4	5	6	7	8	9	10	11	12	13	14	15	16	17	18	19	20	21	22	23
10	90	89	88	87	86	85	84	83	82	81	80	79	78	77	76	75	74	73	72	71	70	69	68	67
11	90	89	88	87	86	85	84	83	82	81	80	79	78	77	76	75	74	73	72	71	70	69	68	67
12	90	89	88	87	86	85	84	83	82	81	80	79	78	77	76	75	74	73	72	71	70	69	67	66
13	90	89	88	87	86	85	84	83	82	81	80	79	78	77	76	75	74	73	72	70	69	68	67	66
14	90	89	88	87	86	85	84	83	82	81	80	79	78	77	76	75	73	72	71	70	69	68	67	66
15	90	89	88	87	86	85	84	83	82	81	80	79	78	77	75	74	73	72	71	70	69	68	67	66
16	90	89	88	87	86	85	84	83	82	81	80	79	78	76	75	74	73	72	71	70	69	68	67	66
17	90	89	88	87	86	85	84	83	82	81	80	78	77	76	75	74	73	72	71	70	69	68	67	66
18	90	89	88	87	86	85	84	83	82	81	79	78	77	76	75	74	73	72	71	70	69	68	67	66
19	90	89	88	87	86	85	84	83	82	80	79	78	77	76	75	74	73	72	71	70	69	68	67	66
20	90	89	88	87	86	85	84	83	81	80	79	78	77	76	75	74	73	72	71	70	69	68	67	65
21	90	89	88	87	86	85	84	82	81	80	79	78	77	76	75	74	73	72	71	70	69	67	66	65
22	90	89	88	87	86	85	84	82	81	80	79	78	77	76	75	74	73	72	71	69	68	67	66	65
23	90	89	88	87	86	85	83	82	81	80	79	78	77	76	75	74	73	71	70	69	68	67	66	65
24	90	89	88	87	86	85	83	82	81	80	79	78	77	76	75	74	72	71	70	69	68	67	66	65
25	90	89	88	87	86	84	83	82	81	80	79	78	77	76	75	73	72	71	70	69	68	67	66	64
26	90	89	88	87	86	84	83	82	81	80	79	78	77	76	74	73	72	71	70	69	68	67	65	64
27	90	89	88	87	86	84	83	82	81	80	79	78	77	75	74	73	72	71	70	69	67	66	65	64
28	90	89	88	87	85	84	83	82	81	80	79	78	76	75	74	73	72	71	70	68	67	66	65	64
29	90	89	88	87	85	84	83	82	81	80	79	77	76	75	74	73	72	70	69	68	67	66	65	63
30	90	89	88	87	85	84	83	82	81	80	78	77	76	75	74	73	71	70	69	68	67	66	64	63
31	90	89	88	86	85	84	83	82	81	79	78	77	76	75	74	72	71	70	69	68	66	65	64	63
32	90	89	88	86	85	84	83	82	81	79	78	77	76	75	73	72	71	70	69	67	66	65	64	63
33	90	89	88	86	85	84	83	82	80	79	78	77	76	74	73	72	71	70	68	67	66	65	63	62
34	90	89	88	86	85	84	83	82	80	79	78	77	75	74	73	72	71	69	68	67	66	64	63	62
35	90	89	88	86	85	84	83	81	80	79	78	77	75	74	73	72	70	69	68	67	65	64	63	62
36	90	89	88	86	85	84	83	81	80	79	78	76	75	74	73	71	70	69	68	66	65	64	62	61
37	90	89	87	86	85	84	82	81	80	79	77	76	75	74	72	71	70	69	67	66	65	63	62	61
38	90	89	87	86	85	84	82	81	80	79	77	76	75	73	72	71	70	68	67	66	64	63	62	60
39	90	89	87	86	85	84	82	81	80	78	77	76	74	73	72	71	69	68	67	65	64	63	61	60
40	90	89	87	86	85	83	82	81	80	78	77	76	74	73	72	70	69	68	66	65	63	62	61	59
41	90	89	87	86	85	83	82	81	79	78	77	75	74	73	71	70	69	67	66	64	63	62	60	59
42	90	89	87	86	85	83	82	81	79	78	76	75	74	72	71	70	68	67	65	64	63	61	60	58
43	90	89	87	86	85	83	82	80	79	78	76	75	73	72	71	69	68	66	65	64	62	61	59	58
44	90	89	87	86	84	83	82	80	79	77	76	75	73	72	70	69	67	66	65	63	62	60	59	57
45	90	89	87	86	84	83	81	80	79	77	76	74	73	71	70	69	67	66	64	63	61	60	58	56
46	90	89	87	86	84	83	81	80	78	77	76	74	73	71	70	68	67	65	64	62	61	59	57	56
47	90	89	87	86	84	83	81	80	78	77	75	74	72	71	69	68	66	65	63	61	60	58	57	55
48	90	89	87	86	84	83	81	80	78	76	75	73	72	70	69	67	66	64	62	61	59	58	56	54
49	90	88	87	85	84	82	81	79	78	76	75	73	72	70	68	67	65	64	62	60	59	57	55	53
50	90	88	87	85	84	82	81	79	77	76	74	73	71	70	68	66	65	63	61	60	58	56	54	53
51	90	88	87	85	84	82	80	79	77	76	74	72	71	69	67	66	64	62	61	59	57	55	53	52
52	90	88	87	85	83	82	80	79	77	75	74	72	70	69	67	65	63	62	60	58	56	54	53	51
53	90	88	87	85	83	82	80	78	77	75	73	72	70	68	66	65	63	61	59	57	55	53	52	50
54	90	88	87	85	83	81	80	78	76	75	73	71	69	67	66	64	62	60	58	56	54	52	50	48
55	90	88	87	85	83	81	79	78	76	74	72	71	69	67	65	63	61	59	57	55	53	51	49	47
56	90	88	86	85	83	81	79	77	76	74	72	70	68	66	64	62	60	58	56	54	52	50	48	46
57	90	88	86	84	83	81	79	77	75	73	71	69	68	66	64	62	60	58	55	53	51	49	47	44
58	90	88	86	84	82	81	79	77	75	73	71	69	67	65	63	61	59	57	54	52	50	47	45	42
59	90	88	86	84	82	80	78	76	74	72	70	68	66	64	62	60	58	55	53	51	48	46	43	41
60	90	88	86	84	82	80	78	76	74	72	70	68	65	63	61	59	57	54	52	49	47	44	41	39
61	90	88	86	84	82	80	78	75	73	71	69	67	65	62	60	58	55	53	50	48	45	42	39	36
62	90	88	86	84	81	79	77	75	73	71	68	66	64	61	59	57	54	51	49	46	43	40	37	34
63	90	88	86	83	81	79	77	74	72	70	68	65	63	60	58	55	53	50	47	44	41	38	34	31
64	90	88	85	83	81	79	76	74	71	69	67	64	62	59	57	54	51	48	45	42	39	35	31	27
65	90	88	85	83	80	78	76	73	71	68	66	63	61	58	55	52	49	46	43	40	36	32	28	22
66	90	88	85	83	80	78	75	73	70	67	65	62	59	56	54	50	47	44	41	37	33	28	23	16

Dip of a short horizon

To be used when the sea horizon is obscured by land

Arguments are observer's height of eye in metres and distance to the land in nautical miles. Dip is in minutes of arc, always subtracted. This table replaces the dip table in the *Nautical Almanac*.

	Height of eye (metres)								
Distance (miles)	2	3	4	5	6	7	8	9	10
.5	7.6	11.3	15.0	18.7	22.4	26.1	29.8	33.5	37.2
.6	6.4	9.5	12.6	15.7	18.8	21.8	24.9	28.0	31.1
.7	5.6	8.2	10.9	13.5	16.2	18.8	21.4	24.1	26.7
.8	5.0	7.3	9.6	11.9	14.2	16.5	18.8	21.2	23.5
.9	4.5	6.6	8.6	10.7	12.7	14.8	16.8	18.9	20.9
1.0	4.1	6.0	7.8	9.7	11.5	13.4	15.2	17.1	18.9
1.1	3.8	5.5	7.2	8.9	10.6	12.2	13.9	15.6	17.3
1.2	3.6	5.1	6.7	8.2	9.8	11.3	12.9	14.4	15.9
1.3	3.4	4.8	6.3	7.7	9.1	10.5	11.9	13.4	14.8
1.4	3.2	4.6	5.9	7.2	8.5	9.9	11.2	12.5	13.8
1.5	3.1	4.3	5.6	6.8	8.0	9.3	10.5	11.7	13.0
1.6	3.0	4.2	5.3	6.5	7.6	8.8	9.9	11.1	12.3
1.7	2.9	4.0	5.1	6.2	7.3	8.4	9.4	10.5	11.6
1.8	2.8	3.9	4.9	5.9	6.9	8.0	9.0	10.0	11.1
1.9	2.8	3.7	4.7	5.7	6.7	7.6	8.6	9.6	10.6
2.0	2.7	3.6	4.6	5.5	6.4	7.3	8.3	9.2	10.1
2.1	2.7	3.6	4.4	5.3	6.2	7.1	8.0	8.8	9.7
2.2	2.6	3.5	4.3	5.2	6.0	6.8	7.7	8.5	9.4
2.3	2.6	3.4	4.2	5.0	5.8	6.6	7.4	8.2	9.0
2.4	2.6	3.3	4.1	4.9	5.7	6.4	7.2	8.0	8.7
2.5	2.6	3.3	4.0	4.8	5.5	6.3	7.0	7.7	8.5
2.6	2.5	3.3	4.0	4.7	5.4	6.1	6.8	7.5	8.2
2.7	2.5	3.2	3.9	4.6	5.3	6.0	6.6	7.3	8.0
2.8	2.5	3.2	3.9	4.5	5.2	5.8	6.5	7.2	7.8
2.9	2.5	3.2	3.8	4.4	5.1	5.7	6.4	7.0	7.6
3.0	2.5	3.1	3.8	4.4	5.0	5.6	6.2	6.8	7.5
3.1	2.5	3.1	3.7	4.3	4.9	5.5	6.1	6.7	7.3
3.2	2.5	3.1	3.7	4.3	4.9	5.4	6.0	6.6	7.2
3.3	2.5	3.1	3.7	4.2	4.8	5.3	5.9	6.5	7.0
3.4	–	3.1	3.6	4.2	4.7	5.3	5.8	6.4	6.9
3.5	–	3.1	3.6	4.2	4.7	5.2	5.7	6.3	6.8
3.6	–	3.1	3.6	4.1	4.6	5.2	5.7	6.2	6.7
3.7	–	3.1	3.6	4.1	4.6	5.1	5.6	6.1	6.6
3.8	–	3.1	3.6	4.1	4.6	5.0	5.5	6.0	6.5
3.9	–	3.1	3.6	4.1	4.5	5.0	5.5	6.0	6.4
4.0	–	3.1	3.6	4.0	4.5	5.0	5.4	5.9	6.4
4.1	–	3.1	3.6	4.0	4.5	4.9	5.4	5.8	6.3
4.2	–	3.1	3.6	4.0	4.5	4.9	5.3	5.8	6.2
4.3	–	3.1	3.6	4.0	4.4	4.9	5.3	5.7	6.2
4.4	–	–	3.6	4.0	4.4	4.8	5.3	5.7	6.1
4.5	–	–	3.6	4.0	4.4	4.8	5.2	5.6	6.1
4.6	–	–	3.6	4.0	4.4	4.8	5.2	5.6	6.0
4.7	–	–	3.6	4.0	4.4	4.8	5.2	5.6	6.0
4.8	–	–	3.6	4.0	4.4	4.8	5.2	5.5	5.9
4.9	–	–	3.6	4.0	4.4	4.8	5.1	5.5	5.9
5.0	–	–	3.6	4.0	4.4	4.8	5.1	5.5	5.9

GLOSSARY

Navigational Terms in Five Languages

English	French	German	Dutch	Spanish
Across	en travers	hinuber	dwarsover	al costado
Abeam	par le travers	querab	dwarsscheeps	por el traves
Aground	echoué	auf Grund	gestrand	encallado
Ahead	en avant	voraus	vooruit	avante
Almanac	Ephemerides	Jahrbuch	Almanak	Almanaque
Alongside	à couple	längsseit	langszij	al lado
Anchor	Ancre	Anker	Anker	Ancia
Anchorage	Mouillage	Ankerplatz	Ankerplaats	Fondeadero
Anchoring prohibited	Défense de mouiller	Ankern verboten	Verboden ankerplaats	Fondeadero prohibido
Anemometer	Anémomètre	Windmesser	Windmeter	Anemómetro
Around	autour	herum	rond	alrededor
Astern	en arrière	achtern	achteruit	atras
Bands (horizontal)	bandé	waagrechtgestreift	horizontaal gestreept	fajas horizontales
Bar	Barre	Sandbank	Drempel	Barra
Bay	Baie	Bucht	Bocht	Bahia
Beach	Plage	Strand	Strand	Playa
Beacon	Balise	Bake	Baken	Baliza
Bearing	Relèvement	Peilung	Peiling	Marcacion
Before	devant	vor	voor	antes
Bell	Cloche	Glocke	Mistklok	Campana
Between	entre	zwischen	tussen	entre
Black	noir	schwarz	zwart	negro
Blue	bleu	blau	blauw	azul
Breadth	largeur	Breite	breedte	ancho
Breakers	Brisants	Brecher	Brekers	Rompientes
Breakwater	Brise-lames	Wellenbrecher	Dam	Escollera
Bridge	Pont	Brucke	Brug	Puente
Buoy	Bouée	Boje	Boei	Boya
Calm	calme	glatt	kalm	en calma
Canal	Canal	Kanal	Kanaal	Canal
Cape	Cap	Kap	Kaap	Cabo
Channel marker	Bouée de chenal	Fahrwasser-tonne	Markering van de vaargeul	Boya de canal
Chart	Carte	Seekarte	Zeekaart	Carta nautica
Chart table	Table à cartes	Kartentisch	Kaartentafel	Mesa de cartas
Chequered	à damier	gewürfelt	geblokt	damero
Chimney	Cheminée	Schornstein	Schoorsteen	Chimenea
Church	Eglise	Kirche	Kerk	Iglesia
Cliff	Falaise	Klippe	Klip	Acantilado
Coast	Côte	Küste	Kust	Costa
Compass	Compas	Kompass	Kompas	Compas
Compass adjuster	Compensateur de compas	Kompensierer	Kompassteller	Compensador de compases
Conical	conique	kegelförmig	kegelvormig	conico
Creek	Etier	Bach	Kreek	Arroyo
Current	Courant	Strömung	Stroom	Corriente
Danger	Danger	Gefahr	gevaar	peligro
Dark	foncée	dunkel	donker	obscuro
Degrees	Degrés	Grad	Graden	Grados
Depth	Profondeur	Tiefe	Diepte	profunidad
Diamond (shape)	losange	Raute	ruitvormig	rombo
Diaphone	Diaphone	Kolbensirene	Diafoon	Diafono
Dividers	Pointes sèches	Stechzirkel	Passer	Compas de puntas

English	French	German	Dutch	Spanish
D/F Radio	Radio-gonio	Funkpeiler	Radio-richtingzoeker	Radio-goniómetro
Dock	Bassin	Dock	Dok	Dique
Dolphin	Bouée de corps-mort	Dalben	Dukdalf	Boya de amarre
Downstream	en aval	flussabwärts	stroomafwaarts	rio abajo
Draught	Tirant d'eau	Tiefgang	Diepgang	Calado
Dries	assèchant	trockenfallend	droogvallend	en seco
Dunes	Dunes	Dünen	Duinen	Dunas
East	Est	Ost	Oost	Este
Ebb (tide)	Marée descendante	Ebbe	Eb	Vaciante
Echo sounder	Sondeur	Echolot	Echolood	Eco sonda
Entrance	Entrée	Einfahrt	Toegang	Entrada
Estuary	Estuaire	Mündung	Zeegat	Estuario
Fairway	Chenal	Fahrwasser	Vaargeul	Canal
Ferry	Ferry	Fähre	Veerboot	Ferry
Fixed light	Feu fixe	Festfeuer	Vast licht	Luz fija
Flag	Pavillon	Flagge	Vlag	Bandera
Flares	Fusées éclairantes	Leuchtsignale	Hand-stakellichten	Bengalas
Flashing light	Feu à éclats	Blinkfeuer	Schitterlicht	Luz de destellos
Flood (tide)	Marée montante	Flut	Vloed	Entrante
Fog	Brume	Nebel	Mist	Niebla
Gale	Coup de vent	Sturm	Stormachtig	Temporal
Green	vert	grün	groen	verde
Hand bearing compass	Compas de relèvement	Handpeilkompass	Handpeilkompas	Compas de marcar
Harbour	Port	Hafen	Haven	Puerto
High water	Pleine mer	Hochwasser	Hoogwater	Pleamar
Hill	Colline	Hügel	Heuvel	Colina
Horn	Nautophone	Nautofon	Natofoon	Nautofono
Index error	Erreur de collimation	Indexfehler	Indexfout	Error de indice
Inner	interieur	inner	binnen	interior
Island	Ile	Insel	Eiland	Isla
Jetty	Jetée	Steg	Steiger	Malecon
Latitude	Latitude	Breite	Breedte	Latitud
Leading light	Feu d'alignment	Leitfeuer	Geleidelicht	Luz de efilación
Leeward	sous le vent	Lee	aan lij	sotavento
Left (side)	gauche	links	links	izquierdo
(Sea) Level	Niveau	Wasserstand	Waterstand, Peil	Nivel
Lifeboat	Canot de sauvetage	Rettungsboot	Reddingboot	Bote salvavidas
Light	Feu	Feuer	Licht	Luz
Lighthouse	Phare	Leuchtturm	Vuurtoren	Faro
Light vessel	Bateau-feu	Feuerschiff	Lichtschip	Buque faro
Lock	Ecluse	Schleuse	Sluis	Esclusa
(Patent) Log	Loch enregistreur	Patentlog	Sleeplog	Corredera mecanica
Logbook	Journal de bord	Logbuch	Logboek	Cuaderno de bitacora
Longitude	Longitude	Lange	Lengte	Longitud
Low water	Basse mer	Niedrigwasser	Laagwater	Bajamar

English	French	German	Dutch	Spanish
Marina	Marina	Marina	Jachthaven	Puerto deportivo
Mast	Mât	Mast	Mast	Palo
Mean (average)	moyen	mittlere	gemiddeld	media
Minutes	Minutes	Minuten	Minuten	Minutos
Moon	Lune	Mond	Maan	Luna
Mooring prohibited	Accostage interdit	Anlegen verboten	Verboden aan te leggen	Amarradero prohibido
Mountain	Montagne	Berg	Berg	Montana
Mud	Boue	Schlick	Modder	Lodo
Neap tide	Morte eau	Nipptide	Doodtij	Aguas muertas
North	Nord	Nord	Noord	Norte
Obstruction	Obstruction	Hindernis	Hindernis	Obstrución
Occasional	occasionnel	gelegentlich	facultatief	ocasional
Occulting light	Feu a occultation	Mischfeuer	Onderbroken licht	Luz de ocultacion
Orange	orange	orange	oranje	naranja
Outer	avant	äusser	buiten	exterior
Overfalls	Remous	Stromkabbelung	Stroomrafeling	Escarceos
Parallel ruler	Règle parallele	Parallel-lineal	Parallel-lineaal	Regla paralelas
Peninsula	Peninsule	Halbinsel	Schiereiland	Peninsula
Pilot	Pilote	Lotse	Loods	Piloto
Pilot book	Instructions nautiques	Seehandbuch	Zeemansgids	Derrotero
Pilot cutter	Bateau-pilote	Lotsenboot	Loodsbooot	Barco del practico
Planets	Planètes	Planeten	Planeten	Planetas
Pole Star	Etoile polaire	Polarstern	Poolster	Estrella polar
Port (side)	Babord	backbord	bakboord	babor
Port tack	babord amure	auf steuerbord-bug*	over bakboord	con amuras a babor
Protractor	Rapporteur	Winkelmesser	Gradenboog	Transportador
Pencil	Crayon	Bleistift	Potlood	Lapiz
Pontoon	Ponton	Ponton	Ponton	Ponton
Quay	Quai	Kai	Kade	Muelle
Radiobeacon	Radiophare	Funkfeuer	Radiobaken	Radiofaro
Radio receiver	Poste récepteur	Empfangsgerät	Radio-ontvangtoestel	Receptor de radio
Range (of light)	Distance	Reichweite	Bereik	Alcance
Range (of tide)	Amplitude	Tidenhub	Verval	Repunte
Red	rouge	rot	rood	rojo
Reef	Récif	Riff	Rif	Arrecife
Right (side)	droit	rechts	rechts	derecha
River	Rivière	Fluss	Rivier	Rió
Rocks	Rochers	Felsen	Rotsen	Rocas
Rough (sea)	dure, agité	rauh	ruw	agitado
Round	circulaire	rund	rond	redondo
Rubber (Eraser)	Gomme	Gummi	Vlakgom	Goma
Sand	Sable	Sand	Zand	Arena
Seaward	vers le large	seewärts	zeewaarts	hacia la mar
Seconds	Secondes	Sekunden	Seconden	Segundos
Sextant	Sextant	Sextant	Sextant	Sextante
Shoal	Haut-fond	Untiefe	Ondiepte	Bajio
Shore	Côte	Land	Kust	Costa

English	French	German	Dutch	Spanish
Shoreward	vers la terre	landwärts	kustwaarts	hacia tierra
Sight reduction tables	Tables de navigation	Höhentafeln	Zeevaartkundige tafels	Tablas rapidas
Siren	Sirène	Sirene	Mistsirene	Sirena
Slipway	Slip	Slip	Helling	Varadero
Spring tide	Vive eau	Springtide	Springtij	Marea viva
Squall	Grain	Bö	Bui	Chubasco
Square	carré	viereckig	vierkant	cuadrangular
Stand (of tide)	Etale	Wasserstand	Stilwater	Margen
Star	Etoile	Stern	Ster	Estrella
Starboard	Tribord	Steuerbord	Stuurbord	Estribor
Starboard tack	Tribord amure	auf backbord-bug*	over stuurboord	con amuras a estribor
Steep	raide	steil	steile	empinado
Stones	Pierres	Steine	Steenen	Piedras
Strait (narrows)	Détroit	Meerenge	Straat	Estrecho
Stripes (vertical)	raiée	senkrecht gestreift	vertikaal gestreept	fajas verticales
South	Sud	Süd	Zuid	Sur
Sun	Soleil	Sonne	Zon	Sol
Surf	Surf	Brandung	Branding	Resaca
Swell	Houle	Dünung	Deining	Mar de fondo
Temporary	temporaire	zeitweilig	tijdelijk	provisional
Tide tables	Table des marées	Tidenkalender	Getijtafels	Tabla de mareas
Topmark	Voyant	Toppzeichen	Topteken	Marea de tope
(a) Tow	Remorque	Schlepper	Sleep	Remolque
Tower	Tour	Turm	Toren	Torre
Town	Ville	Stadt	Stad	Ciudad
Triangle	Triangle	Dreieck	Driehonk	Triangulo
Tug	Remorqueur	Schlepper	Sleepboot	Remolcador
Upstream	en amont	flussaufwärts	stroomopwaarts	rio arriba
Water	Eau	Wasser	Water	Agua
Wave	Vague	Welle	Golf	Ola
Weather forecast	Prévisions météo	Wetterbericht	Weers-voorspelling	Pronostico
West	Ouest	West	West	Oeste
Whistle	Sifflet	Heuler	Fluit	Silbato
White	blanc	weiss	wit	blanco
Wind	Vent	Wind	Wind	Viento
Windward	au vent	luv	aan loef	barlovento
Wreck	Epave	Wrack	Wrak	Naufragio
Yacht club	Yacht-club	Yachtclub	Watersport-vereniging	Club nautico
Yellow	jaune	gelb	geel	amarillo

*N.B. Note different terminology in German

INDEX

Page numbers in *italic* refer to illustrations.